The Boy Next Door

"Staley, a gifted storyteller, weaves a delightful tale of the intersection of politics and friendships with the melodies of memory and music. She draws on six decades of lived experience and shares the observations and lessons learned from growing up in Hot Springs, meeting President Kennedy at Girl's Nation, college teaching, leading the Arkansas Arts Council as a department head under Governor Clinton, employing her voice to celebrate Clinton's gubernatorial and presidential inaugurals, running for the state legislature, and a life of giving and public service. Throughout it all, Staley holds dear the role of music in everyday life, shaping her own experiences and of a growing friendship between her family and the Clintons – Bill, Hillary, and Chelsea. For presidential historians, Arkansas history buffs, and any intellectually curious citizen, this book is informative, insightful, and an easy read about events and relationships that would otherwise be unrecorded and lost to future readers and scholars. We are all in Carolyn Staley's debt for such a fascinating story well told."

—Stephen A. Smith, Professor Emeritus, University of Arkansas

"This book is captivating! No previous writer has covered a President's early high school years who actually knew him and his friends! You get to look at a remarkable young boy, you know will grow up to be a remarkable President, and after this amazing book, you know how it happened! I would recommend this book to any person! It is more informative than you can believe!"

—Harry Thomason, TV and Feature Film Director

"Carolyn Staley is an original Friend of Bill (FOB), having known him since their early teens. A love of music, intellectual curiosity, and the search for spiritual uplift have bound them together over the years. Carolyn's insightful recollections give us greater insight into the individual we have come to admire, revere, and love. And she has given us a years-old example of the enduring bond of friendship."

—Rodney Slater, former Secretary of Transportation

"Carolyn Staley describes episodes from Clinton's early life that reflect his kindness, thoughtfulness, competitiveness, ambition, and desire to seek opportunities for service that he hoped could make life better for people both in this country and beyond."

—David Stricklin, writer, historian,
& former head of the Butler Center for Arkansas Studies.

"Carolyn comes with a unique perspective on Bill Clinton's life, having been next-door neighbors in Hot Springs, Arkansas, and close friends for over sixty years. The memories and stories she shares with her readers offer a rare look at Bill Clinton's many years in public service and beyond."

—David Pryor, former Arkansas Governor
and three-term United States Senator

"Carolyn Staley's wonderful memoir captures not only the uniqueness of her 60-year friendship with Bill Clinton, but the richness of the values they share, and the power of friendship and faith in underpinning a purposeful life. A trip down memory lane for me, and an uplifting read for anyone!

—Mack McLarty, Clinton's first White House Chief of Staff,
and later Counselor to the President
and Special Envoy for the Americas in the Clinton Administration

"Exemplifying the words from the 1983 song *Friends Are Friends Forever*, Carolyn Staley insightfully writes about a special friend who became President of the United States. In the years to come, when scholars and historians take in-depth looks at the life and work of Bill Clinton, Carolyn's book will be a valuable resource."

—James L. "Skip" Rutherford III, Dean Emeritus,
University of Arkansas Clinton School of Public Service

"In her fun, hard-to-put-down book that offers readers a fresh view of a much-chronicled figure, Carolyn Staley gets extra points for an unvarnished portrait of Bill Clinton. This funny, poignant, and full-of-surprises memoir is a platonic love story with the central character a young Bill Clinton, charismatic, brilliant, and ambitious, wanting to change the world. done. The Boy Next Door is a rewarding read, and one that confirms that the boy from Hope and Hot Springs never left them far behind."

—Janis F. Kearney, former presidential diarist, and author of *Conversations: William J. Clinton: from Hope to Harlem, Daisy: Between a Rock and a Hard Place,* and *Only on Sundays: Mahalia Jackson's Long Journey*

"Carolyn Yeldell Staley was Bill Clinton's neighbor, classmate, confidante, and pal—Carolyn has been there since the beginning. I met her on my first trip to Hot Springs, Arkansas, in the summer of 1965. Her joy, her powers of observation, keen insight and extraordinary recall make this book essential reading for all of us FOBs as well as anyone seeking a deeper understanding of one of the towering political figures of our era."

—Tom Campbell, Bill Clinton's roommate at Georgetown University

The Boy Next Door

My sixty-year friendship with Bill Clinton

Carolyn Yeldell Staley

Parkhurst Brothers Publishers
MARION, MICHIGAN

www.parkhurstbrothers.com

Consumers may order Parkhurst Brothers books from their favorite booksellers, expecting prompt delivery. Parkhurst Brothers books are distributed to the trade through the Chicago Distribution Center. Trade and library orders may be placed through Ingram Book Company, Baker & Taylor, Follett Library Resources and other book industry wholesalers. To order from Chicago Distribution Center, phone 1-800-621-2736 or fax to 800-621-8476. Copies of this and other Parkhurst Brothers Publishers titles are available to organizations and corporations for purchase in quantity by contacting the Special Sales Department at our home office location, listed on our website. Manuscript submission guidelines for this publishing company are available at our website.

Printed in the United States of America

First Edition, August 19, 2025

Printing History: 2025 2026 2027 2028 2029 16 15 14 13 12 11 10 9 8 7 6 5 4 3 2 1

Library of Congress Cataloging in Publication Data: [Pending]

ISBN: Hardback 978162491-208-5
ISBN: e-book 978162491-209-2

Parkhurst Brothers Publishers believes that the free and open exchange of ideas is essential for the maintenance of our freedoms. We support the First Amendment of the United States Constitution and encourage all citizens to study all sides of public policy questions, making up their own minds.

Cover design by Will Staley
Text design by Harring Book Design
Acquired for Parkhurst Brothers Publishers
And edited by Ted Parkhurst

082025

Dedicated to

My husband Jerry, my partner for 54 years, who always cheers me on;
Our dear children, Sarah, Mary, & Will,
and their spouses, Charles and Misti;
Our grandchildren, Georgia, Scarlett, Timothy,
and our deceased Freeman and Pearl Luna;
My parents, Walter and Kay (Boswell) Yeldell,
my siblings Lynda, Walter, and Deborah,
The great cloud of generations who took risks, persevered in faith,
and gave me strength to do the same;
My friend, Bill, for a lifelong friendship that has enriched each day;
And to God, who made us neighbors and friends;
With thanks and gratitude.

Acknowledgements

Authoring a book is a group project, I quickly learned. I wish to thank several Beta readers who gave me invaluable advice and guidance, particularly in the first few drafts. They include our children Sarah Staley Shenk, Mary Staley Chappelow and Will Staley, my siblings Lynda Yeldell, Walter Yeldell, and Deborah Yeldell McAfee who read and gave suggestions. Thanks to my family for sharing memories of life next door to the Clintons and photographs as well.

Candace Wellman, historian, author of *Interwoven Lives*, *Peace Weavers*, and *Man of Treacherous Charm*, and distant cousin in Bellingham, Washington generously gave untold hours of her time to read every chapter and make suggestions for edits and clarification. She helped me create the book proposal and query letter for agents. Candace emailed many times a day for months as the book drafts continued to be edited. Words are inadequate to thank her. Candace is the author of two award-winning books from WSU Press, "Peace Weavers: Uniting the Salish Coast through Cross-Cultural Marriages" and a companion volume, "Interwoven Lives: Indigenous Mothers of Salish Coast Communities.

Author Bitty Martin, fresh off her successful book publication *Snake Eyes*, gave me very helpful early advice as she read many chapters of drafts. Bitty also read the query letter and book proposal draft and gave helpful suggestions.

Margaret Pugh O'Mara, professor of history at the University of Washington and successful author of Code, *Cities of Knowledge*, and *Pivotal Tuesdays* and friend from many years as neighbors in downtown Little Rock's Quapaw Quarter, read and gave helpful advice and encouragement.

David Stricklin, former director of the Clinton studies division of the Bobby Roberts Library of Arkansas History and Art of the Central Arkansas Library System, were generous to read and give comments and encouragement that kept me buoyed a long time. Glen Whaley, assistant at the Roberts Library also read and gave suggestions about other possible readers. Glenda Cooper, high school friend read early chapters for me as well and gave suggestions.

Deep appreciation to friend and neighbor, photographer Tom Krellwitz for many hours given to this project in editing all the photos and giving them new life.

Thanks to our son Will Staley, graphic designer and director of Thrive, Inc. for designing the book jacket. Thanks to Judy Hughes Freeman for reading the final proof.

Thanks to countless friends who encouraged me to tell the story of our friendship as part of the public history of Bill Clinton, not only our years as friends since high school, but also as a glimpse into his human side that few have had the privilege to experience through a long friendship.

Thanks to friends and Clinton associates who read chapters of the book and provided helpful comments for the book jacket. They include Tom Campbell, Janis Kearney, Mack McLarty, Governor David Pryor, James "Skip" Rutherford, Sec. Rodney Slater, Steve Smith, David Stricklin, and Harry Thomason.

Thanks to my publisher Ted Parkhurst for sending me suggestions when I first floated the idea of writing a memoir. Before I started writing in earnest in 2020, he outlined helpful tips for a successful writing process. His publishing has been familiar to me since the 1980s when I was Director of the Arkansas Arts Council and he led much-in-demand story-writing and poetry workshops in public schools.

Thanks to Ted for agreeing to read the book proposal and offering to have Parkhurst Brothers publish the book. I am grateful for his belief in me and the book idea.

Thanks to Bill Clinton for the lifetime of shared experiences and the many memories of friendship for over sixty years. Thanks to him as well for reading the first draft and encouraging me by telling that it was very good and to keep going. Major thanks for writing the foreword to the book.

Thanks to my husband Jerry who supported me during the many hours, months and years as I wrote the draft memories.

Finally, thanks to God who gave me the friendship with Bill that has allowed me to have so many memories to share.

Table of Contents

President Clinton and Carolyn Staley chatting at the White House.
(Photo by Jerry Staley)

A Note from Bill Clinton

Carolyn Staley and her family, the Yeldells, lived next door to us in Hot Springs on Scully Street. The houses on our block-long street faced an empty lot of the same length, about half a block wide, which thanks to a neighbor just to the south of us, was filled every spring with a massive bed of beautiful peonies. So we lived in a small neighborhood where we all got to know one another.

Carolyn was the oldest of four children in a family headed by a Baptist minister and his warmhearted, quick-witted wife who welcomed us into their home, where Carolyn and I bonded over our shared love of music. I was a pretty good saxophone player and she was a gifted pianist with a beautiful soprano voice.

One day I walked over and rang the Yeldell's doorbell to ask her if she would accompany me on my saxophone solo at the upcoming state band festival, which was held in Hot Springs. Soon I found myself regularly in the Yeldell's living room playing my contest pieces and other music, from classical to gospel to jazz. It was an especially proud moment when we conquered the 5/4 beat of Dave Brubeck's "Take Five." Usually, the accompanist was better than the soloist!

We were also both members of the student council, and after our junior year were chosen to attend the American Legion Boys State and Girls State programs, where we were each elected as one of the two senators to represent Arkansas in Washington at Boys Nation and Girls Nation, a formative experience for both of us. We were both elected to class offices. I was president and she was secretary of the class of '63.

Soon, the association which accredited Arkansas Schools imposed strict limits on the number of extracurricular activities students could enroll in. For example, because I was my band's student conductor, I couldn't run for class or student body president. In one of the dumber political moves of my life, I allowed my name to be put up for class secretary by a friend as a protest against the new activity restrictions. Carolyn already had the job and defeated me handily, as she should have. And I learned a valuable lesson: Never to run for an office you don't really want and don't have a good reason to hold. Carolyn knew what was going on and never held the foolishness against me.

After high school, Carolyn and I kept in touch with letters and hung out during holiday and summer breaks with the rest of our group of life-long friends.

Carolyn studied voice at Indiana University and met her future husband, Jerry Staley, a talented photographer and marvelous man. She had the talent to become a professional opera singer, but didn't want the rigorous lifestyle that came with it, including moving to Europe for a few years to join opera companies there. Instead, she kept a busy schedule teaching, singing locally, and raising a young and growing family. Meanwhile, after finishing my formal education, I met and married Hillary and began my political career in Arkansas.

When I became Governor in 1979, I asked Carolyn if she would be interested in moving from Indiana back to Arkansas to join my administration. She did and served admirably, first for the Arts Council and later leading our efforts on adult literacy. The added bonus was that we became neighbors again, as she, Jerry, and their family bought and renovated a great old house about three blocks from the Governor's Mansion. For 12 years, Hillary and I visited often for parties, games, and singing around the piano. When Chelsea was born, Carolyn wrote a beautiful song welcoming her to the world which she played and sang for us at the Governor's Mansion. The Staley house also hosted a celebratory brunch for my family and closest friends the morning after I was elected President in 1992. The picture of all of us standing on the front porch was carried in newspapers across the country. It's one of my favorite photos and was included in my memoir, *My Life*.

After I became President, Carolyn and her family moved to the Washington area where she went to work for, and later led, the National Institute for Literacy. Her efforts made a big difference in countless lives. Meanwhile, I was blessed to have the frequent letters and faxes that she sent to the White House to keep me connected to the real world and to my old friends outside the

"White House Bubble." Best of all were the jokes she sent, which kept me laughing amidst all the challenges the Presidency brings. Thanks to her and many others, I never felt far from home.

One of the qualities I've always admired most about Carolyn is that she is constantly looking for new ways to learn, grow, and serve. Perhaps nothing embodies this more than her decision after leaving government service to join the ministry. As the daughter of a pastor, her faith had always been a big part of her life—and by following it into the ministry, I believe she found her true calling. After she retired, she continued to speak at small churches who didn't mind listening to an intelligent, knowledgeable, female pastor.

The older I get, the more I realize what a gift it is to have friends with whom you have shared every phase of life. Today, I still see Carolyn when I'm in Little Rock, usually on visits to my Library and Presidential Center. For years the members of our crew played cards in the apartment atop the Library while eating barbecue and discussing current events, giving updates on our kids and grandkids, and spending a lot of time laughing.

It's almost impossible to put into a few words what our friendship of more than 60 years has meant. There are so many stories, you'd have to write a book. I'm grateful to Carolyn for doing just that: telling a story that reveals an observant eye, a big heart, and a giving spirit.

Bill Clinton

President of the United States, 1993-2001

From the Author

I have written this account to tell the story of my friendship with Bill Clinton, beginning at age 15 (in 1961) when we became next-door neighbors in Hot Springs, Arkansas. The story continues to the present day. Few people have been fortunate enough to have such a long-lasting friendship with a United States president, and especially as a next-door neighbor during high school and college. Our friendship continues today through regular visits and communication.

I have written a brief biographical synopsis of the years of my life before 1961 in chapter one. There, I recount documents about my childhood, education, musical interests, and my family life in a minister's family. I believe this history reveals the fascinating foundation of how our friendship was developing with common interests and strengths that prepared us for friendship even before we met in 1961.

I hope this story of friendship with Bill Clinton affords a glimpse into our lives in the 1960s as high school and college students, our mutual interest in music and regular practice for saxophone/piano performances, our shared involvement in student government and leadership, our family life and related experiences, and Bill's entry into politics as it continued through his presidential years 1993-2000, extending through the years since the presidency and our continued friendship. We've shared experiences in working for racial understanding. Our faith matters to each of us and underpins our lives and actions.

The book covers over 60 years of our lives and our nation's history. Bill and I remain in touch and visit regularly in person when he is back in Little Rock. In between times we text and share notes and phone calls.

I have been deeply honored to be called one of Bill Clinton's closest friends. I am certain that he is that to me. My hope is that sharing these memories and experiences will offer students of history and of the Clinton presidency new insights into areas of life not often written about. He has read the book and said he has enjoyed it very much as it has also helped him relive many memories. He recently told me, "Your book is very good."

I am thankful for the experience of having our church parsonage next door to the Clinton's home, for a shared love for music and student leadership, and for continued friendship these six decades and beyond. I am deeply grateful. With equal thanks for my incredible family and all the experiences of life and love through the years, there aren't pages adequate to contain the love and memories we share.

Carolyn Yeldell Staley
Little Rock, Arkansas
Fall 2022

My Life as a Preacher's Kid

I am a preacher's kid, born in Owensboro, Kentucky September 7, 1946, after my dad, Walter L. Yeldell, returned home from Germany where he served as a US Army chaplain in WW II. He had attended Southern Baptist Theological Seminary in Louisville, Kentucky, and met my mother, Emma Katherine Boswell, when he preached revival services at Yellow Creek Baptist Church in Daviess County, Kentucky, outside Owensboro and where she was in the choir. They were married in 1944, just before my father left to serve in the war.

During my father's Army tour, my mother Kay lived with my grandparents on a large homestead farm near Thruston (Daviess County), Kentucky, where my grandfather raised tobacco. As a young girl, mother walked behind his plow, punching holes in the dirt with a stick to plant small tobacco plants that my grandfather placed along the rows. She had an idyllic childhood living among peach trees and rolling farmland in a house that was once the earliest log house on record in the county. Dad and Mother lived there after his return from WWII. My first home was there. I lived with my extended family, including my mother's parents, Edward and Georgia Boswell, and great-grandmother, Emma Ellis Bell Thornsberry. I called Emma "Grandmother Twosie" because I had two grandmothers.

Our family, always interested in genealogy, has traced my maternal ancestors back thirteen uninterrupted generations to the American Revolutionary War and to our patriot, Stephen L. Ellis. The family came from England, where the names Boswell, Ellis, and Bell are well-known. After my ancestor, Lewis Craig, a pastor in Fredericksburg, Virginia, was imprisoned for his faith in Virginia, he loaded covered wagons and set out for Kentucky. He had heard land was available cheap in Kentucky. Craig established the first Baptist church there.

A chapter in the Baptist history, *The Traveling Church*[1] chronicles the family's journey. We have a family will from Kentucky that lists the names of enslaved people bequeathed to heirs. I am particularly pleased that my father's Baptist ministry and my own continue the legacy of these early Baptist minister pioneers in America.

My father's ancestors trace back to William II of England. They settled in Philadelphia as a Quaker tinsmith and family, then moved to South Carolina, where they became slaveholders. We are in touch with relatives, both white and African American, as we explore our family history. Joseph Yeldell was a well-known city councilman when he lived in Washington, D.C., and one day the split headline of the Washington Post heralded news about Clinton and Yeldell. Finding that amusing, I sent a copy to the president. I also found a Yeldell campaign button at an antique shop outside the District. What a fascinating keepsake!

My chaplain-father was assigned to an Army medical corps in Germany and Austria. He provided pastoral and paramedical care to the sick and dying, prepared graves for burial, and conducted funerals. He could never talk about the war because of the trauma he experienced. He told mother about seeing oil drums filled with amputated limbs. I remember seeing pieces of shrapnel in my mother's cedar chest, and a black and white photo of a heap of emaciated corpses at Dachau that was taken after liberation. I have a copy of that photo and it became more special to me when I visited Dachau forty years after the war. While there, I led a memorial service with Lutheran students, and also as I served as soloist in Jewish temples for thirty years.

My father was a handsome, imposing man towering over most others at 6'3" and about 250 pounds. His blonde hair started thinning early while in the US Army, and eventually he was mostly bald on top. Daddy had a huge, easy smile, and everyone loved him. A constant whistler, his return home was announced by his cheerful, whistling as he approached on foot.

When Daddy left a church pastorate, it was not uncommon to see people cry. He grew up very poor in southeast Arkansas, the eldest of five children, and the first in his family to attend college. He played football and wrote to the governor to ask for shoes so he could play the game. Soon, he received the needed shoes in the mail.

My mother was exceptionally beautiful. As a young woman, she had several beaus. One Christmas before marrying Daddy, she received three watches from the young men. One boy gave her an unripe persimmon as they walked the country lane one afternoon and suggested she take a bite. It caused her to pucker up, just as he planned. She was the eldest of three children in the Boswell household. Her little brother, George, age 10, died of a childhood disease which devastated her family. As an adult, Mother was ladylike, smart, and a gifted teacher and leader. She gets a trophy in my book for raising four children as a pastor's wife, particularly while we were all teenagers. She made wonderful coconut pies and an extra one when she and Daddy had a fuss.

In 1947 when I was a toddler, our family moved from Kentucky to Clarksville, Arkansas, nestled in the Ozark Mountain foothills. My father began his pastorate at First Baptist Church, a moderate-size church with about 200 members, but the largest church in town. My siblings Lynda (1948), Walter (1950), and Deborah (1952) were born in Clarksville. They were a source of great fun during our childhood. Deborah and I are look-alikes and are often mistaken for each other. Lynda has been a corporate comptroller and Walter has worked in tourism and managed large hotel properties in Arkansas and Gatlinburg, Tennessee. Deborah is an English professor at the historically black Arkansas Baptist College in Little Rock. We are close friends and neighbors.

As a child, I showed a natural gift for music. I started playing the piano by ear at the age of four. I was overweight at the age of six and endured kids' bullying, but I was basically happy. I was competitive, welcomed leadership opportunities, enjoyed meeting people of different races, and had a strong theological bent.

Church was the center of our lives. I walked into the kitchen one morning and told mother I was going to heaven that day. She worried I had a premonition about the dreaded polio epidemic and said, "Oh Carolyn Ann, don't say that!" I'd heard so many sermons about "human beans" (I later understood my father was saying human *beings*) enjoying eternal life that it sounded like a happy place. My siblings and I played church instead of playing house.

My maternal grandparents, E.J. and Georgia Boswell of Kentucky, gave our family a piano as my sister and I began lessons. Going to church to practice was inconvenient and having a piano at home meant I could play for hours. Daddy and Mother took great pride of our musical talents and asked us to perform when friends visited.

I also had an early interest in acting. I sometimes went to Mr. Woodard's carpentry shop with daddy when he worked on furniture. Woodard was a short man with a scruffy beard and had an under-bite in his lower jaw that moved in a funny way as he talked. I practiced making that same expression. I also noticed the overbite of our Sunday school teacher, Miss Philpot. I remember looking in the mirror-finish stainless-steel toaster on our kitchen table and making faces as I impersonated this pair. Mother and Daddy chuckled at my talents. I sometimes went to my bedroom after supper, stood on a small stool in front of a mirror so I could see myself. Then I'd put a *Little Golden Books* record on the small record player nearby and listen to the story. I looked in the mirror and tears welled up as I listened to the sad story. What a dramatic little girl I was, already showing glimpses of the future stage and opera performer I'd become.

Clarksville introduced me to the racial tensions. My sister and I became friends with a black man, Junior, who lived behind the Hobbs' house and walked his cow to town some days. Henry who lived next door commented, "Here comes a chocolate milkshake walking a cow." Muriel Hobbs said, "One day we're going to find a cross burning on our front lawn" because of our being friendly to Junior. Oscar Hobbs also had a black shoeshine man named Chicken who worked at his barber shop, and I liked chatting with him. I learned then about the Ku Klux Klan activities around the country. The activities were particularly strong in neighboring Mississippi where the White Citizens Council and the Klan worked against the Student Nonviolent Coordinating Committee, and where the murders of young Emmit Till and civil rights activist Medgar Evers were highly publicized. There were whispers of fear and unrest across the south about race.

While Dad was pastor of First Baptist Church, Clarksville, he worked alongside the carpenters to build our Gothic-style church. When I sang at a church anniversary as an adult, one of the members told me as they were remodeling the sanctuary, they found Dad's scrawled note on a beam over the baptistery, "God, I love this place." I was midway through third grade when we moved. I had no idea what the new city would be like, but I hoped so much they would have a Peach Festival like Clarksville had every summer. After we moved, I asked someone, "When is your Peach Festival?" The person looked at me quizzically and answered, "We don't have a Peach Festival. But we do have a big

Cotton Carnival in Memphis every year." I learned that West Memphis was considered a stepsister to the big city of Memphis just across the Mississippi River. The Delta was certainly a change from the Ozarks.

We moved to West Memphis in 1954 for Dad to pastor First Baptist Church. The town was home to Southland Greyhound Park, a dog racing track. Gambling was rampant and people came from all over the south to the races. Word had it that people came from Memphis to West Memphis to do their "dirty work." There was an uncomfortable crime rate in the town. As we drove across the bridge into Memphis, we passed large cotton fields dotted by ramshackle farm worker houses. Cotton was king and a farmer with a great deal of land could become very wealthy indeed.

I accompanied our junior high choir and the director Mr. Lindenmeyer told me about a piano competition at the Arkansas State Band festival in Hot Springs, Arkansas and suggested I enter. My piano teacher helped me select a Haydn Sonata to perform. Riding on the school bus with the band to Arkansas's popular tourist town was an adventure. We stayed at lake cottages, saw the famous Hot Springs bathhouses, and visited Hot Springs High School for the festival. I didn't know then that my future was about to change. I would soon meet my new neighbor who would become my best friend and future President of the United States, Bill Clinton.

"We're Moving!"

Walking back home across the street from school after the Hot Springs music competition, my little sister Deborah raced up the sidewalk, shouting, "We're moving! We're moving!" I looked at her through exhausted eyes. I was tired from the trip but still jubilant after receiving a gold medal and judge's praise which was a boost to my self-esteem and future hopes of being a concert pianist. This news as I arrived, still on a cloud, was a real setback. Deborah was excited, but I felt as though my world was ending. My best girlfriends lived here and we'd already planned our lives.

The largest Baptist church in Hot Springs had called Dad to be their pastor. We would move in the summer of 1961 for him to lead Second Baptist Church, and

I would begin my sophomore year at Hot Springs High School in the fall. It never occurred to me to protest. This was a serious decision made after much consideration. My disappointment would heal with time. We would adjust to this new adventure. It seemed a bit uncanny that we were moving to Hot Springs, the city where I had competed and heard a concert performance with Bill Clinton performing.

I grew so much in these years in West Memphis. Music was my passion and I dreamed of a concert career. I ran for Student Council and won school contests for magazine and PTA membership sales. I won essay and poster competitions and Bible memory contests as well. Music, student government and a competitive streak gave me good self-esteem and an identity.

My father said, "When your mother dies, she won't go to heaven, she'll go to Memphis!" Mondays were days free from lunch preparation because Dad had Rotary Club. So she went to Memphis with friends and Goldsmith's was her favorite department store. She found beautiful clothes for us, and also bought us Madam Alexander "Cissette" dolls for Christmas.

Dad laughed and said, "We're graduating from dog racing in West Memphis to horse racing in Hot Springs." Our family was moving on to "big time" gambling. We didn't know yet about the Vapors and Southern Club, about slot machines and organized crime, nor that my father, as the newly-elected president of the Arkansas Baptist Convention, would lead opposition to gambling, making this a stressful time in his life and ministry. We certainly had no idea that our future next-door neighbor would be Bill Clinton and that his mother Virginia would be a racetrack fan, going to the races nearly every day and often winning the "daily double."

As the moving van pulled away from our home in West Memphis, we left behind a new parsonage, special friends of a lifetime, the thrill of living near Memphis, and opportunities to attend major concerts. We left the Mississippi Delta and culture, the Cotton Carnival, hayrides along the levee, and cotton fields, and headed into the unknown.

[1] *The Traveling Church*, Center for Baptist Heritage & Studies, Richmond, Virginia, 2007

CHAPTER ONE

My New Neighbor, Bill Clinton

The doorbell rang, and I answered the door. Standing there was a tall, good-looking guy I'd heard so much about. He was now my new neighbor. We hadn't met yet, but I remembered seeing him outside geometry class as I stopped for a drink at the water fountain. I remembered him chatting with a friend nearby, suddenly looking my way. He had raised his voice and said, "And *she's* going to be my new neighbor." It was slightly indirect as a first interaction. He didn't approach me to speak but wanted me to hear what he said.

Now, he was standing in front of me, looking at me through the screen door. The classmate I'd wanted to meet was *right there*. I was slightly stunned to see him, and my mind raced for a second. His presence at my door was so unexpected that I was unprepared for a personal introduction. I was excited to see him face-to-face, and while I was self-confident, I was also at a momentary loss. Why was he here?

I hadn't dwelled on it, but I was curious to meet this classmate. I had wondered how, when, and where I would meet this guy I'd heard so much about. Now, he was standing there, right in front of me. I didn't have to hope for an introduction or wonder any longer about meeting him. He was at my door.

He shouldn't have had to come to our door to meet. I hoped my mother had been over to greet the Clintons and welcome them. We were also new to the neighborhood, but it was customary to say hello to new neighbors and deliver homemade muffins or brownies. Mother hadn't told me if she'd done it.

He smiled slightly, probably as unsure about our first meeting as I was. I hoped I looked ok. I smiled, opened the door, said hello, and invited him in.

We stood at the door to talk, and he got directly to the point. "Hi, I'm your new neighbor. I have a favor to ask. I need a piano accompanist for my saxophone solos at the state band competition. I wondered if you would be my accompanist."

Sure, I'll be happy to," I said, feeling a tad nervous because I'd never accompanied an instrumental soloist. But I felt sure I'd manage. We agreed it would be easy, as he could just come over to practice any time.

We both breathed, smiled, and seemed pleased to have this new partnership in place. The conversation started to flow more easily. We talked about when we might begin, and he said he'd bring the music over for me to practice.

Life is funny. You think about things you hope will happen. You wonder about when, where, and how—and then, in an instant, the moment comes. You open the door. If you are lucky, the answer is in front of you. It was for me. I met Billy Clinton.

ɛ ɞ

Hot Springs: Beauty, Friends, Segregation

Our family's move to Hot Springs gave us a beautiful new hometown. Hot Springs National Park still offers a verdant landscape nestled by surrounding Hot Springs Mountain, North Mountain, and West Mountain, beautiful old hotels, scenic vistas, and the steam rising off the thermal display springs on Bath House Row. It was the first National Park named by Congress in 1921 and the first natural area designated by Congress in 1832 for preservation.[1]

The observation tower atop Hot Springs Mountain overlooks the forested mountains. Its museum includes an exhibit about Bill Clinton, filled with memorabilia I lent the city. I loved the beautiful, bricked Promenade that stretched from the Arlington Hotel to the end of Bathhouse Row and the men playing checkers at concrete game tables along the way. Shiny cars idled near mineral spring fountains where people filled jugs with steaming water. It was like no other place I'd been. Hot Springs differed from the Arkansas Delta in nearly every imaginable way: the flatland of the delta was no match for the undulating landscape of Hot Springs, and the rural, small towns of the delta could not compete with the urban feel of Hot Springs.

My new hometown was rich with the cosmopolitan accents of visitors from all over the world. I often asked my mother to let me walk the short distance from high school along the promenade to the Arlington Hotel before picking me up after school. I heard people from Europe and other parts of the USA sitting and chatting on the veranda. I went to the Tack Room Grill on the ground floor for a pink lemonade. I sat in the writing rooms off the lobby with ornate walnut "partner desks" (and hotel stationary) to do my homework. I felt regal in the splendor of the grand old hotel. Later, I strolled along Central Avenue and visited the imported foods delicatessen with strange offerings like chocolate-covered ants.

Lake Hamilton, Lake Ouachita, and Lake Catherine, just outside town, added to the beauty. Camping, picnicking, fishing, and hiking were all new options for us. Boating and water skiing were friends' favorite pastimes, and invitations to spend afternoons on party barges made Hot Springs seem more promising. We had a steady stream of out-of-town friends coming to visit, and my mother became a seasoned tour guide as she showed guests all the beauty.

We settled into the church parsonage. It was lovely but not as special as the newer one in West Memphis. While it is now the practice of churches to allow their pastor to purchase a home, it was routine at that time for churches to have a parsonage. Our family couldn't afford to buy a home to fit our needs. The parsonage was a ranch-style house at the corner of Wheatley and Scully Streets. It had three bedrooms, but we'd enjoyed four in West Memphis. We wouldn't have a guest room, and kids would need to share rooms. Lynda and I were assigned the primary bedroom with a bath and large closets. My brother Walter and sister Deborah shared a room until I went to college three years later.

Most of the time, I was home, practicing piano for hours, doing homework, and helping my mother with housework. Living in the parsonage meant being ready for church members to drop by unannounced, so we kept the house spotless. We enjoyed TV in the evenings and Saturday mornings. Dick Clark's Dance Party was a favorite when Dad wasn't home. He didn't approve because of Baptist views against dancing. Being in a Baptist pastor's family was not easy. Church members could be critical. Shopping, movies, or fishing in the creek were unthinkable for us on Sundays. We children tried to keep life as easy as possible for our parents.

Undoubtedly, raising a family of four teenagers was difficult, especially as a Baptist pastor. Rock and Roll was in full swing. Elvis, Chuck Berry, Jerry Lee Lewis, and all the gyrating hips on the screen were big distractions. Dancing wasn't allowed, but we loved the music. In high school, I went to sock hops at Lee School after ballgames to be with friends. I served on the decorating committee for our Junior Prom at the Arlington Hotel and attended but didn't dance.

There were only three houses on Wheatley Street. The Shuberts lived across from us in a house where high school friend Mike Thomas lived later. Mike was one of those who would pay the ultimate sacrifice in Vietnam. Mr. Wheatley lived up the hill and behind his house was a small pond where my brother Walter, Roger Jr., and Will Shubert fished. Our dog, Missy, always tagged along. A creek nearby at the corner of 7th Street provided fun for Walter and Deborah as they fished for crawdads and imagined they were in a faraway place.

During the summer of 1961, a new house sprung up next door to ours, just around the corner on Scully Street. As I later learned, it was a speculation house and would be the new home for the Clintons, who were moving from the Hot Springs downtown resort district. It was called a "Gold Medallion" home and had an insignia on the steps to note the electrical futuristic furnishings. Somedays after the crew left, I walked through to explore and see the built-in vacuuming system and latest appliances. The large pink master bath had a luxurious sunken bathtub, a seated vanity with wall-to-wall mirrors, and an enclosed toilet.

Across from our carport was a lot that Mr. Wheatley planted with peonies. The field supplied local florists and was a marvel to see around Mother's Day, when it exploded with pink, deep rose, and white peony blooms. We posed for pictures with the flowers every year.

Many other friends lived on Scully Street: Mike Karber, the Hassin family including Guido, Anna Ruth, Florice, Teresa and Alberta, Millie Weger, John Wilson, and others. We enjoyed the Hassin's parties when Woodrow cooked for days to prepare a feast. Their garage sometimes housed a garage band. The Hassins and Karbers were next-door neighbors. The Karbers spent their free time reading. Michael Karber was very smart and my sister's boyfriend. The Hassin family was outgoing. Woodrow Hassin was a chef, and Gina was a stay-at-home mom. Gina was Italian, and Mr. Hassin was Syrian. The Hassin kids were brilliant. Guido earned his doctorate in biology. He died tragically of cancer as a young adult and left his wife, Valerie Neal, and son, Bryan Guido. Dr. Valerie Neal, Guido's widow, retired in 2020 as the curator of Space History at the National Air and Space Museum of the Smithsonian Institution. She helped develop the Udvar Hazy Center at Dulles International Airport in VA in 2003 with exhibits, including the Space Shuttle Discovery, the Enola Gay, and the Gemini 7 space capsule. Our son Will was an intern design assistant at the Air and Space Museum in Valerie's office. He assisted with graphic design for the Udvar Hazy Center and designed the exhibit cart for education specialists.

Uppermost in my mind that summer of 1961 as a newcomer to Hot Springs was getting ready to enter Hot Springs High School in the fall. The school had a large student body, about 900 students, sophomores through seniors. It was a magnificent school built in 1914 in the Late Gothic Revival style. Hallways teemed with students visiting along the railings of the open stairwell between classes, looking over four levels. Light flooded the building from rooftop windows. Open classroom windows let breezes into the un-air-conditioned rooms. The front entrance was imposing, and the sidewalk featured a large painting of our school mascot, a Trojan warrior. The rule was that no one walked across the Trojan head. Lance's sandwich shop across the street was a favorite for lunch during our 40-minute lunch break, and others walked to the Club Café. The cafeteria also provided a full lunch at 50 cents. After lunch, we often sat on the edge of the stage in the auditorium to sing folk songs that I accompanied on my ukulele. *The Cruel War is Raging*, and *Michael Row the Boat Ashore* were favorites. Our teachers were true professionals, and several older women were lifelong teachers. We had younger teachers, too, who added a youthful balance and energy.

I wanted to meet as many people as possible so that I could feel at home before the start of school in only two months. I was keenly aware that I needed to meet people quickly to integrate with the school community fully. As I'd done in West Memphis, I aspired to run for student council. Knowing student leaders would help me get involved faster, so I signed up for every activity I could that summer to meet friends and get a head start on having a successful school year.

School and Church Segregation and Race Relations

Hot Springs High School and all Arkansas schools were segregated. The 1957 Little Rock Central High School crisis led to the integration of all Arkansas schools, but school districts had ten years to develop an integration plan. Second Baptist Church, one of the largest churches in town with 2500 members, was segregated as well, as were most churches at the time. However, future school integration plans made churches concerned they might face integration first, and churches began to discuss how to handle it.

Our church held a business meeting to discuss the hypothetical issue of seating Blacks who wanted to come to worship. While the situation had not arisen, demonstrations were happening across the south, and churches were steeling themselves to prepare. There were occasional city-wide race relations worship services, but they weren't the norm. Churches all over town were asking the question: "Should we seat Black people who come to church to worship with us?"

As a high school teen, I sat near the back of the sanctuary for the discussion. My father moderated and had not shared his opinion beforehand. He asked anyone wishing to speak to stand and voice their opinion. There were no heated outbursts, for which I was thankful, and I know my dad was too. Most comments focused on the question of the "true desire" to worship as opposed to the visitors wishing to make a statement about race. Some people said they would hate to see our church in that public limelight, but since we were the largest church in town, we would likely be a target. It was a difficult discussion, and tension hung in the air.

After everyone spoke, I raised my hand to be recognized. A gnawing discomfort had been growing as I listened to the debate. I'd never spoken at a business meeting before. My father, seeing my raised hand, called on me. "Carolyn Ann," he said, "do you have something you'd like to say?"

"Yes, I would like to speak, thank you." I spoke quietly and calmly. "I would just like to say that this doesn't seem right. I can't imagine a church turning people away, regardless of their race. Most of all, I can't imagine that Jesus would turn anyone away from a worship service. Haven't we been taught that Christ's message is for everyone? And that Jesus loves everyone? And it isn't our place to judge a person's motivation for coming to worship. No one asks each of us that question. We're taught that only God knows our hearts. I just would hate for our church to be known as a place where anyone is unwelcome to come and experience God's love." Then I sat down. I remember my father looking down for a few moments, and then he looked up and said with a slight smile, "Thank you, Carolyn Ann." I hoped he'd been proud of me. Then he asked if anyone else had anything further to add. Seeing no hands, the vote was taken. I believe I was the only vote in favor of seating Black visitors.

Our classmate David Leopolous' family belonged to St. Luke Episcopal Church, where members discussed integration as well. His mother, Evelyn, spoke up to say she was dismayed that the question had even arisen for discussion. "If you have to vote on this matter, I don't need to be at this church." We were all troubled that churches were having these complex discussions. But churches were, after all, simply microcosms of our larger community and reflected the time in which we lived. Sadly, the primary guiding principle was fear of change, fear of what a new society would look like, and fear of what the future might bring.

Years later, when our family lived in Little Rock in the early 1980s, we were members of the integrated Second Baptist Church downtown. We also had women deacons, women ministers, and a full array of social outreach programs for the poor, elderly, and marginalized. My Dad came to worship one Sunday evening, and the pastor called on him for the benediction. Before he prayed, he recalled that one of his favorite college professors at Ouachita Baptist University had been a pastor at Second Baptist, and he spoke of the impact he made on my Dad's life as a budding pastor. He said something I had never heard him say. "Surely this church is an example of what Christ meant for a church to be, a church open to all people." I believed then that I had seen my father's heart and knew that he felt our Hot Springs church should have faced integration. The issue never arose, but I was grateful to hear him speak these words.

"You need to meet Billy Clinton for sure."

As the summer went on, I researched people I needed to get to know. I inquired about who the popular school leaders were and why. "You need to meet Billy Clinton for sure," I was often told. He was a leader, interested in music, an outstanding student, and very popular. He was active in student government, popular with all the students, and well-rounded. He was a band member. I also heard he was popular with girls. It sounded like we had interests in common, especially music, and I hoped our paths would cross.

Many people were on my list to get to know, mostly girls my age. I joined Pep Squad to meet classmates, and many became new lifelong friends, including Claire, Mauria, Anne, Kenny, Mary Jo, Glenda, Gail, and others. I also met David Leopoulos, Ron Cecil, and Joe Newman, who were good buddies with Billy Clinton and provided great comic relief. Students dressed nicely for school. Girls wore skirts or dresses, sweater sets, loafers or oxfords, and the guys wore jeans and shirts, loafers, and usually white socks. There wasn't a dress code, but we followed the popular teen fashion trends we saw in *Glamour* and *Seventeen* magazines.

I hoped to get involved quickly in the school music program. I auditioned as a piano accompanist for the 350-voice Trojan Chorus and was selected. I was assistant pianist in my sophomore year and principal accompanist during my junior and senior years. Our choral director was a dynamic woman, Dora Jane Ledgerwood Ellis. DJ, as we knew her, was a short, blonde powerhouse who wore beautiful clothes and signature rhinestone eyeglass frames. She was a Hot Springs native trained as a classical singer in New York City. She studied voice with opera diva Marjorie Lawrence of the Metropolitan Opera, who made Hot Springs her home while convalescing from polio. DJ was a true professional and musically demanding. She selected challenging pieces, ranging from classical works to musical theater and pops. The school also had smaller auditioned choral groups I accompanied, the female Troubadours and the male Toreadors.

In my sophomore spring of 1961, my geometry class was about to begin, and teacher Miss Burma Bryan was standing in the doorway waiting for the bell to ring. I was at the water fountain for a quick drink before class when Bill and a friend were standing nearby. As they talked, Bill raised his voice, turned toward me, and said, "And *she's* going to be my next-door neighbor." I looked his way (I don't remember responding), but I acknowledged I heard him and went on into class. I hadn't met Bill yet, but I clearly remember that moment and wonder what it might mean for my life. I had a strong hunch this was going to be a game-changer. Now I knew who my new neighbors would be: Billy Clinton and his family.

Bill said, "And she's going to be my next-door neighbor."

The Clintons' move in the spring of 1962 took place almost without notice. Virginia and her sons Billy and Roger, Jr. were our new neighbors. I didn't meet them right away as we had been traveling when they moved in. Spring and summer for us always meant trips to the Southern Baptist Convention location, a trip to Owensboro, KY, to see my maternal grandparents, Edward and Georgia Boswell, and also church youth camp.

We began to learn more about the Clinton family. Not long after Virginia, Bill, and Roger Jr. moved in, my mother noticed Virginia's former husband, Roger, sitting in his Buick out front and saw Virginia go out to sit with him. Eventually, they reconciled, and Roger moved into the house with the family. Virginia was surprised and hurt to learn that Roger didn't actually own their house on Park Avenue in Hot Springs but rented it from his brother. They'd moved there from Hope, and Roger began working with his brother Raymond at Clinton Buick Company. Bill was a first-grader at St. John's Catholic School. Finding out they didn't own their home made her feel financially insecure and eroded her trust in Roger. She asked for a divorce and moved to her new home with her sons. Soon, Roger rejoined the family.

I first remember meeting Bill when he came to our house one afternoon and asked if I'd accompany his saxophone solos. I told him I'd be happy to. Bill had heard me play piano accompaniments for the choral programs at school, and I hoped he had been favorably impressed. At least he felt I had the skills to accompany his band solos. The state band competition was coming up, the same annual event I'd attended from West Memphis while in Junior High. He gave me the music for his solo, and we began to rehearse. I was initially nervous, but the music was not too difficult, and I enjoyed the new friendship. I was, after all, still getting acquainted in a big school. And Bill was one of the guys I'd been told I needed to know.

I met Virginia for the first time when Bill invited me over. Her appearance stunned me because her makeup and hair were unlike anything I'd seen. She had a white streak in the front center of her short black hair, perfectly coiffed, teased, and sprayed. Her eyebrows were drawn with a soft silver-gray pencil and applied in a high, pointed arch. She wore false eyelashes. Her upper lid had black liner. Her skin was flawless and creamy. She used bright red lipstick to match her fingernails and toenails. She was striking and glamorous.

She wore a crisply starched nurses' uniform to work, and I never saw her in scrubs.

I also met "Little Roger," as Bill's family and friends called him, to distinguish him from his dad, Roger Clinton, Sr. Ten years younger than Bill, he was a handsome boy and pleasant to be around. Bill was his caregiver after school before Virginia or Roger got home. Virginia worked early morning surgeries at Ouachita Hospital or St. Joseph Hospital, so she left home early.

Roger was always with Bill and his friends. Roger joined in any activity we were enjoying if he wanted to and went with us to the movies or to run errands. I remember going with Bill and Roger to the Arlington Hotel Park for the annual Christmas pageant, to movies, and being together many times.

Roger enjoyed outside adventures with friends in the neighborhood. He played with my sister and brother, Deborah and Walter, and they fished in the nearby creek or at the Wheatley's pond. They found crawdads or mudbugs and had a great time outdoors. One day, Deborah went over to see if Roger could play. He didn't answer the door, but after several doorbell rings, he appeared at his bedroom window. The window was high, and he balanced his footing on his headboard to look out. Deb kept asking him to come play, and he kept mouthing something Deb couldn't understand. He finally yelled at her at the top of his lungs, "I can't come outside. I have diarrhea!" He tried so hard to be discreet.

Any discussion of the Clinton family must include their German Shepherds. The first was named King, who spent time both inside and outdoors. He was gentle and loved by all the neighbor kids. The Clintons added other German Shepherds named Prince and Duke to the household through the years. The dogs frequently joined backyard touch football games, romping and playing with Bill and Roger.

Bill's faith has always been central to his life

The Clintons weren't regular church attenders, but from childhood, Bill was allowed to go if he desired. As a boy, he attended Park Place Baptist Church when his family lived on Park Avenue. At age 9, he decided to be a Christian and was baptized there. Friend Bert Jeffries, who later died in Vietnam, was baptized at the same service. The guys had a memorable baptism as the woman baptized before them had a near-sinking experience. As Rev. Fitzgerald lowered her into the water, her foot flew up and caught on the glass splash guard that protected the choir below. It took a while for the pastor to free her, but all ended well. It provided a moment of comic relief for Bill and Bert as they nervously awaited their turn.

☙ ❧

Throughout our years of friendship, it became clear that Bill's faith was as important to him as mine was to me. While he didn't talk about it much or get heavily involved in the church except for choir, his faith was a solid underpinning in his decision-making and leadership.

As this memoir of our friendship unfolds, many faith-related experiences interlace the decades. Both of us are progressive Christians and believe that following Jesus means adhering to his teachings to care for the poor and downtrodden, the sick, naked, hungry, and the immigrant. It means a life that flows from love rather than hate, judgment, and intolerance. Our Christian church experiences spanned from liturgical Catholicism to spirit-filled Pentecostalism, from white churches we attended to African American celebrations, from tent revivals with sawdust floors to vaulted cathedrals.

Faith is a source of strength and comfort for us and our families. Music favorites reflect Bill's faith, and he often listens for peace and comfort. My life as a preacher's kid meant that faith and prayer came naturally. It became more apparent in our adult years that we shared this source of strength. We regularly interacted with Jewish friends, a few Buddhists, Christian Science, and other faith traditions and respected all faith backgrounds. I was a temple soloist for 35 years, taught in a Catholic university, was music director in a Lutheran church, and later was a Methodist minister. We have been enriched as we have shared faith in our friendship.

I was welcome anytime, whether they were home or not.

Bill's house eventually became my home away from home. Virginia told me I was welcome anytime, whether they were home or not. Any time I could steal away from my house chores, I'd go next door. Sometimes no one was home. If the garage door was up and the kitchen door was open, I knew I was welcome.

I enjoyed walking next door, just looking around and learning more about Bill and his family. I was fascinated because they were unlike anyone I knew. Bill was gifted, poised, mature, and talented, and I was curious to know him better. I was amazed that my neighbor had a common interest in music and leadership. But I also knew we lived in different worlds.

The Clinton's home was a ranch design. It had a long living and dining room along the front of the house. The paneled kitchen and family room spanned the back of the house, mirroring the living and dining room. The family room had two recliners facing the television. A TV and shelves for books filled the back wall. Off the den was a patio where Virginia sunbathed. Later the Clintons enclosed the patio to make a pool room for Roger.

A long hallway led from the den to the bedrooms. Bill's room was the primary bedroom, the largest of the three with a shower. Virginia wanted the large pink bathroom, so they gave Bill the primary bedroom. His furnishings were a double bed, dresser, desk, and a music stand for saxophone practice. A large closet held his school wardrobe, a suit for dress-up, and his band uniform. He had one pair of black dress shoes and one pair of brown dress shoes. Once he was invited to a friend's wedding out of town and arrived with one brown shoe and one black shoe. I never heard how he managed it, but it sure gave his mother a laugh. Bill had a black and gold Trojan winter coat, longer than a football letter jacket. Virginia took my picture once with Bill wearing that coat and me in a red double-breasted jacket that we got at Ripley's Factory outside Memphis, a favorite coat-shopping spot. I treasure that photo.

The Clinton's living room furnishings were comfortable, with a sofa and a couple of upholstered chairs. A chest stood against the foyer wall with a large portrait of Bill over it. Later Virginia framed Bill's band medals and hung them next to his portrait. Friends called this spot "the shrine." Virginia redecorated the living room with red and black velvet Mediterranean-style furniture. Above the sofa hung a large frame with stallion heads on a black and red velvet background. Roger and I visited one day and I remarked that the living room had been redecorated. He said, "Mother chose this furniture so Bill and I wouldn't fight over it when she dies!" The décor matched Virginia's flair perfectly.

The dining area, where we sat to play cards and do homework, had a teak Danish-modern table and upholstered chairs. A matching china cabinet with a sliding glass top section stood against the wall. A second cabinet for silver had a large mirror over it, and this cabinet is where I first saw the Bible displayed with the name "William Jefferson Blythe" engraved on the front. I didn't know Bill had another surname. Was this my friend Bill? I knew him only as Billy Clinton. Later, I learned about his father's death in a car accident as he was traveling home to Hope from Chicago in May 1946. His automobile tire blew out on a wet road near Sikeston, Missouri. He was thrown from the car into a drainage ditch filled with water and drowned at age 28 before Bill was born in August. Bill started using the Clinton name in grade school, making it legal as a teen. He initiated the adoption and went to the courthouse to apply. The courthouse staff called Virginia for her approval. Bill told her he thought it would be easier for Roger and everyone else if they had the same last name.

Beneath the dining room picture window was a stereo with a section for albums. Overflow records leaned against the wall. The living/dining room was so long that Bill put his new Christmas golf putting green there to practice. The entire house had beige carpet and walls.

The house's exterior was orange brick with white trim and black wrought iron columns at the front door. The garage door had a basketball hoop above the door, and Bill spent his free time shooting baskets. Climbing red roses trailed up the wrought iron columns at the front. Virginia also planted rose bushes around the back patio. My sister Deborah, age 10, pulled her red Radio Flyer wagon up the street to the Housley's horse barn for manure for Virginia's roses. She made a dollar a load and felt rich. Virginia spent many happy hours tending her roses while sunning in her tube top and shorts. Bill and Roger mowed the lawn. Virginia stayed tan and in good shape. I marveled at the deep, beautiful tan she achieved with her olive complexion. She used tanning lotions although I don't think we knew much yet about SPF numbers. She was always health conscious.

My father trimmed the high hedge that separated our properties. There was a narrow pathway between the hedge and the Clinton's house. My dad stood on a step ladder to trim the hedge and would spot Virginia tending her roses in her tube top and shorts. They'd have a good chat. My Dad often said, "The first sign of spring isn't the robin. It's Virginia working in her yard!"

He said, "No, just keep it. We'll get around to playing it someday."

I got to know Bill better as our sophomore year rolled along. He performed with our high school band, the Pep Band, at ball games, pre-game parades, and in the Stardusters stage band. I thought my friend Candace "Kenny" Maschmeyer was lucky to be the Starduster soloist and perform *My Funny Valentine*. Bill conducted the band as a senior when he was Band Major. He was naturally gifted and took band seriously.

One of the band appearances was the annual Hot Springs Christmas parade. The Hot Springs High School band marched in the parade, as did the all-Black Langston High School band. The Langston drum section alone was worth going to the parade to hear. Their drum cadences were rhythmic and catchy, syncopated and lively. We could hardly wait for them to come by. They had the crowd dancing.

Bill also led the Trojan Pep Band in parades through the Hot Springs business district on Central Avenue before football games. The Pep Band's white jumpsuits and Bill leading the way sporting a giant sombrero were a sight to behold. They were great musicians and fired up the crowd before games. David Leopoulos, not a Pep Band member but a friend who sat with Bill and the band, came up with a cheer for the football team when the game was particularly gruesome. The band would start the cheer: "Mary had a little lamb, its fleece was white as snow, and everywhere that Mary went, GO TROJANS GO!" They'd break into peals of hysterical laughter. Sadly, our Trojan team was pretty terrible and suffered losses except for one memorable victory in our junior year, thanks to team stars Phil Jamison and Jim French.

Bill and I became closer friends through high school and bonded through our love for music. We were naturally competitive and always wanted to win top honors in the solo competitions at the state band festival. I competed in the solo piano competition and accompanied Bill in his saxophone solo competition. As the competition ended, we both watched for the scores and were elated when either of us earned a first-place gold medal. One year, Bill checked the scores and tracked me down to excitedly report that I was awarded first place for the Chopin *Polonaise Militaire* and was very proud of me. He'd gotten a first place, too.

It was convenient to be next door to Bill and be able to practice anytime. He just walked over with his saxophone, and we played whatever he wanted to practice until he settled on a piece for the competition. Director Virgil Spurlin helped Bill select pieces to showcase his talent. Many were transcriptions for saxophone from classical literature. He always played very well. Years later,

I found his music to *Rhapsody in Blue* for saxophone and piano and offered to return it. He said, "No, just keep it. We'll get around to playing it someday." It's still in my music chest.

Bill won the coveted First Chair position for the tenor sax in the Arkansas All-State Band. It meant he was the best in the state and section leader. Through band, Bill amassed a wealth of friends who later became election supporters. Once, when he was president and planning a trip, a White House staff member called to ask if a name sounded familiar. Someone who lived where the president was traveling heard he'd be there and wanted to see him. The person claimed they knew the president from Arkansas Band Camp. I didn't recognize the name but felt confident no one would make that up.

I kept some of my band competition score sheets, comments, and the judge's critiques that were helpful to me. Playing the piano was something I'd taken for granted since elementary school. I had much to learn about music besides memorizing notes, including theory, musical form, and analysis. I grew tremendously as a musician through the band contests.

A friendly competition raged among band members about who had the most gold medals. Letha Ann Wooldridge was Bill's main competition. They had a running battle about who could earn the most. The medals were pinned to the band uniform front, and it was impressive when a student had many of them. Pianists just stored them away. Bill amassed an extensive collection. A funny experience happened when a new academically-competitive student decided to wear to school medals he had earned at the Colorado School of Mines. Not to be outdone, Bill and Letha Ann wore their medals to school the next day. It was hilarious. We hoped the new student was not offended; it was all in good fun.

Bill loved to read piano music. Many days after we practiced, Bill would sit next to me, and we'd play and sing about anything we could think of. He played the melody, and I filled in the bass harmonies. Bill had an excellent ear for music and could play almost anything.[2] He also loved to sing *The Green, Grass of Home* recorded by Tom Jones. My mother would sing along with us and cry. At our local music shop, I found music for Dave Brubeck's *Take Five* album, and we enjoyed these pieces for saxophone and piano. Bill loved to play *Blue Rondo a la Turk*, and we proudly tackled the complicated five-beat measures in *Take Five*.

Bill and I both loved soul music. Bill collected every Ray Charles and Nancy Wilson album he could find, and we listened to them for hours. I have albums by Stan Getz and Judy Collins he gave me. Bill also loved symphonic band works written by Ouachita University composer Francis McBeth, who conducted the state festival band. I heard them play *Chant and Jubilo* in 1964, and it was thrilling. Bill loved *Crown Imperial* by American composer William Walton and had a recording of Dvorak's *New World Symphony* that we nearly wore out. Music was always playing, whether on his stereo or in my living room, with saxophone solos and piano singalongs.

"I did it! I beat McDougal on a math test!"

After school hours, Bill did homework and practiced the saxophone. His light often shone late at night as he studied. He wanted to make the top grade in every subject and was willing to go the extra mile to rise to the top. Other students were naturally gifted in some classes, but that inspired Bill to work harder. Math and science sometimes gave him a challenge, and some whiz kids pushed him. Virginia said Bill came home one day exclaiming, "I did it! I beat McDougal on a math test!" Jim McDougal was brilliant at trigonometry and calculus and Bill was not happy until he topped Jim's test score.

Bill loved Lonnie Warneke's Honors English class. A young teacher fresh out of college, she took the class on a field trip to Jasper, Arkansas, which was Bill's first experience seeing parts of rural Arkansas. He also took physics taught by Thural Youngblood, a new teacher from Grannis who had a thick country accent. Youngblood peppered his teaching with colloquialisms that made us double over in laughter, but we mastered the basics.

Bill's world history teacher, Paul Root, was a wonderful man who later served as Bill's education advisor when he was governor. My history teacher was Phillip Leasure and our honors class was held in Lee School, a former elementary school that provided overflow classrooms. My classmate, Tommy Young, was a poet and sent missives down the aisle to me. He was later killed in Vietnam.

Bill's foreign language class was Latin. A photo of him in a Latin class drama seated on a throne in a toga was taken for the yearbook but not published. As a yearbook staffer, I got to keep leftover pictures and grabbed that one as a keepsake. After his presidential election, it disappeared, and I hope it's under lock and key somewhere. Bill also was in the cast of drama department plays including *Arsenic and Old Lace* and *Gentlemen Prefer Blondes*. He liked learning new skills and having fresh opportunities.

Bill and I shared an interest in leadership and served on the Student Council. He was president of the Junior Class, and I was treasurer and senior class secretary. He was president of the Latin Junior Classical League, vice president of Math Club, and president of Beta Club as a senior. He was elected Band Major and was a student conductor for concerts. It was a well-accepted fact that no one was a better-rounded student than Bill Clinton, and I did my best to keep up the pace.

I heard my Dad's voice, "Carolyn Ann, it's time to come home." We were asleep in our chairs

Bill and I enjoyed spending free time with other friends, including David, Joe, and Ronnie, who were pals since the Clintons lived on Park Avenue. In grade school, they walked to the Polar Bar after school for a treat. Ronnie's dad was the manager, and the guys could order whatever they wanted—usually a chili cheeseburger and a shake. This must've been heaven for them.

After many high school days, friends gathered in Bill's kitchen and watched as he made one of his signature sandwiches. He had three favorites, each starting with cottage rye bread. One was peanut butter with banana slices. Another was with tuna salad, which Virginia kept in the fridge. The third was a hodgepodge creation that started with slices of deli meat and cheese, then a slathering of peanut butter to top it off. We'd never seen such a sandwich. A big glass of milk usually followed. A special treat was a platter of fried pies with fruit filling made by the Clintons' housekeeper. The only food Bill didn't like was chocolate, which started when he was a boy, but he's not sure how it was triggered.

We talked about everything and shared silly jokes. Ronnie Cecil and David Leopoulos kept us in stitches. Ronnie told us about trying on a pair of slacks at a local shop. When the clerk asked how they fit, he said they reminded him of the Velda Rose ballroom. She replied, "The Velda Rose doesn't have a ballroom." Ronnie said, "These pants don't either." We collapsed laughing.

We usually went to the dining table to play hearts or gin rummy. We competed and played to win. Bill was the strategist and kept a mental count of the cards. This ability drove everyone else mad, but it also made everyone a better player. We always had a favorite record on the stereo, too.

Sometimes, on the way home from school or on weekends, Bill and I stopped by the music store to browse through new records. We also watched lots of ten o'clock "Late Show" movies on TV. Bill checked the newspaper to see what was on with a 4-star rating and hoped for a classic. Starting a 2-hour movie that late could sometimes lead to nodding off before the movie ended. One night, I heard a knock on the Clinton's carport door and my Dad's voice calling, "Carolyn Ann, it's time to come home." We were asleep in our chairs. Mother found us asleep watching a late movie in our den, too. She knew the movie should be over, so she checked and found us asleep. The minute she entered, Bill would pop straight out of his chair in a daze and walk home.

We rarely had spending money so staying home was always the best option. No one dated much because our group enjoyed doing things together as friends. Virginia welcomed Bill's friends and visited with us when we were together. She told me later that the reason she loved being with us was that she recognized this was a special group that would remain important in each other's lives. She took pictures and home movies of our antics.

When we did go out to eat, it was usually to the Burger Chef for a fifteen-cent hamburger. We loved barbeque when we could afford it from McClard's or Stubby's. We also enjoyed Cook's Ice Cream parlor with its dozens of homemade flavors. Huge, upholstered booths lined the walls, and each had a jukebox coin box. After Burger Chef, we would go to Putt-Putt for miniature golf. Bill took the game very seriously and worked to perfect his skills. The rest of us just did our best to make a decent score. Sometimes, we went to the bowling lanes nearby, where the guys bowled and gals watched. The boys also played pinball machines and Bill was amazingly good at the games. As governor, he had a pinball machine installed in the basement of the Governor's mansion.

My house was a popular destination for girls interested in Bill. Friends with a crush on him parked near our drive with the car in sight of Bill's window so he could see they were at my house. Soon, we'd hear the backdoor open, and Bill would pop in. My home helped advance several relationships. Two friends who dated Bill during high school were Mary Jo and Mauria. Mary Jo asked Bill to escort her to the Homecoming dance when she was a homecoming maid, and Mauria went with Bill to prom and our graduation party. They both had a great fondness for Bill, and he for them. We remained friends throughout our lives. Mary Jo died of cancer after Bill's presidency. We grieve Mauria's recent death as we recall that she and her husband Bob visited with Bill and other old high school friends when he was in Little Rock. Bill also dated Susan from Benton for a short time. I couldn't believe he drove thirty minutes each way for a movie!

Some wondered why we never were romantically linked, and I think there were several reasons. We had a special friendship, and dating might risk that friendship. My father was a preacher, and I was on some kind of pedestal. I was not little and cute like other coeds. It just wasn't something we explored. Mike Karber told me he thought 'Carolyn Clinton' would be a nice name. But we found we just enjoyed the time as friends. I knew Bill was a big catch. After he was President, one high school coed told a reporter that all mothers secretly hoped their daughters would date Billy Clinton.

Sometimes neighbors Mike Karber and Guido Hassin joined David and Joe for touch football games in Bill's backyard. Band pals Jim Case and Jimmy Walker came over too. The guys enjoyed spending time together. Ron eventually moved to Florida, but David and Joe still live in Little Rock, and we see Bill when he's in town.

In high school, Bill always came over when out-of-town guests visited. I thought even then he was adding potential voters to his Rolodex for future political plans. When my aunt and uncle from Philadelphia visited, he came over, and eventually, everyone turned his way to listen. They commented after he left about what an impressive young man he was. Who knows how many of those he met in the 1960s remembered Bill Clinton in 1992? No doubt he garnered many early votes just by being friendly and meeting everyone possible.

Bill has always been generous. In high school, he gave me nice gifts for Christmas and birthdays, including *Toujours Moi* cologne and a silver musical jewel box. He gave me many records. I still have the Stan Getz and Nancy Wilson albums, Glen Yarbrough's *The Lonely Things*, Richard Harris' *MacArthur Park*, Ray Charles, Judy Collins, and more. Books he gave me included *The Family of Man*, a photo overview of humanity from all walks of life. He also gave me *Let Us Now Praise Famous Men* by Walker Evans and James Agee. It was filled with stunning photos of the Depression captured in 1936 and focusing on the lives of sharecroppers. It helped me understand the hardships the Depression-era poor endured. I gave him books and records, too, including a recording of Robert Frost reading selections from his poetry and Carl Sandburg reading from his work, *Lincoln*. In college, I gave him a sweater and the pale blue necktie and thought I recognized at my wedding years later.

She cautioned me that jealousy is a "green-eyed monster" that would destroy any relationship.

Virginia ran a tight ship at home and made sure her sons were well cared for. She was a proud mom and really doted on them as the light of her life. She attended every school and community activity they were part of.

Virginia became concerned about her husband Roger's drinking as he became abusive. She told me after his death about horrific experiences with his violent anger. People have expressed surprise that I never knew anything about tensions in the Clinton's home, but when Bill and friends got together we never talked about family issues. It became commonplace in later years for friends to share problems, but we simply enjoyed being together. It wasn't avoidance, but it simply wasn't the norm to talk about family problems.

Roger Sr. was often home when I went next door to visit and was always nice to me. He complimented me on the party food I made when Bill and I hosted parties, such as trays of tuna salad sandwiches, crackers and cheese, and other snacks. He said, "Someone is going to be awfully lucky to get you as a wife." I never observed Roger inebriated or hostile when I was in their home. He usually was watching TV with Virginia. "Big Roger," as we knew him, was an alcoholic, and it eventually spilled over into their home life. Roger Jr. once came next door to our house to ask Bill to come home, crying that his dad was going to hurt Virginia. He was so young and frightened. Eventually, the tense family situation settled, and Bill is reported to have warned Roger never to touch his mother again.

Many mornings during racing season, Virginia came home from the hospital to change clothes and head to Oaklawn Race Track. She was always chic and always wore her gold necklaces and charm bracelet filled with tokens, such as the lucky horseshoe with a diamond in the center. She'd hop in her Buick convertible with the top down and go place her bets, never more than $2 each. Mother was in the backyard hanging clothes one morning when she saw Virginia leaving. "Are you going to that old filthy racetrack, Virginia?" Mother called to her. Virginia smiled and waved and shouted back, "Let's just call it a fellowship, Kay, and we'll all be happy!"

While I was in high school, my father was elected President of the Arkansas Baptist Convention. It was a big honor but also brought a new level of stress. He had to balance church ministry and be the leader of the largest denomination in the state. Illegal gambling had exploded in Hot Springs from the mid-1950s to the spring of 1964. Pastors organized to plead with Governor Faubus to end gambling. Faubus had a permissive view of gambling, and it expanded unchecked. The tourism industry argued that businesses would suffer without gambling. From the time Faubus became governor in 1955 until March of 1964, there was no state interference with the Hot Springs casinos or bookie joints. By the early 1960s, as many as 89 different restaurants and clubs were paying the annual city gambling tax, including several fraternal and veterans' organizations. There were over 440 slot machines in operation in the early 1960s. Gambling establishments were supported and run by respected business leaders and even church-goers. Gone were the bad old days of the 1930s when visiting gangsters were regular guests.[3]

Things began to change in the early '60s as the federal government looked into illegal gambling in Hot Springs. Churches that had long opposed gambling added their criticism. Things took a turn when a bomb exploded at the Vapors in January 1963, followed by three additional bombings in later weeks. No one was ever charged, but the primary suspect was an organized crime syndicate from out of state.[4] Voters in 1964 rejected a constitutional amendment to legalize gambling. Dad was leading the fight for Baptists, and it was a tough time for him and our family. We heard there were people praying for my Dad to die. To the best of my knowledge, my parents never had a conversation about this with Virginia, although my Dad's high profile as state Baptist president kept him in the news. Their friendship remained strong, but this was an area of life where there were likely to have been disagreements. Friendship won out.

As Bill was elected Governor of Arkansas and president, my mother, and Virginia shared a sister-like love and great pride in his accomplishments. Virginia also helped my mother through some difficult hospitalizations and illnesses. When Virginia died, my mother drove to Hot Springs to be with Bill,

Roger, Dick, and family. She felt almost like a mother to Bill and Roger and wanted to be a source of strength and comfort.

Through the years and our many visits, Virginia gave me advice on life. She cautioned me about jealousy, calling it a "green-eyed monster" that would destroy any relationship.

Before the era of walk-in nail salons, Virginia showed me how to polish my nails. Her nails were always bright red and perfectly manicured. She also advised that it's a good idea to put your make-up on first thing in the morning and get your hair perfectly coiffed. She said once that's done, you're ready for anything the day brings. As a young boy, Bill used to sit in her bathroom and watch her apply her makeup with great precision.

She once talked with me as an older college student about why she thought it was a good idea sometimes for couples to live together before marriage. She said it was an opportunity to get to know each other and to be sure they were compatible before making the commitment to marry. That was shocking to me, but I listened and processed through my own life lens. As I considered a singing career, Virginia told me I should do whatever was necessary, including living in Europe if required, even leaving my children for a period. I understood this later in terms of her own life and her decision to leave Bill with her parents to study anesthesia in New Orleans. It was a hard decision, but it allowed her to provide for her family and live her career dreams.

She was a strong woman. I loved Virginia, and she became like a second mother to me. As long as I was away from home, I sent her a Mother's Day card addressed to "my other mother." She told me she looked forward to receiving them and how much they meant.

One day, Virginia came by to ask if I'd like to ride to the hospital with her. I asked my mother, grabbed a book to read while I waited, and was happy to get out for a bit. Virginia parked at Ouachita Hospital and went inside. I was reading when a staff member came out to say Virginia wanted me to come inside. I followed him to the operating area, put on surgical scrubs and joined Virginia and the team assisting with a baby delivery. They casually chatted about life while keeping a close eye on the patient. It all stunned me. Why was I here? Was this actually happening? The patient received an anesthesia commonly called "twilight sleep, a standard practice at the time that allowed the mother to help with delivery but not feel pain. The hospital wasn't air-conditioned, and windows were open. I wondered why I hadn't heard the woman's labor pain screams outside in the convertible with the top down.

As we drove home, Virginia asked what I thought of the experience. She said she thought it would be good for me to understand the childbirth delivery process. My mother wasn't so sure this was an appropriate field trip, but no harm was done, and no ill feelings resulted. I remember thinking that seeing the child's birth was an amazing, spiritual, highly unique experience, and I was most grateful. It made me feel a close bond with Virginia. She wanted me to live, learn, and experience life to the fullest. In everything she said and did for me, I knew it was from a heart of love. She didn't have a daughter and she certainly made up for it with me.

As hard as she worked, Virginia was also a wonderful homemaker and mother. She was a good cook and always prepared hot meals for the family. Sometimes, the housekeeper also prepared the evening meal or made fried pies, but Virginia was the chief cook. After dinner, Virginia would disappear to her room to change into tailored, long cotton pajamas and slippers. When she entered the room looking Hollywood glamorous, she'd say, "You know something, nobody has told me all day how cute I am!" This always got a laugh and usually a compliment, too. She'd sit in her favorite den chair, enjoy a cigarette, do her nails, and watch television with the family, then go to bed early, knowing she had surgeries the next morning.

As I spent more time with Virginia, I got to know her better and to love her. She was a remarkable woman. Many days, she came home from work to find Bill's friends gathered at the dining table. She'd toss her purse on a chair and make a pot of drip coffee. She told me her recipe for good coffee was "One spoonful of coffee per cup plus one for the pot."

"It's just not fair!" she would often begin. She would talk about her day and the injustices she saw, particularly in healthcare as a nurse anesthetist. She told us what she'd seen and heard and what we needed to know about life. Maybe it was politics, maybe something just on her heart and mind. She wanted us to learn and to grow up and do something to make our world better. Often, when the conversation ended, she would close by saying, "Well, like the old boy said, 'It ain't right but it's so.'" She helped foster within Bill and his friends a sense of responsibility to change things for the better. She said there was no dream too big, and there was nothing we couldn't accomplish if we really put our minds to it. She had endured painful obstacles in her life and had chosen to overcome them rather than be a victim. Virginia impressed me with the mature way she spoke with Bill. She trusted him and expected him to act as an adult, to do what was right, and always to do his best.

After Bill's election to public office, I often thought about how those conversations with Virginia and friends could easily have been practice arenas for his press conferences. Bill was adept at engaging friends in discussions on a variety of topics. No doubt, the hours we spent talking about issues during high school and college built a strong foundation for future town hall meetings, campaign stops, and press conferences. As I listened to him as governor and president, it seemed like only yesterday that we were talking about what needed to be done in America.

The only bad habit Virginia had was smoking. I found it odd that she worked in healthcare and yet smoked so much. I saw where she stored her cigarettes in a kitchen drawer. One day, I took a cigarette and matches. I walked to a large vacant lot off Seventh Street and lit it up. I had always wanted to try smoking. Fortunately, I didn't have a good experience.

Mother and Virginia became closer after Bill and I left for college. Many mornings after surgery, Virginia perked a pot of coffee and brought it over to visit with Mother. I'm sure Mother was busy sewing, baking pies, getting lunch ready for Dad, or preparing a church program. She was an exceptional teacher and began studying her Bible lesson on Monday for the following Sunday. Virginia brought Mother up to date on Bill's life at Georgetown. Mother said she could barely get a word in because of Virginia's news, but I'm sure sometimes Virginia felt the same about Mother's reports of my early life.

Virginia and my mother Kay became good friends and coffee-drinking buddies. They were about the same age but from very different circles of life: the preacher's wife, who spent her time at home and church, and the career woman, who loved the racetrack and nightlife. They could not have been more different, yet they shared a common strength in their love for and pride in their children. The unlikely pair became lifelong friends.

"So help me, if you beat me for this, I'll never forget it." Was he serious?

In the summer of 1963, Bill attended the Arkansas All-State Band camp in Fayetteville. I thought it was amazing that his mother let him drive there for camp week. He later made a trip to California to drive a car back for the Clinton Buick Company. Bill enjoyed meeting everyone possible at band camp including some girlfriend interests. He talked about the clarinetist from DeQueen and thought she was probably such a good player because there was little else to do in her town besides practice. He also met a girl named Candy from Fayetteville who came to Hot Springs for a visit. His love-interests were always "lookers."

Later, musing about the importance of music in his life, Bill said for a short time, he'd considered making music his career. But he ultimately decided he didn't want the late nights, didn't like "mixing up his days and nights," and didn't particularly enjoy the jazz club culture. He also doubted he had the talent needed to succeed. Virginia told the story about taking pre-teen Bill to the Vapors Club to hear a performer, but he felt uncomfortable and asked if he could walk back home. He thought about a music major but ultimately decided to attend Georgetown University to study foreign affairs and prepare for a career in public service.

I spent hours at home playing the piano. I didn't drive yet and my parents liked for us to be home anyway. One afternoon, I was playing JS Bach's *Jesu, Joy of Man's Desiring* and didn't realize Bill had come into the living room to listen (my back was to the room as I sat at the piano}. When I finished playing, he began applauding. I was startled and turned around to see Bill sitting there on the loveseat. I was always glad when he dropped by.

The story of Bill sitting on that loveseat listening to me play became famous in our family. My great-grandmother Emma Ellis Bell Thornsberry gave the loveseat to my mother. It was given to Emma by her Sunday School class at Maceo, Kentucky, and passed on to my mother. Mother had just had the loveseat reupholstered in gold velveteen. Bill sat on the loveseat after an afternoon jog, and the perspiration on his legs left marks on the fabric. The new fabric showed slight marks but it is a nice memory now as I have the chair in my home and remember how Bill sat there to hear me play.

Before junior year Bill got his driver's license and began driving to school. Bill asked if I wanted to ride to school with him. I was, after all, right next door, and he had plenty of room in his black Buick four-door sedan. The car was huge and seemed like a block long with fin tails. Bill also drove the family's "Henry J" convertible some but not to school. I gave Bill two dollars each week to help pay for gas, although he didn't ask for the money. Bill filled up the tank at the Esso station in front of St. John's Catholic Church. We left early for school many mornings so Bill could go to the band room to drop off his sax, see Mr. Spurlin, and look over sight-reading selections or possible competition solos. We also sometimes had Student Council meetings before school. Somedays on weekends Bill would be on his way to run a few errands and would stop and ask if I wanted to ride with him. I enjoyed getting out of the house and spending time with him, just going to the post office or whatever was needed.

Before riding to school with Bill, I rode with Michael Karber in his Willy's Jeep with Guido and Anna Ruth Hassin, and my sister Lynda. We were jam-packed for rides to school during sophomore year, so it helped to ride with Bill. Lynda and Michael started dating and he began taking her to school, and the Hassins rode with them as well. After school some days, Bill gave Joe Newman a ride home. One day, Joe was in the backseat, and because it was raining, Bill pumped the brakes to make sure they weren't wet. The jerking movement made Joe carsick, and he asked Bill to stop. Bill did it again just to tease, and Joe became mad, and he jumped out of the car and walked home. Most drives home after school were easygoing. We'd listen to the radio, and I especially liked the popular Neil Sedaka, who sang *I'm Living Right Next Door to an Angel*. Bill referenced that song when he wrote in my high school yearbook our senior year, and I just found a similar note in our junior yearbook, "To Carolyn, the greatest girl I know. I really do live next door to an angel. God bless you, Bill."

The first time Bill got angry at me, I was stunned, but I deserved it. For Christmas, he received a new saxophone case made of gray leather with a handle at one end. When we returned to school after the Christmas holidays, Bill dropped me off at the side door, and he parked near the band room. He asked me to take the case out of the back seat, and as I picked it up, I lost my grip. It tumbled out of my hand, hit the street, and bent the handle. I was horrified, and he was upset. He was so proud of that new case and didn't even have the opportunity to show it off at school before I banged it up. I felt terrible. I mentioned the incident to him many years later, and he replied, "Yeah, I'm still mad at you about that."

Most of the rides to and from school were just routine. The radio was usually on, and we'd chat, and maybe not. I'd hop out at the carport when we got home, and he'd go home to check on Roger, get a snack, start homework, and practice saxophone. Sometimes, he'd shoot basketball hoops. It all was just a normal high school daily routine.

I was elected as the Student Council class representative in our junior year. I got to know the upperclassmen who were leaders at school. Bill was also on the student council. The council organized classroom Thanksgiving baskets for needy families. I felt good to be involved in community service. The student council nominated a candidate slate for student council offices each year and nominated me for treasurer. Their support was not a guarantee of victory because anyone could run, but it sent a strong signal. I felt I had made a solid beginning in my new school. When Mother picked me up after school, I was excited to tell her that I'd been nominated. I'll never forget her reaction, "Oh Carolyn, no!" I couldn't understand why she'd react that way, but she knew, I imagine, that being new in school meant I would likely lose and be disappointed. Still, I was happy and felt uplifted to be recognized after having just moved to the school a year earlier.

My opponent was Ronnie Cecil, who had been a classmate of most students since elementary school. David Leopoulos was his campaign chairman, and they wrote a funny campaign skit for the class assembly. Mine was more traditional and serious. I hung lots of posters and banners throughout the school that friends, including Bill, helped make. I got to school early to get good spaces before they were filled by other candidates. I campaigned hard and felt I had at least a solid chance. The day of the election, I was feeling butterflies all morning, hopeful but unsure. The announcement of the results came over the intercom while I was in Mr. Duncan's chemistry class. "The winner of the position of treasurer is .... Ronnie Cecil." My heart sank. I asked to be excused and went into the hallway and shed a few tears. I was able to get myself together and go back to class soon, but that loss really hurt.

During the spring of our junior year, an assembly was held to elect senior class officers. A new leadership-booster policy was in place that assigned a point value to positions. As Band Major, Bill couldn't run for Senior Class president. He held other club leadership positions, too, in Beta Club, Latin Club, Math Club, and these added points. As nominations were made, it was pointed out that the only position Bill and I could run for was secretary. We were nominated. Although he later admitted he really didn't want the job, it was the only spot he could vie for. As the votes were counted, Bill and I were in a runoff. We stood in the hallway awaiting results.

Bill looked at me and said, "So help me, if you beat me for this, I'll never forget it." Was he serious? I felt sure he was just joking to break the tension, but I also knew he played to win. The votes were tallied, and the announcement was made: "Carolyn is the winner for class secretary!" Bill and I never talked about it again. The stereotype of girls being secretaries probably helped me clinch the position. We'll never know. But presidential reporters and historians have enjoyed pointing out that I beat him in an election.

Years later, as senior class officers planned class reunions, I remarked from the stage at a reunion, "Mr. President, when we ran for class office, and I won senior class secretary, we had no idea these elections were for life!" He enjoyed a hearty laugh as a term-limited US president.

"Guess we'll never forget this, me with my arthritis of the face! It was wonderful, wasn't it?"

It's often said, "Nothing ventured, nothing gained." I discovered from my student council election loss came new opportunities and new recognition. My teachers noticed my interest in leadership. Fellow classmates saw that I wanted an opportunity to serve, and the opportunities began to open. I learned that if you work hard, even if you don't win the contest you hoped for, other rewards will come as a result of your effort. I shared that advice with our children and grandchildren through the years, telling them to just get out there and try. People will notice and think of you as a leader. Later that spring, students were selected by teachers for Arkansas Girls State, and I was on the list. To top it off, our school's attendees unanimously voted to nominate me for Governor of Girls State. I was so honored. We made campaign materials and hoped to make our principal, Johnny Mae Mackey, proud. She was a giant of a leader at Arkansas Girls State. I didn't win the race for Governor, but the counselors noticed during the week that I was a leader in the making. I'd also had a high profile being on stage each day as camp pianist for assemblies. At the close of camp, I was elated to learn that I'd been chosen by the counselors as one of two girls selected to be senators at Girls Nation in Washington, DC, later in the summer.

A week earlier, Bill attended Arkansas Boys State and was elected to several positions. The delegates elected Mack McLarty, Bill's childhood friend from Hope Kindergarten, as governor. Bill was elected to attend Boys Nation in Washington, DC, and had the opportunity to meet our state Senators and see our federal government at work. Bill also "won" by meeting all the young men at Boys State who would be voters as Bill entered public service in the '70s.

Bill drove to Girls State at the end of the week, and I enjoyed introducing him to girls I'd met. He was thrilled that I was selected for Girls Nation. Only two boys and two girls from each state were selected to attend as senators, and two of us were next-door neighbors. What an honor and an exciting time for us to share.

Boys Nation and Girls Nation weeks were powerful events in our lives. We spent the week in the metropolitan DC area on college campuses, with Girls Nation at American University and Boys Nation at the University of Maryland at College Park. We ran for state and national party positions as Nationalist or Federalist Party members. We visited the Capitol and spent time in the offices of our state Senator. I was elected on the first day as Senate Minority Whip. I planned to run for other offices but learned afterward that we could only be elected to one office. I was disappointed my campaigning was over.

As Minority Leader, I met my liaison, Senator Everett Dirksen of Illinois, and learned about the workings of his office. This was a distinct honor. I also met Arkansas senior Senator John McClellan, a giant of a man and wonderfully welcoming. I'd heard about him from my parents. Later, as an adult, I had the opportunity to know his daughter, Mary Alice McDermott, and her family, who were members at Pulaski Heights Baptist in Little Rock. I shared memories of meeting Senator McClellan and what an impression he made.

Taking the Senate elevator was a memorable experience, and I rode with Vice President Lyndon Johnson a few times. We also rode the members' underground tram between Senate office buildings and the Capitol. It was an up-close experience designed to encourage us to run for national office someday, and they rolled out the red carpet for us.

Girls Nation week included a tour of the White House. We wore a hat and gloves for this occasion. Afterward, we went into the Rose Garden where President John F. Kennedy welcomed us and spoke. We were honored to meet him and shake his hand, and as I was about to speak to him, Kennedy turned to look away at another girl in the group. I did get to meet him and have a handshake, but my souvenir picture is my profile, smiling at the back of Kennedy's head. Bill got a great picture of his handshake with Kennedy. He remembers wanting to be on the front row to be sure he had this opportunity to meet his hero.

During Clinton's presidency, I visited the Rose Garden on several occasions. Once was in 1994, when President Nixon died, and I was at the White House with other friends. President Clinton invited Phil Jamison, Jim French, and me to accompany him to the Rose Garden to announce to the nation that Nixon had died. I thought about that day in 1963 when I stood there to meet President Kennedy and when Bill had met him as well. How amazing that life had come full circle. It struck me how truly right it all seemed, both then and now, that Bill Clinton would be in the Rose Garden as our President.

The photos of Bill and me meeting Kennedy were published in the high school *Old Gold Book* yearbook. Next to our pictures with President Kennedy, Bill wrote, "Guess we'll never forget this, me with my arthritis of the face! It was so wonderful, wasn't it? Bill"

Bill and I were invited to speak to the American Legion and its auxiliary programs about our DC experiences. We also were invited to a Democratic Party event on Petit Jean Mountain and Bill drove us there to speak about our experiences. Bill was not really keen on going but agreed to make the trip. On the way home, we pulled into a gas station for gas, and Bill drove over a big rock that scraped the muffler and tailpipe. It really made him mad, probably because he feared he'd damaged the car, but all was fine.

As we got close to home, I summoned a tremendous amount of courage and scooted across the car seat to sit closer to him, and he chuckled quietly. Of course, nothing came of it, but he saw right away that I wasn't afraid to take a risk. I was just happy we had the Boys and Girls Nation experiences, and that we'd had that opportunity to tell about it. Maybe I had a schoolgirl crush on him, but maybe I just admired him tremendously. We got home, I scooted out and walked into my house, and we never talked about it.

The Boys State and Girls State, Boys Nation, and Girls Nation experiences were deeply valuable. Both Bill and I met people from all over the state and nation. We got a rare glimpse of state and national political life and learned about our system of government. We were inspired to run for office—an inspiration that Bill quickly fulfilled in his run for Arkansas Congress, Arkansas Attorney General, Governor of Arkansas, and President of the United States. I was inspired, too, and one of the reasons I wanted to move back to Arkansas after working in DC from 1994-2005 was to run for office, and I did in 2010. Most of all, Girls Nations affirmed the idea that the boy next door would be president someday, and I thought about it often. When I visited DC, I pictured him living in the White House and working the US Capitol. I selected birthday cards with the White House in the design. He had everything it took to be a great leader—heart, mind, spirit—and I knew someday it would become reality.

Girls and Boys State and Nation programs were during the summer of 1963. Little did we know that that same November, our hero, President Kennedy, would be assassinated in Dallas. After hearing the news that President Kennedy had been shot and killed, our principal, Mrs. Mackey, called students to the auditorium to share the news. Bill and I were particularly shaken, having just met Kennedy a few months earlier. We watched every minute of televised news of his death and funeral. We hadn't known such horror in our youth, and it was a personal jolt.

When Bill ran for president in 1992, the photo and video of him meeting President Kennedy featured prominently in campaign materials. Now my high school belief he would someday be president was coming true.

She urged us to run for office and said it was a noble profession and high calling.

During our junior year, Johnnie Mae Mackey was named principal of our high school. She was the first woman principal in 42 years and followed Mr. Terry Humble. Mrs. Mackey was bigger than life. A large woman with a ready smile that students knew not to mistake as softness, she was one of the strongest women I ever knew. She ruled with a firm hand but was always fair. She was a patriot and taught us the importance of honoring the flag, how to salute, and that we must always stand when the flag enters a room or stadium. She urged us to run for office and said it was a noble profession and high calling.

Mrs. Mackey led our pep rallies in a rousing cheer called "Hullabaloo." She started slowly in a calm, low voice for the first time through, then the second time was chanted as loudly as possible, with fists high in the air. The cheer was: *"Hullabaloo kanick kanick, wahee wahie, we win or die, ching chang chow chow, bing bang bow wow, Trojans, Trojans, rah rah rah!"* Even to this day, when our class reunions are held, we sing our Alma Mater and chant "Hullabaloo."

Patriotism was a hallmark of our lives and times. Mrs. Mackey promoted it, but it was also generally accepted as a spirit of love for country. We never heard anyone speak disrespectfully about our president or country. My grandmother once said, "I may not have voted for him, but once he's elected, he's my president, and I support him."

Flag Day was an important day for Mrs. Mackey. She called a student assembly in the spring to honor it. Flag Day is celebrated on June 14 to commemorate the adoption of the flag of the United States on June 14, 1777. I will always remember Mrs. Mackey's speech about the women and men, her husband Harris included, who gave their lives for our freedoms.

She told us that the American flag is a sacred symbol and that we were to respect it. When the flag is carried into a room, people are to stand and salute the flag until it passes. She recounted the day she attended a University of Arkansas Razorback football game at War Memorial Stadium in Little Rock. As she sat in the stands, she saw the color guard enter and march onto the field. Everyone continued to sit and chat. Finally, frustrated and angry, Mrs. Mackey stood up and turned to everyone in the stadium and, in her huge, booming voice, called out, "If there's a red-blooded American in this stadium, STAND UP!" And she said, "You know what happened? They stood up. They all stood up!" The lesson was that anytime our flag entered a room, we were to stand and salute. I remember it to this day and do my best to always honor her teaching as well as her sacrifice and legacy.

One of the hallmarks of Mrs. Mackey's tenure was her work to build young leaders. She created a point system for school offices and students could earn ten points. The idea was ahead of its time, and ours was the only school I knew with the policy. When our daughters attended college, there was a push on many campuses to build leaders, but we were trying it early. The goal was to expand leadership opportunities throughout the student body and not limit them to a few. The program made students look for new leaders and encouraged students to run for election. It was novel and effective as well.

Mrs. Mackey took me under her wing as a senior, arranging speaking opportunities at civic clubs and urging me to enter contests such as the Elks

Club Youth Leadership competition. I felt honored to have her support. She also took Bill under her wing and scheduled speaking opportunities for him, so many in fact that he often missed class.

It was formative for me to see strong women in leadership. Mrs. Mackey served as chairman of Arkansas Girls State, chair of the Garland County Library board, and twice was named the Arkansas Business and Professional Women's Club "Woman of the Year." Virginia Clinton was another strong woman in my life. And I had already experienced the leadership of my own mother, Kay Yeldell, seeing her teaching and organizational skills in church programs. Her skills in speaking and motivation were unparalleled. She excelled at creating visual teaching materials. Her devotion to excellence in all things made a lasting impact on my life.

He often responded, "A duck can waddle!"

Bill and I shared a concern about weight. Since childhood, I had been the tallest of my classmates, and I struggled with weight. In high school, I dieted to slim down and wished I could be more like other girls in height and size. I later learned to celebrate my height, but it took a while. Bill sometimes mentioned his weight and how he wasn't happy about it. When I told him I thought he looked good, he often responded, "A duck can waddle!" We didn't work out, and personal fitness hadn't become a craze. He got exercise shooting baskets at the garage door hoop and played golf and caddied when the PGA tournament was held at Hot Springs Country Club.

During our junior year, I was invited to be a "hostess" for the spring Trojan Band Banquet. My parents let me shop for a beautiful new dress, and I found a black crepe one with a flowing tea-length skirt, sleeveless, and a sheered bodice. I had lost weight that year and felt pretty. The banquet was at the Velda Rose Hotel, and Mickey Rooney, the current headliner at the Vapors nightclub, spoke at the banquet.

I was always trying to lose weight. Virginia bought an exercise bench called a Stauffer. The center section was motorized and vibrated the hips. I'm not sure what anyone thought this would accomplish, but the Stauffer was the current rage. I was invited to use it anytime, and Bill was never home when I did so. I also started walking in our neighborhood and got good results from climbing the steep hills around. I lost more weight simply by cutting my food intake. I also had a college-age boyfriend and that helped my success. Bill was concerned that I was dating an older guy and had slimmed down. He wanted me to look and feel good but also wasn't sure I should be dating college men.

He spotted it right away and whispered, "Hey, let me see that."

During our senior year, the local Elks Club held a youth leadership essay contest. Students submitted essays about what it meant to be an American and the responsibilities of service and leadership required of every citizen. Bill won and received scholarships, nice trophies, and public recognition with yearbook photos and speaking opportunities.

Bill was active in the Masonic program for young men called Demolay, whose purpose is to develop leaders of young men aged 12 to 21 and named for Jacque Demolay, the last member of the Knights Templar. Bill was chosen leader of the Hot Springs Demolays and got to select a "Girl Friday" and a "Demolay Sweetheart." The sweetheart was someone who represented the ideal of womanhood. I was honored that he selected me as Sweetheart and, for the installation ceremony, gave me a gardenia corsage. Having this respect from him was special indeed.

As we continued our senior year, Bill was unsure about where to apply for college. His delay was making guidance counselor Edith Irons a nervous wreck. One day before Physics class I was in Mrs. Irons' office and spotted the Georgetown University catalogue. I checked it out and took it to class, where I sat across from Bill. I made sure the catalog was on top of the books under my desk. He spotted it right away and whispered, "Hey, let me see that." He wound up applying to Georgetown as his only choice. Concerns mounted that a young man from Arkansas, a non-Catholic without legacy ties, might not be admitted. Virginia asked him a practical question: "What do you think the chances are that Georgetown, a Jesuit school, will accept a Southern Baptist boy from Arkansas?" Fortunately, he impressed the admissions staff, and his formal introduction to DC began.

The highlight of my senior year and musical life thus far was playing a two-piano arrangement of George Gershwin's *Rhapsody in Blue* for choir and piano with our high school chorus. It was challenging and co-pianist Letha Ann Wooldridge and I rehearsed feverishly. Only later did I realize what a compliment it was that DJ chose this piece to showcase her accompanists' talent. Bill loved the performance and told me afterward how well I played.

Bill was a National Merit Semifinalist and was selected for the Academically Talented Student Award in 1963. At the end of our senior year, when grade point averages were tallied, Bill came in third place in our class. However, his greater achievement was in his overall scholarship, leadership, and community service. He was a highly distinguished graduate.

In May 1964, our high school graduation day arrived. Commencement took place in an outdoor ceremony at our beautifully decorated football field. A Baccalaureate service was at our Second Baptist Church a few days earlier, where my Dad gave the sermon, and our senior picnic took place on Lake Hamilton. We anxiously watched the dark clouds gather before graduation and knew rain was imminent. The three hundred seniors in grey caps and gowns, honor students wearing a gold cord and tassel, lined up for the processional, *Sine Nomine* by Ralph Vaughn Williams. The light rain didn't dampen our experience.

As a top graduate, Bill was a program participant. He gave the benediction and it was a beautiful prayer that our lives would be caring about the ills of our world and that we'd not stand idly by. He prayed, "God, leave within us the youthful idealism and moralism which have made our people so strong. Sicken us at the sight of apathy, ignorance, and rejection so that our generation will remove complacency, poverty, and prejudice from the hearts of free men…Make us care so that we will never know the misery and muddle of life without purpose and so that when we die, others will still have the opportunity to live in a free land."[5] The commencement program listed the colleges students would attend and scholarships. Bill was on his way to Georgetown University in Washington, DC. I was going to Baylor University and been awarded a music scholarship. We were headed out into the big world.

Our graduation party was held on the lake at Arc Isle, and while a date wasn't required, I wasn't sure I'd go. Virginia was a chaperone and asked me to go with her. I was glad I celebrated our big day with friends. Hot Springs High School had given me a great start in life in many ways.

The time of old friends splitting up and going separate ways to college was exciting and sad. The future looked bright, but we knew a special time was ending. Virginia echoed that years later as she talked about our group and said she felt privileged to share it as we were at her home so often.

With graduation behind us, the reality of college set in. Life was changing, and the people we had been with every day for three years would no longer be in our daily lives. Big changes lay ahead. As much of a dream the years had been, there were fresh new experiences awaiting us, with new memories to be made and prophecies to be fulfilled.

---

[1] Hill, Mary Bell. *Hot Springs National Park.*, Charleston, SC: Arcadia Publishing. 2014

[2] We loved to play *Summertime, What Child is This* and *A Taste of Honey*. We sang folk songs by Peter Paul and Mary including *Leaving on a Jet Plane* and *All My Trials*. We also played hymns and *Amazing Grace* was a favorite. We loved Ray Charles' *Georgia On my Mind, Yesterday, I'll Be Seeing You* and *Love Walked In*. He also loved sax greats John Coltrane, Boots Randolph, Stan Getz and works by Thelonious Monk, Ramsey Lewis and Isaac Hayes.

[3] Farrar, Clay, "The Heyday of Casinos," Dallas, TX: Texas Historical Society. *The Amateur Historian*, April 2018

[4] Dillard, Tom, Arkansas Democrat Gazette, Opinion, "Hot Springs' Notorious Casinos," April 2019

[5] Clinton, Bill, Benedictory prayer, Hot Springs High School Graduation ceremony, May 29, 1964

CHAPTER TWO

College Goodbyes and Ties

Bill was on his way to Georgetown University to study foreign affairs. I found a newsstand that sold Foreign Affairs magazine, with its familiar gray paper cover and bought a copy for him. I was interested in what he would be learning and wanted to be conversant on the topic. It was probably also a bit like buying baseball magazines as a preteen to impress boys with stats I memorized.

I planned to major in music, although I wasn't sure I wanted a career in music, as much as I loved it. I listed psychiatry as my major, hoping to help people as a mental health professional. I was also interested in public service, but as time drew closer and the need for scholarship assistance loomed, my natural major was music. I applied to Baylor University and received a music scholarship.

Through the summer, a pall seemed to hang over our home. Did my parents not want me to go to Baylor? Were they sad their first child was going far away to school? I thought they'd be happy that I was going to a Baptist school. My Dad was the first in his family to graduate from college, and his years at Ouachita Baptist University were life-changing. OBU was a small church-affiliated university located in Arkadelphia, Arkansas, with a history spanning 135 years. Ouachita had 1,500 students and was nationally ranked as a small university. My Dad was on the Board of Directors but didn't insist I attend. I didn't understand the lack of enthusiasm for what I expected would be a family-approved college choice, but I didn't feel their joyful support.

Sometime that summer, I changed my mind and decided to go to Ouachita

University. I wasn't sad about it; it was a relief. I could tell Dad was excited because he got out his Army footlocker and freshened it up with a coat of battleship gray paint. He wanted to send it with me as my blanket storage. I was happy he was getting excited about the fall, but I was speechless when he added pink swan decals to the top of the footlocker. Who decorated with pink swans? Wasn't that a bathroom motif? I was mortified to imagine how my roommates would react. Still, I hated to hurt his feelings. Mother suggested he find another option, and he decided on red geraniums. At least that was better. They were trying to help me prepare for college however they could, and I appreciated it. At least now, there was some excitement in the air.

Bill thought dating a senior was too much, too soon for the young, inexperienced girl next door.

My father's college friend, Neno Flaig, was Dean of Women at Ouachita, and she arranged housing and roommates for me. I lived in Johnson Hall in a large corner room on the second floor with two roommates. Beverly from El Dorado was a wild child. The other girl was from a small rural town in Arkansas—its name no longer in my memory. I arrived after Beverly moved in. She said in amazement, "Look at the closet. She doesn't have *one piece* of madras!" Indian Madras plaid fabric was the fashion rage in 1964, and Mother made a couple of wrap-around Madras skirts for me, plus I had a Madras blazer. Also in fashion were Peter Pan collar blouses, oxford cloth shirts, and circle pins or "virgin pins." We wore teased hairdos with a flip or a shorter do. We filled the air with hairspray by the cans-full and always needed more.

Dean Flaig asked me as my junior year approached if I would be willing to take a Black roommate if needed, and I told her I'd be happy to. The opportunity never arose, but I was honored she felt she could ask and was comfortable with the idea. Ouachita had already admitted a few Black students. Four were enrolled during my freshman year, and a dozen by my junior year. Several were local residents, so they likely would have lived at home rather than in a dorm. There were also a few African and Asian mission students. Otherwise, the campus was all white. I didn't mention the possibility of new living arrangements to my roommates because we were happy living together, and I didn't want to create concern. They wouldn't have been shocked; we all knew integration was a critical corrective step for society.

As I was starting to date in college, Bill took an interest in who I was going out with. Jim Case, a high school bandmate of Bill's, was at Ouachita and kept Bill informed on my dates. My steady as a freshman was a senior named Max from Magnolia. One evening, as I walked to the dorm, Max slowed down as he drove past in his red VW Beetle, rolled down his window, and called to me. After introducing himself and asking my name, he shouted, "Yeldell, I think I love you. I crave your bod." Goodness, I was stunned! Laughing it off, I went inside. Later, he called and asked for a date. Ever the gentleman, he was happy, though our relationship did not include any "bod" involvement. College dating was markedly innocent in the 1960s, at least for my dates and me.

Young people today are floored to learn couples dated back then and didn't have sex. As Christian girls, we'd been taught "to save ourselves for the man we'd marry." In fact, I wasn't aware of any girls who were sexually active. No one was on the pill, as far as I knew, and the fear of getting pregnant was an ever-present concern. Most girls and guys I knew clearly knew where to draw the line. Max became jealous when I started dating another guy, found me in the music school, surprised me with a big kiss, and asked, "Can *he* kiss you like that?"

I'd never had guys fighting over me before.

Max was studying pre-med, with a particular interest in audiology. He was a small-plane pilot. I never flew with Max, but he sometimes took a plane from the Arkadelphia airfield to Hot Springs and flew low over our house to earn hours toward his pilot's license. If he spied my mother in the backyard hanging laundry, he thought it was great fun to fly low over our house and "buzz" the rooftop. It terrified Mom but was all in good fun.

Bill thought my dating a senior was too much, too soon for the young and inexperienced girl next door. He asked his friend Jim to keep an eye on things. I thought that was funny and felt mildly complimented by his concern.

Bill and I exchanged letters frequently in college; it was always a banner day when his latest letter arrived. I treasured his newsy updates. Now, of course, I wish I'd kept them. I remember lots about them, however. Bill's letters were always full of news about his experiences, the courses he was taking, and the new friends he was meeting. They were often also philosophical about the future, his studies, and the responsibility each of us had to do our God-given best in life. I loved hearing about his roommates and the girls he was dating. He sometimes told me he was so happy my letter had arrived. Once, I recall him saying he had saved it to take to a quiet place when he had time to savor it. I bought light blue Crane paper with matching envelopes for my letters and loved using a fountain pen. He always encouraged me in my writing. More than once, he said he thought I should consider a writing career because I wrote such good letters.

Bill yelled, "Where are they? Where are they?"

Some of the happiest times during college were going home for holidays. Seeing old friends, hearing about college experiences, and comparing notes on our studies was exciting. Bill didn't come home for Thanksgiving of our freshman year because of travel costs. We missed him. I'll never forget our freshman year Christmas vacation back home in Hot Springs. Virginia told David Leopoulos and me that she was going to the airport to meet Bill's plane and invited us to wait at home until they arrived. David and I decided to make it a Christmas homecoming to remember. We painted a huge "Welcome Home Bill" banner to greet him. When we heard the car enter the garage, we ran to hide in Roger Jr.'s bedroom closet. Bill walked in, yelling, "Where are they? Where are they?" As we heard him walking down the hallway, we got tickled and started laughing. Bill threw open the closet doors, and we fell into a huge huddle. We laughed and nearly cried for joy. Christmas could now begin!

During our Christmas break, we spent lots of time together. There were parties, shopping for gifts, movies, card games, and backyard football. Virginia was always ready for Christmas early. Her decorations were up, and gifts were wrapped before anyone else. The tree in their living room sparkled with lights and silver tinsel. Colorful gift boxes were piled high underneath.

Bill and I enjoyed working on the daily *Hot Springs Sentinel-Record* crossword puzzle. He'd call some mornings and say, "Come over and bring your copy of the paper." We had orange juice and competed to finish the crossword first. We always had records on, often the latest by Ray Charles, Nancy Wilson, Stan Getz, Dave Brubeck, or jazz drummer Buddy Rich.

Virginia and I visited after Christmas, and she was laughing hysterically. "I have to tell you the funniest thing." Roger had been waking up for several nights complaining about his room being too hot.

He said, "Daddo, I'm burning up!" She thought maybe he had a fever, but it was normal. Roger was wearing his new Christmas pajamas. Virginia decided to check the label. She discovered that she had unknowingly bought him thermal pajamas. She laughed at her mistake and Roger's unfortunate misery.

During my freshman year at Ouachita, I'd gotten into good shape, thanks mainly to swimming classes. Also, I was on the cafeteria meal plan. That and the fact that my roommates and I didn't snack much positively affected my physique. When I came home for Christmas, Bill was surprised to see me slimmer. I bought a pair of tartan plaid slacks, and Mother suggested I model them for him. He was seated in the den and agreed to critique my new outfits. He was complimentary as I modeled. Then, Mother teasingly told me to put on the powder blue negligee that my paternal grandmother Daisy gave me for graduation and model that as well. When I walked in, Bill exclaimed, "That does it!" He was shocked! We enjoyed a good laugh.

I invited friends to go caroling. We stopped by our high school principal, Johnnie Mae Mackey's house. She was touched when we came by and said we were a special group and our class was one of a kind. Many of our classmates showed leadership and a gift for making a difference in our world. Mrs. Mackey challenged us to live up to our God-given potential and said she expected to hear great things about us.

Indeed, our class did produce world-class leaders. We had many who served in Vietnam and four who died there. Our class included several doctors and scientists, including Jim French, a plastic surgeon who settled in DC and later did cleft palate surgeries in Haiti and Africa. Barney Bond and Jim Ashabranner practiced medicine in-state. Phil Jamison was a Navy commander and worked for the US State Department on the nuclear arms limitation SALT treaty after retirement. Rick Silverman became a renowned surgeon, and Peggy Keaton and Jim Moshinskie became college professors. Joe was a successful accountant, and David was a technology specialist. Anne, Kenny, and others were teachers. Claire was a bank examiner, and Mary Jo was a businesswoman. Many I haven't mentioned, but their camaraderie faded over the decades. We responded to the challenge of service and tried to live it to the best of our abilities.

During the Christmas season of our freshman year in college, Claire Callahan hosted a beautiful party for friends. We gathered at the piano to sing holiday songs. We were happy to be together again, and our cheer was enhanced since Claire's mother gently "spiked" the celebratory punch. I wore a new blue velvet dress with a Christmas tree brooch. Debutante season kicked off with parties that culminated in the debutante ball. Some parents gave them the choice of making a debut or traveling to Europe. The "freer spirits" among them chose to travel. After all, we knew each other, so there was no need to make a debut. I was invited to be a debutante but declined due to cost and the required father-daughter dance that would have been impossible for my Baptist pastor dad.

There were church services, parties, midnight mass with Claire and her family at St. John's Catholic Church, the Hassin family's Christmas Eve party, and endless joy-filled days. Bill never understood why our family opened gifts on Christmas Eve. His household rule was, "We open gifts on Christmas morning, not before!" I explained to Bill that when your dad is a preacher, and Christmas falls on Sunday, it's challenging to open gifts and get to church on time. I continued, "Because we are *exceptionally good* children, Santa comes to see us early." There were always parties on Christmas Eve, and my family missed them unless we could go after Santa came.

We talked about what was on our hearts and minds after a semester of college. Bill and I had conversations with friends and family about the inequality of our segregated community. He had experienced so much as a young boy living in Hope with his grandparents as his mother attended nursing school in New Orleans. He'd witnessed his grandfather's friendships with Black community members, extending credit at his store so they could buy what they needed, and how he demonstrated kindness and color-blind treatment of all people. The equality of the races was deeply ingrained in him. To Bill, even as a young adult, equal rights and opportunities were simply the right way of living.

Bill, our friends, and I felt we missed a rare opportunity in high school by not having an integrated educational experience. Our worlds were completely separate from the students at all-Black Langston High School. The closest we came to participating in anything together was the Hot Springs Christmas parade, in which both Black and white area school bands marched and played.

Bill was also struck by the wide breadth of educational backgrounds of students he'd met at Georgetown. He thought about it frequently and was beginning to formulate a future education policy. During a memorable conversation, Bill reflected, "You know, when babies are born, they are basically the same no matter where they come into the world. There are differences in genetics, economic status, environment, and other factors. Some of these things the child has no choice about. However, one of the largest factors in that child's life is the education they receive because of where they were born and where they live. The one thing that could truly give all Americans a chance at a more level playing field in life is a high-quality education."

Later, as Governor of Arkansas, Bill made education reform a priority. Those words from the Christmas vacation of our freshman year came back to me. As his future wife, First Lady Hillary Rodham Clinton, chaired the hearings for Arkansas educational reforms, I thought it likely that his commitment to academic excellence for every child had taken root during his first year at Georgetown.

He was astounded at the possibilities ahead.

My sophomore and junior years at Ouachita continued to prepare me as a musician. They also widened my exposure to humankind as I met people from around the state, nation, and world. My roommate, Margie, and suitemates, Virginia and Jenny Lou, were a joy. We shared life, love, and discussions about how times were changing. Male friends were being drafted to serve in Vietnam, and the women's movement was growing. The Sixties were years of great unrest in our nation, with the Vietnam conflict filling the news daily and sending young men home in coffins. We lost several high school classmates in the war. Many were considering ways to avoid the draft during college, even moving to Canada.

Things were changing for women, and norms were turning upside down. Ripples were felt as far away as rural Arkansas. When I started as a freshman at Ouachita, my roommates and I discussed how we envisioned our future. One thought she'd be a music teacher and use a spare bedroom for a music studio to earn "pin money" to help support the family. Most expected to be homemakers and give music lessons. Nobody envisioned being full-wage-earning partners.

In just a few years, all that had changed. The world was open to women for careers outside the home, and more women were making that choice. I was living on the cusp of the women's revolution and a historical time for equal rights. I don't remember discussing this dramatic societal transition in our dorm rooms. It took place slowly without much fanfare and would significantly impact our lives.

I continued music studies during the spring of my freshman year and made a discovery. My voice-major roommate said the Opera Workshop needed more singers and suggested I join. I told her I'd never sung because I was always the accompanist for choirs and soloists, but I went along to be a good sport. The director, David Scott, taught voice and invited me to audition. Much to my surprise, he told me he thought I had a good voice hiding inside. He encouraged me to take voice lessons. Little by little, I discovered the joy of singing. I learned the basics and sang in repertoire classes each week. Mr. Scott told me in one lesson to just let go and "sing like a big, fat opera singer!" His wife Frances, also a voice teacher with a studio next door, came bursting into my lesson exclaiming, "Who is this WOMAN singing?" They put me at ease and coaxed my budding voice into a newfound gift.

❧ ☙

Early in my Sophomore year, I decided to double-major in piano and voice. I soon discovered this meant twice the practice and required recitals. As I grew more excited about singing, I basically sight-read through piano lessons, much to Ms. Bowden's dismay. I was able to memorize several piano pieces to play in the recital but found that my heart had moved to singing. In my sophomore year, I sang the title role in Gian-Carlo Menotti's opera, *The Medium*. In my Junior year, I sang the role of the Mother in Menotti's *Amahl and the Night Visitors*—the first opera performance I had ever attended when my piano teacher Lillian Faulk took me to hear it in Memphis as a junior high student. My music theory professor came backstage afterward with tears in his eyes and said how moving he had found it. I was eager to learn opera arias by Mozart and Verdi. Often, when I performed, the voice faculty would glance at each other and smile, amazed and amused at what was transpiring for this piano major. I still loved the piano, but the new joy of singing was winning my heart.

❧ ☙

Ouachita Baptist University gave me opportunities to grow in many aspects. I was active in campus leadership and was awarded the Freshman Leadership Award. The Hot Springs Business and Professional Women selected me as "Arkansas Career Young Woman of the Year." As much as music meant, I felt destined to grow into adult responsibilities, including leadership and public service. Music was a core expression of my life, but I wanted to explore all possibilities.

Meanwhile, Bill was experiencing a significant growth period at Georgetown, where he met students from around the country and the world. He told us at Christmas that he was amazed at many of his classmates' educational opportunities. He observed the difference that a good education can make. His professors were both thrilling and demanding. He was having new experiences and was astounded at the possibilities ahead.

Roger looked at me and said, "You drive carefully."

One of my many summer jobs was working with Bill at Clinton Buick Company, taking inventory in the parts department that Bill's stepfather Roger managed. Counting hundreds of nuts, bolts, and screws in tiny pull-out drawers seemed endless. Bill climbed a ladder, did the counting, and called out the number, which I then entered on the paper inventory report. Up that ladder, Bill had to deal with larger items like gaskets, mufflers, and tailpipes. It was a hot, dusty challenge, but we earned some money and spent time together, too.

Bill was out of town for one week, and I continued taking inventory. On Tuesday morning of that week, Roger greeted me and pointed to the back lot where a wrecker had just unloaded a badly damaged car. He told me to "go take a good look." When I neared the car, I was shocked and sickened to see flesh dangling from the twisted steering column. I knew he'd sent me out there to see first-hand what an auto accident could do. A relatively new driver, Roger knew that young people sometimes take driving too casually. As I walked back into the parts department with a pale face, Roger looked at me and said, "You drive carefully."

꧁ ꧂

During my freshman summer, I worked at the college library. My sister Lynda was entering Ouachita, and Dad found jobs for us. We lived at Cone Bottoms Hall, which provided summer housing for girls on the OBU campus.

My main job at the library was shelving books. I spent hours in the stacks, returning books to their assigned places. If I had not been so easily distracted by intriguing titles, I would have been more efficient. Bill wrote and asked me to please check out *I and Thou* by Martin Buber for his required reading before returning to Georgetown in the fall.

When my library job occasionally became tedious, my co-workers and I found ways to stir up a little fun. A wall-sized, air-intake grate allowed us to see into the reading room. We could see friends studying, but they couldn't see us. One day I stood at the grate and whispered loudly, "Pssst, it's God. I see you. I know what you're thinking. I know what you've done." Eyes opened wide. Self-conscious head-turning and throat-clearing reactions were hilarious. My bravery in impersonating the almighty was short-lived. I only pulled that trick a couple of times. Those moments of youthful impertinence were memorable breaks from book shelving.

The library job helped me learn a good deal about life. Mike Makosholo from Nigeria was a regular at the library who came to OBU through missionary connections. Mike taught us a Nigerian song in the Yoruba language. We still sing it today. Arkadelphia, Ouachita's location, was still segregated, as was most life in the mid-1960s. Friends on campus were saddened to learn that when Mike asked to join the First Baptist Church in town, the congregation refused him because of his race. I couldn't imagine a greater injustice. The policy changed in time, but it was a sad reminder of the times in which we lived. I also met Ho Soo Byun from Korea. When I was assigned to the library front desk, he came by to teach me basic Korean. I enjoyed our lessons and still try the phrases when I meet Korean friends. I learned, "Hello, how are you, friend?" and "Goodbye." But he also taught me practical phrases any homemaker would need, like, "Would you like tea or coffee? Would you like some rice?" "You are beautiful," and "I love you."

During election-year summers, Bill worked in campaigns. He helped the 1966 Frank Holt for Governor Campaign organize the "Holt Generation" of young voters, register them, and enlist them as volunteers. One of Bill's jobs was to drive Holt's wife and daughters around Arkansas to campaign. His daughter Lyda told me years later that Bill sometimes spoke at events and that crowds were riveted by his remarks. His campaign speaking skills were being honed for future years.

The Holt campaign brought into stark contrast the competing forces of good and evil in civil rights. It was a time of significant change. Orval Faubus was stepping down after six terms as governor. Holt served as attorney general for two years, leaving the post after being elected in 1962 to the Arkansas Supreme Court. In 1966 he resigned to run for governor. Holt told voters that change was coming in racial issues. He said the days of Plessy v. Ferguson "separate but equal" were over, and a new day of equal access to education and the benefits of life should be extended to every citizen. The frontrunner, Jim Johnson, was a white supremacist and avid segregationist. Holt finished as runner-up in a crowded seven-man field but lost the run-off to Johnson by 15,000 votes. Johnson eventually lost to Winthrop Rockefeller. The campaign job gave Bill valuable political experience and insight into issues.

Rockefeller made his first run for governor in 1964 against Faubus. I volunteered for Rockefeller even though he was a Republican. My opposition to Faubus stemmed largely from memories of the 1957 Little Rock Central High Crisis and the embarrassment Faubus brought our state. Our family experienced anti-Faubus sentiments on a family trip in 1962 to California. My father always backed our car into parking spots, so our Arkansas car tag wasn't visible. I helped the campaign by making posters and calls. When Rockefeller visited Hot Springs, I organized a "conga line" down Central Avenue and we chanted, "One two three four Conga, Rockefeller is the strong-uh, Faubus is no long-uh." I became a "Young Republican" and attended a Young Republican convention. I learned GOP views at "The Freedom Forum" at Harding College in Searcy. I was getting a full dose of conservative dogma. It lasted only long enough to see Rockefeller elected in 1966. Then I returned to the Democratic Party. I was happy to help end the Faubus era that was a black eye for our state and a bad memory for our family.

I should have known Bill and Tom would plan some surprise as they dropped me at school.

Summers home from college meant time with friends. We were like a small family and always together. Bill loved to get us together to talk, read, enjoy music, and play card games. David Leopoulos called me once and asked if Bill had called me, too. "So, do you want to go over and watch Bill read?" he asked. We laughed but knew it didn't matter what we were doing as long as we were together. David didn't have a car, so Bill drove across town to pick him up. We continued working crossword puzzles, and Bill still works the *New York Times* crossword puzzle and has upped his skills by working it in ink. He also created a puzzle for the *Times* after his presidency.

Bill and I usually planned a reunion party with friends during summer break at Bill's house. I prepared simple snack foods, and we shopped for groceries. My father had a fit when he realized I was spending my earnings on food for the party. It was traumatic. My mother asked, "Who do you think you are? Mrs. Astor?" Money was tight for our family with kids in college. For my tonsillectomy, Dad used $100 from the money I earned as a pianist for a summer youth revival. Still, we moved ahead with the party to catch up on friends' college life and future plans. We didn't drink, but inevitably, someone brought beer and drank it outside on the driveway. Virginia and Roger arrived home once after the party was in progress, and we were relieved the drinking was outside. They would have strongly disapproved of underage alcohol use.

Bill's Georgetown roommates visited Hot Springs during the summers. Tom Campbell and Tom Caplan visited a time or two, as did others. By his graduation in '68, Bill had forged a lifetime of lasting friendships. Tom Campbell came for a visit in 1966, and Bill and Tom offered to drive me to Ouachita for my junior year. When we arrived, friends remembered Bill from high school band, Boys Nation, and Girls State visits. My roommates had heard about my next-door neighbor, Bill. It was also always exciting to hear the warning call, "Men in the hall." I told Bill and Tom about the day a maintenance worker came to our dorm and knocked on the door of a coed just getting out of the shower, a towel wrapped around her. "I've come to fix the knobs on your chest," he explained. We howled.

I should have known Bill and Tom would plan some prank when they dropped me at school. As they packed my things in Bill's trunk, they hid a partial bottle of whiskey in one of my shoeboxes. After they left, I opened the box and gasped. Drinking on campus (or off-campus, for that matter) was strictly forbidden, and anyone caught was expelled. My roommates and I grabbed the bottle and raced down to the creek behind our dorm. We poured out the whiskey and found a safe place to ditch the bottle. What a couple of jokesters! I am sure they roared all the way home just thinking about the reaction we would have when the bottle was discovered. Fortunately, we weren't found out. I think I could've explained my way out of the situation if pressed. I was on the dorm judicial council and had seen coeds in hot water. But we avoided this ordeal, thankfully, and made a fun memory.

When Bill ran for Georgetown student body president, he was busy with his campaign preparations while home for the summer. He was president of his freshman and sophomore classes and now took on this campus-wide race. He showed us posters / fliers he had made to post around campus and enlisted friends to make more. We spent lots of time at his dining room table to help. He won the election due in large part to his affable style, Southern accent, and charm. But he was also exhibiting a strong talent for politics and organizing that would soon come in handy.

I told him I'd received a written marriage proposal.

During my junior year at Ouachita, a new opportunity opened for me. A couple from First Baptist Church, West Memphis, Bill and William Spears, offered to help pay my college expenses. They said since they had no children, they had the ability to help our family. Dad told me that if I wanted to change schools, this would be my opportunity. (I always wondered how Mrs. Spears came by the name 'William' but never inquired, probably thinking it would be disrespectful at my young age.) Ouachita was excellent but felt small, and I wanted more competition and exposure to the performing arts at a larger school. He loved Ouachita, but he wanted me to grow.

I considered both the Juilliard School in New York City and Indiana University with its famous music school. I applied to both and chose Indiana for a liberal arts education rather than strict conservatory training. As a result of my solid music education at Ouachita, I passed all entrance exams in theory, sight reading, music history, and literature. In the summer of 1967, I began a new college chapter.

Later in the fall, Roger Sr. was diagnosed with cancer and died while Bill was at Georgetown. He and Bill had reconciled after the home struggles caused by alcohol. Bill spent many weekends at Duke University Hospital, where Roger was receiving treatment. I was at Indiana University when Virginia and Bill told me he was near death. Bill came home to say his last goodbyes, but I couldn't go home for the funeral because of my recital. They didn't expect me to come, although I wanted to be there. Virginia had a lovely gold bracelet engraved with Roger's name and date of death and gave it to me as a keepsake and one to Mary Jo Rogers. Both of us enjoyed a special friendship with Roger. It was a touching remembrance.

Bill and I kept up our letter writing during his senior year at Georgetown, and his letters were always full. I shared everything too about my life. I told him I had received a written marriage proposal from one of the senior "preacher boys" at Ouachita whom I barely knew. He outlined the reasons why marrying him would be a good idea and that I'd be a perfect preacher's wife as a singer, pianist, and leader. I took the letter home, shared it with my parents, and watched my father's expression as he read it. He broke into a big grin and chuckled with my mother. I wonder if it made him think of himself when he was a college "preacher boy" and looking for the perfect preacher's wife.

Bill kept himself informed about my family from his mother's letters as well as my own. When he heard that my sister Deborah was engaged to a boy he didn't think was quite good enough for her, he wrote to me with concern. "If ever there was a time to preach, it is now! Preach, preacher's daughter, preach!" The engagement eventually ended, much to his relief.

We grew closer that Christmas.

I looked forward to going home for Christmas and seeing Bill and our mutual friends again. We always enjoyed catching up about our lives and plans. Of course, the crossword puzzle contests continued, as did games of hearts, trips to the bowling alley, and the miniature golf course. Some Christmases when I sang in worship, Virginia, Bill and Roger would come. She loved *O Holy Night* and asked me to sing it at holiday parties when Bill was governor.

Senior year 1967, I arrived home for Christmas a day or so before Bill. On the evening of his arrival, Virginia asked if I'd like to ride with her and their friend, Marge Mitchell, to the airport to pick Bill up. My folks jealously guarded my time while home, but they approved. I got in Virginia's Buick wearing a new tweed suit. Marge and I waited in the car while Virginia went into the terminal to meet Bill. They finally arrived and loaded the luggage into the trunk. It was wonderful to see him home for Christmas. On the drive home, we sat in the backseat together and talked about his trip and Christmas plans.

Over Christmas vacation, Bill and I spent a lot of time together. We were experiencing a new kind of relationship. We enjoyed the annual Cotillion Club ball at the Velda Rose Inn. At the party, Bill danced with other girls. I heard one fellow ask Bill, "Aren't you going to ask Carolyn to dance?" He replied, "Her dad is a Baptist preacher, so she doesn't dance, and my dad sells Buicks, and I don't drive a Ford." I thought that was a caring response. We also went to Little Rock for a dance; otherwise, we just enjoyed being with friends, watching TV late movies, and talking about where life seemed to be heading.

Spending time together during Christmas brought us closer in ways we hadn't experienced. During the Christmas holidays, we were sitting at Bill's kitchen table one night, and he asked if I'd thought about what the person I married would be like. I said I wanted him to have strong values, a good sense of humor for tough times, be a Christian, and be a peaceful, kind person. He said he had always thought his wife would have a substantial career identity outside the home and that her work would be as important to her as his work was to him. I thought it was interesting that he had developed this idea about his future mate. He asked, "Have you ever thought about what your life will be like when you are married? Will you work outside the home?" I was surprised by the question but told him I'd always thought I'd work, maybe teaching and singing, but also caring for the family and home.

We didn't discuss marriage and future partners again, but I replayed this conversation many times. His mother had a career plus her role as mother, and that was the model he knew. I envisioned that I'd continue the role I'd grown up with, seeing my mother at home, tending to the house and family, being involved in church, community, and school activities, and keeping things running well. Thoughts of what kind of life and career I might have soon changed radically. After marriage, I had seven part-time jobs, including being a college voice professor at two schools, a church and temple musician, a university residence hall director, a wife, and a mother. I experienced my first and only migraine headache that crippled me for a day or so because I was trying to do too much. We were saving for a home down-payment but I found my limit. I had no idea when Bill and I talked that my future would involve juggling multiple jobs plus family.

When Bill worked for Senator Fulbright while at Georgetown, he observed the senator's relationship with his wife and was impressed with their marriage. They spent time together reading and simply enjoying each other's companionship. Bill was always watching and learning about every aspect of life.

This Christmas was magical and memorable. Bill offered to drive me to the airport to fly back to Bloomington. When he came to get my bag, Virginia was with him. She and my mother stood in our den, hugged, and shed a few tears. I didn't know why, but I assumed it was because we were going back to school and growing up fast. Bill stayed with me at the airport, and we read the paper while waiting for our departure. We were an "old hat" duo, taking our relationship in stride and knowing we'd see each other again. It felt comfortable and right.

He saw* Glamour *and* Vogue *magazines on the table, and he asked me, "Do you read these magazines?"

Bill called sometimes, and we also continued to write. I was a live-in nanny for an Indiana University professor and his wife. My friend Nancy Nedwell lived there, too, and it was great having free housing in exchange for helping with the girls. Bill's picture was among those of other friends on my desk. I told all my friends he would someday be president and to remember his name. Don, Robin, Donna, Carol, and Mary heard many long stories about our friendship and how I'd predicted for years that he'd be president one day. It was a great occasion when Don Lollar, a friend and Baptist Student Union director, was invited to meet the president and have a photo taken in the Oval Office years later.

Bill invited me to Georgetown for a senior dance called the Rose Ball, which delighted me. It meant I would miss a chamber literature test, but the professor said I could take it later. What a thrill to visit my friend, Bill, to see Georgetown University, and to tour DC again. I bought a new black dress and flew to DC. Bill met me at the airport and drove to the house at 4513 Potomac Avenue that he was renting with roommates Tom Campbell, Tom Caplan, and Jim Moore. Bill gave me his bedroom, and he slept in Tom's room next door. The dance was a gala event with the Peter Duchin Orchestra entertaining. We sat at a large round table for dinner with Bill's housemates and their dates. Each girl received a long-stemmed red rose.

Bill's housemate, Kit Ashby, was dating a Georgetown coed, and she invited me to tour the National Gallery of Art. We spent most of our time in the early Italian galleries, paralleling her art history studies. We focused on the works of Titian of the Venetian School, Fifteenth and Sixteenth Centuries.

Bill took me by the house where several Georgetown girls lived, including Denise Hyland, whom he dated earlier. She met us at the door carrying a wide-brimmed straw hat and a picnic basket as she and a beau were leaving. I could tell there was still a special bond between Bill and Denise.

While Bill and I were in their living room, he saw *Glamour* and *Vogue* magazines on the coffee table, and he asked me, "Do you read these magazines?" I told him that I enjoyed them regularly. Maybe he was asking to be sure my fashion knowledge was up to par with the cosmopolitan young women at Georgetown, but I thought I was holding my own. He was likely checking that I was interested in the same things the Georgetown women did. I asked if he read *Esquire* and *Gentleman's Quarterly*, and he laughed and said, "Yes."

Bill took me to dinner at the famous Georgetown Blackie's House of Beef. He wanted to hear more about my music studies and transition from piano to voice major. I told him I loved singing and was getting some opera roles. I explained I was looking forward to our steak dinner because I needed to be a strong, big girl to sing opera.

"So I need to feed you more?" he asked. We both laughed at this revelation.

One afternoon, Bill's housemates and I sat together in their living room. They apologized for the shabby furniture in their rental house. "Look at the sofa falling apart," one of the guys remarked, pointing to the sofa arm falling off. I studied the situation and suggested that they move the sofa to another wall so the limp arm could have support. The scholars were amazed at my resourcefulness.

We were watching TV one evening in the living room, and President Nixon was holding a press conference with his wife Pat at his side. Roommate Tom Caplan was slightly critical of Nixon's comments and remarked that Bill would have handled things differently. I watched quietly and realized Bill's friends also had thoughts of him being president one day.

When Bill was in class, I took the opportunity to tour the Capitol and the White House. Thinking he was destined to be president someday, I had no trouble projecting that image as I toured. At the Capitol, I watched proceedings in the Senate gallery, walked through Statuary Hall, and—spying empty niches—I thought, "Bill's statue will stand there someday." When I visited the White House, I saw the beautiful French furnishings Jackie Kennedy had selected to redecorate the public rooms. I thought, "When Bill is president, he might select some fine early American antique furnishings from Philadelphia, Boston, and New York. Surely, our nation's premiere residence should be appointed with the finest American decorative arts." It was all within my vision of Bill being president one day. He had never uttered a word about this notion, but I knew he was interested in politics, and surely the presidency would be his crowning achievement.

On my way back to meet Bill, I stopped by a bookstore and found a new publication about the American presidency. I bought it for Bill, and he was pleased to receive it.

One evening in DC, Bill and I went to the Georgetown townhouse of some friends. Tom Caplan asked me to play a Chopin *Polonaise*, and I took a turn at it, much to Tom's delight. We were also invited to the home of some married classmates, and after dinner, the group played charades. I drew a card with the title *Til Eulenspiegel's Merry Pranks*. Til was a trickster of German folk legend, and I wasn't sure the group would know his name. Wondering how I could convey this through hand signals, I pantomimed garden hoeing, and someone guessed correctly. It had been a whirlwind and lovely few days

Bill was irritated at me and scolded. "Why do you need your camera? We'll never forget this!"

Later that spring, on April 5, 1968, friends and I went to Philadelphia to do door-to-door canvassing for a new church. I told Bill I was passing through and asked if I might stop to see him on the way. He agreed. The timing for my DC visit was momentous. The day before I left, Dr. Martin Luther King Jr. was assassinated in Memphis. The nation was reeling, but Bill and I didn't discuss canceling my trip. As I flew into DC, I saw the flames rising from the areas where rioting had raged all night. King's death triggered enormous anger that spilled into violence. Georgetown University called in the National Guard to protect the students, and most students stayed on campus. For Bill, the death of King was a call to service. He wanted to be personally involved in this historic moment. He had listened to King's speeches, particularly the "I Have a Dream" address, and had been mesmerized by King's vision.

Bill was very concerned and quiet when he picked me up at the National Airport. He told me he had signed us up to volunteer with the Red Cross, and we would go directly there. When we arrived at the offices, a man approached the car and put a Red Cross sign on Bill's white Buick, his car for his senior year. The men loaded the trunk with food, water, and medical supplies for people who fled their homes and were living in safe spaces. The man told us to put on hats and gave me a scarf to pull over the sides of my face so no one could see my skin color. He told us to follow the lead car, to not stop at traffic lights unless necessary, and to get to our destination as safely as possible. This was a tense and risky assignment. We knew we were driving into the center of the riot-torn area where danger was still present.

We didn't talk as he drove. At one point as the lead car was going through a changing traffic light, Bill was tense. We couldn't afford to stop, and Bill chanted, "Keep going, yes, just keep going. GO, GO, GO!" He continued through the red light, relieved we didn't have to stop. Looting and rioting had spread from 14th and U Streets after Stokely Carmichael's speech at Howard University. The H Street corridor was a tinderbox. We were driving directly into the epicenter of demonstrations and violence. We reached our destination. Someone came to unload the car as quickly as possible. I stayed in the car as Bill assisted.

Afterward, we looked around the area. It appeared deserted and calm. Bill suggested we get out to walk and look around. We parked the car and walked into the area that once featured appliance, furniture, and clothing shops. Now, there was a row of fire-damaged buildings with front windows broken out, inventory looted, and broken glass all over the sidewalk. It was a smoldering wreckage. No one was there in the middle of the day, and it felt surreal to walk around at the destruction scene only hours earlier. Now, it was a silent witness to decades of anger and frustration.

I wished for my camera. I was interested in 35mm black and white photography and enjoyed capturing images and emotions. I knew I'd never forget what I was seeing but still wished I could record it on film. Bill was irritated at me and scolded, "Why do you need your camera? We'll never forget this!" Of course, he was on edge about taking this risk and emotionally torn about the loss we were feeling at Dr. King's death. But he was right, and I never forgot. As we walked, we came to a corner and were about to turn to continue walking. Out of nowhere, a group of men appeared, walking five or six abreast in our direction. They advanced with conviction and purpose. Bill and I turned and walked back to his car without discussion. We kept a normal pace but arrived safely, got into the car, and left the area without incident.

What struck me as somewhat prophetic about the experience was that, even then, Bill seemed aware of the impending leadership role he would one day play in our country's history. It was as though he felt a personal responsibility to contribute to Dr. King's legacy and honor him. Bill knew he had a choice to make about his future, or maybe that the future had already chosen him for a life of public service.

He would play a role in helping continue the work started by JFK, Bobby Kennedy, Martin Luther King, and other visionary leaders of our generation. To Bill, these weren't just historical figures; they were the ones who started the work. He felt called to help continue it. The correct response was not to stay on campus but to act and help where people were hurting and in need. Others could passively watch from the sidelines, but not Bill Clinton. Now, Martin Luther King was dead, and the nation was reeling.

When King's funeral service was broadcast over the radio, Bill, his roommates, and I sat on the front steps of their house to listen with heavy spirits. Mahalia Jackson sang *Precious Lord Take My Hand,* and tributes were delivered. King was remembered as a giant for his risks and arrests, letters and speeches, and his progress in Civil Rights. It was a somber time. A hero who believed in freedom and equality—and worked for it peacefully—was now gone. We had witnessed years of civil rights marches, speeches, arrests, sit-ins, and other demonstrations. All had brought to our collective conscience the truth about the unequal treatment of African Americans in our society. Our lives had been touched, and we mourned King's passing.

Before leaving to join my friends in Philadelphia, Bill asked if I'd type a paper that was due when classes resumed. Although it was late and my train was leaving early the next morning, I said I'd be happy to try it, but I wasn't a good typist. We knew this might be a long night, but I had no idea what a trying circumstance I was walking into.

We went to Senator Fulbright's office, where Bill worked part-time. As Bill wrote the paper, he gave me the manuscript to type. I tried to warm up my skills and get familiar with the typewriter. I discovered the typewriter didn't have a correcting ribbon, and there was no correcting fluid in the desk drawer. How could anyone type a paper without making a mistake? Flummoxed about how this would go, I started typing. When I made a mistake, I'd pull the paper out of the carriage and begin again. This happened over and over. Bill came to check on how the paper was going and saw I was still on page one. "What? What's going on?" I explained the predicament. He sighed, and we plowed ahead.

Somehow, the paper was completed. We were exhausted and went back home for a short rest before I had to be on the train. We overslept. Bill rushed in, telling me to hurry and maybe we could make it. We got to the station, and fortunately, I made the train. Some weeks later, I asked about the paper, and he told me he had made a C. It was not one of his finest projects, and I worried that my typing had played a part. I knew I'd truly tried under difficult circumstances. I hoped maybe his new girlfriend was a better typist.

After graduating from Georgetown, Bill was chosen as a Rhodes Scholar to attend Oxford University in the fall. Virginia and I waited for his interview results with the Rhodes Scholarship committee in New Orleans. After a long wait, I went home. Later, she phoned and said Bill had just called to ask, "How do you think I'll look in Oxford Tweeds?" We were ecstatic about this honor and experience.

The summer of 1968 also held personal new adventures. I went to Venezuela for three months as a student summer missionary. Venezuela was a fascinating experience as I traveled alone around the country to work in Caracas, Maracaibo, Barquisimeto, and jungle villages. Many American oil companies were there, and most churches held services in Spanish and English. I assisted with Vacation Bible School and sang for worship. Pigs and chickens walked through the open jungle church, and gnats spewed from the pump organ bellows as I tried to play and sing. I also visited the beautiful beaches of Los Caracas and met interesting people in both jungle and urban settings. I sent Bill letters and postcards and brought him a handwoven hammock as a souvenir.

I returned from Venezuela in time to serve as Maid of Honor for my sister Lynda's beautiful wedding. My father officiated, and the bridesmaids were friends from Ouachita.

Bill surprised his family by coming home from Oxford for Christmas 1968. He came to our house and waited for me in the living room. His mother Virginia and Jeff Dwire were marrying after the New Year and Bill would be home to celebrate. He sported a full beard and looked very much like the Oxford scholar he was. He brought me a University College blue and gold woolen scarf for Christmas, and I treasured it. Bill and I played piano/sax duets for the wedding, and Roger sang *Just the Way You Are*.

He was distant. I knew something was wrong.

Following JFK's age of Camelot, the presidency of Lyndon Johnson led us into the Vietnam War. The deaths of friends who were drafted, including four high school classmates, marked a time of terrible upheaval. The war seemed unending, and campuses were hotbeds of protest. The "hippy" era dawned with the "summer of love" in California in 1967, and the counter-cultural movement spread across the country. At Indiana University, we had "love-ins" and "sit-ins" and campus protests, class boycotts, and more. It was certainly nothing I'd experienced at Ouachita University. The year was identified by peace symbols, psychedelic colors, easy access to drugs, "tripping out," headbands and flowers in hair, and incense burning in every shop near campus. One classmate came to a lecture wearing a sheet. I didn't get heavily involved in the protest movement but followed the war news with alarm at the growing number of deaths. The strife surrounding Nixon's election in 1968 added to mistrust about the war as the staggering death toll of people our age opened eyes and seemed to test patriotism.

Friends and family were dying. My roommate Nancy's brother was among them. I'll never forget the night her pastors came to our apartment door to bring the news of Bobby's death. Thinking it was an unexpected friendly visit, Nancy was delighted to see them. Then her face dropped suddenly as she saw their downcast expressions. "Oh no! Bobby!" she screamed, and the news began to unfold as we learned of his death in Vietnam.

I didn't see Bill much that summer of '69 because I had stayed in Bloomington for summer classes. I was invited to spend the year in Salzburg, Austria, as a nanny for the family at Schloss Leopoldskron, the von Trapp's home in *The Sound of Music*. It was so tempting, but I had been in Venezuela the summer before and needed a few classes to graduate, so I declined the opportunity. My opera coach told me that not much happened in Salzburg except during the summer festivals. My roommate Nancy took the job instead.

When I got home after summer classes, Bill had met new friends. He called asking to pick me up and took me to meet them. He was dating an older high school friend, Betsy, and was friends with Glenn, an African American young man with whom he formed a rock band. I heard the band was playing a concert at the K-Mart parking lot, and I told Mother I'd like to go. She said someone would see me, the preacher's daughter, and it could also be a dangerous place to be for an outdoor, interracial concert. She was right because a fight broke out, and the police were called.

Bill and Glenn tried to address racial change in Hot Springs that summer. They went to the Hot Springs Boys Club swimming pool and were the first to integrate it. Any step to open doors to justice and equality felt important. It was time for us to take a stand anywhere we could.

Bill and I visited some over those weeks, but he was distant. I knew something was wrong as I heard serious, hushed discussions and phone calls and felt tensions. He was dealing with a troubling personal dilemma about the draft. His baptism friend Bert Jeffries, who wrote to Bill saying to stay away from Vietnam, was, in fact, later killed there. Working for Senator Fulbright and the Foreign Relations Committee gave Bill access to classified information about the Vietnam conflict that proved Americans weren't being given the whole truth. Bill held the military—and those who served in the military—in high regard. Yet, he was conflicted about going to Vietnam. I could feel his personal strain and could only watch and pray for peace in his life and our world.

Bill returned to Oxford knowing his draft number could be called at any time. He has written about this time of anguishing twists and turns. He received his draft notice in April but was allowed to complete his term at Oxford. In June he returned home and accepted the University of Arkansas Army Reserve Officers' Training Corps invitation. Because he couldn't enroll until after he attended summer camp, he would go on active duty after a year of law school. After much angst, he reconsidered and decided to allow himself to be put back in the draft and was classified 1-A. However, a new plan instituted by President Nixon allowed students to complete the school year before reporting, so Bill expected to be drafted after his second year at Oxford. In December, his draft number 311 was called. However, due to the de-escalation of the war in 1970 and troop reduction, he never had to go.

Bill returned to Oxford for his second year as a Rhodes Scholar. He wasn't coming home for Christmas because he wanted to travel as much as possible while in Europe. Virginia tacked a world map on the den wall and put a pin in every place he visited in Europe: Sweden, Finland, Russia, Czechoslovakia,

Germany, and Spain. It didn't surprise me that he stayed with friends he'd made at Oxford at each stop.

Bill asked me to walk with him along the beach. We didn't talk much but just walked for a while.

My life was going well in every way. I was in a serious romantic relationship that began in the fall of 1969. Vocal studies were soaring with my new voice teacher, Metropolitan Opera Wagnerian soprano Margaret Harshaw. Opera roles came my way, with the lead role of Amelia in Verdi's *A Masked Ball*, the role of Flower Maiden in Wagner's *Parsifal* in 1969, and Helmwige in Wagner's *Die Walkyrie* in 1970. This recognition increased my self-esteem, and graduate recitals followed. While I still wasn't sure this was my calling, I believed I could succeed if I chose this path.

The biggest news in my life was that I met my future husband, Jerry Staley. Having grown weary of being in the music building from dawn to dark, I added a minor in art history. In the spring, I took "20th Century Art History," and in the fall, I tried to enroll in "19th Century Art History," only to find the class closed. The advisor told me not to despair because there was an opening in a graduate course, "Art and Architecture of 17th Century Rome." Needing a course, I enrolled. On the second day of class, I took my lunch to the art building. I sat outside the classroom to enjoy it and seated next to me was classmate Jerry Staley. We chatted about Michelangelo, Caravaggio, Bernini, the Vatican, and Roman architecture. I had noticed him in class and thought he was handsome. I especially liked how his eyes wrinkled at the corners when he smiled.

A few days later, I saw Jerry out shopping, and we said hello. Days later, he asked after class if I'd join him for a photo outing in the beautiful Brown County countryside. It was a lovely excursion, and we enjoyed a picnic lunch of ring bologna, cheddar cheese, and Ritz crackers from a country store along the way. We dated steadily through the semester and continued dating through the spring. We both knew love was in bloom. In the spring of 1970, I completed my assistantship and graduate coursework. Only a final recital remained before graduation. The end of grad school was in sight.

I was selected to be a singing waitress on Cape Cod at the Compass Inn for the summer with other opera students from IU. We performed opera arias, musical theater standards, and occasionally a favorite pop or gospel song between waiting tables. I looked forward to going even though it meant I'd be apart from Jerry for a few months. We weren't engaged, but I thought we were getting close. The Cape Cod experience was one I hoped to have before settling down. I'd be in Boston for rehearsals and on Cape Cod for the summer.

After I arrived at South Yarmouth for the summer, I learned of an opening for a voice and theory professor at Brescia College in Owensboro, Kentucky, my birthplace. Brescia College, a Catholic college with about 700 students, was familiar to me because the campus was next to my grandparent's home. This position would be perfect because I'd live close enough to Bloomington to finish my graduate recital and be near Jerry. I flew to Bloomington, Jerry drove me to the interview, and I was hired for the position.

My roommate, Mary, also a voice major, drove me to the Cape and even took my bicycle for me to ride between the Compass and the apartment I would share with four other singers. She returned and drove me back to Owensboro too. What a friendship. I loved being on the Cape. I dieted to save money, eating only blueberry yogurt for lunch and a salad for supper. I drove my bike to a drugstore to weigh myself every day, and when my mother and father brought my car to Owensboro, they said I looked gaunt.

Shopping on the Cape for kitchen pieces Jerry and I admired, I bought two pewter plates and an antique copper pot. I visited the Sandwich Glass factory but dropped and broke my small souvenir. There were wonderful days on the beach, plus lobster for $5 on Fridays. I loved Ferry trips to Martha's Vineyard, Nantucket, and Provincetown. Climbing the dunes at Navy Beach will always stay with me.

While I was at the Cape, Bill came to see me. He was home from Oxford and headed to Yale Law School in the fall. He drove his VW to the Compass, and I met him wearing my orange print uniform because there wouldn't be time to change before work. We drove to Hyannis, where he was staying with Georgetown roommate Tom Caplan at a beach apartment. Tom took us to Hyannis Port to the Kennedy compound and regaled us with stories of his time with the Kennedys, including teaching Jackie to do a popular 1960s dance called The Frug. He made a huge pot of fresh clam chowder that we enjoyed. We talked about his novel writing progress at a desk overseen by a poster of muse Farrah Faucett.

We returned to South Yarmouth, and Bill came to the Compass to hear me sing. Battling laryngitis due to the smoky environment and chilly night air, I got through *O Happy Day* and he enjoyed the crowd favorite. I introduced him to my friends at closing. We visited for a while longer at my apartment, read, and talked. He chatted with my roommates about Oxford life, and they were very impressed with him. We said goodbye and looked forward to seeing each other again. I learned later that he had a minor automobile accident driving back to Tom's apartment in Hyannis the night of our visit. He had forgotten his driver's license, so he was held in jail a few hours before Tom bailed him out. I was sorry for that experience but grateful we'd had a good visit.

Before classes began, Jerry visited Owensboro after our long summer apart. We weren't planning yet about our future but had stayed in close touch all summer. As I watched him walk to my office, I was a bit nervous but eager to be reunited. There were monumental decisions ahead. He invited me to dinner at Gabe's Restaurant, which had a revolving dining room on the top floor and a beautiful Ohio River view. He asked me to marry him and gave me a diamond pendant engagement gift because I once told him I thought I would like to have a simple wedding band with diamonds rather than a set of rings. He asked if I'd be his "Sadie married lady," the title of a song Barbara Streisand sang in *Funny Girl*. Having known from the first that he was The One, I didn't hesitate to say yes. He was gentle, kind, and fun to be with. There was no arguing or tension between us. His temperament was gentle, and I felt we would be compatible. We shared an interest in the arts. He told me he believed love means setting a person free to be all they can be. I was confident that Jerry was the one with whom I could build a home for life.

I had an engagement photo taken for newspapers in Arkansas and Kentucky. I wore my hair in a low bun and admired the classic black and white engagement photos of friends who married before me. No big smile, just a slight one. When my photo appeared in the *Arkansas Gazette*, and Roger saw it first, Virginia told me he called Bill and said, "Bubba, you'd better hurry. You're letting all the good ones get away!" I thought that was a very kind compliment from Bill's little brother.

As Roger Jr. grew older, he became interested in music. He attended Hendrix College in Conway, Arkansas, a fine private school, and majored in political science. However, his love for music took precedence, and he eventually dropped out to pursue his band interests as lead vocalist with the group "Dealer's Choice." The band played local clubs and events. Virginia was his biggest fan and was very proud of him. This was when Bill was beginning his political career and doing well. Roger Jr. was a good-looking young man. Virginia said he had more girlfriends than Bill ever had. My husband Jerry did a publicity photo shoot for his band fliers. I always admired Virginia for giving equal time to her sons. She was genuinely proud of their accomplishments in their chosen fields.

Bill's life was in full swing with great promise of a bright future in public service. Headed to Yale, with Oxford and global trekking behind him, he'd be home soon and on his way to elective office if my predictions were correct. The Vietnam conflict and his potential draft had been a dark period, but his desire to serve his country in other ways was strong and gave him confidence. He'd be home after Yale Law School, meeting his future life partner, and beginning to take the first steps toward the White House, where I envisioned him belonging.

CHAPTER THREE

Marriages, Political Beginning

"Is this where it happened?" It sounded like he was at a crime scene.

Jerry and I were married on a beautifully warm, sunny day, December 28, 1970, in Hot Springs. We felt overjoyed to begin life together. Although my college teaching continued for four months, I planned to move to Bloomington in May as Jerry neared completion of graduate school. Our short distance apart meant we could be together on weekends. We were so happy! My father conducted the wedding ceremony and a few days before we married, he led us through the vows. I respectfully asked that we take out "I plight thee my troth" and hoped we could simply respond with "I will" rather than repeat the vows. I was afraid I might get teary with my Dad conducting the wedding.

I found the perfect wedding dress in Evansville, Indiana—a tailored, ivory knit, knee-length dress with long sleeves and a high neckline. It also had a long rust-colored vest to wear for our departure after the reception. I found beautiful lace for a shoulder-length mantilla. Jerry wore a dark suit and looked very handsome. I had a lovely bouquet of white roses, our mothers wore rose corsages, and Jerry and my father wore boutonnieres.

The Christmas wedding fulfilled my dream of having a wedding just like my parents had—a small ceremony in our living room with immediate family. I hadn't met all our church members, having lived in Hot Springs just three years before college, and a church wedding required inviting all. We wanted to keep it personal. Jerry's mother and sister Terri and my family attended. I tried to do most of the planning to spare my mother the added work during the Christmas season, and she was a wonderful support. We had tall candelabras on either side of a kneeling bench and fresh poinsettias for decorations. A memory candle was on a side table, and at the close of our wedding, we used individual tapers to light the large candle, symbolizing our new life together. We have continued to light the unity candle each year on our anniversary. It was supposed to last 25 years, but we lit it last year at our 50th celebration. I missed not having live music, but the family hummed the *Wedding March* as I entered. Before the wedding, Daddy sampled the nuts on the table, and I detected their scent as he officiated. The postman rang the doorbell during the ceremony with a postage-due letter. I treasured our home wedding, and these fun memories added smiles.

Our friends hosted two beautiful bridal showers. The church-wide party and another hosted by Claire Callahan for a close group of school friends provided a generous outpouring of gifts. Bill joined us at the end of Claire's shower, and we visited with friends and shared news of life. Jerry and I received everything a young couple could dream of to begin our home. The Clintons gave us a large golden wall clock with a sunburst background as a perfect symbol of our timeless friendship.

Mother displayed our gifts in the living room on tables with linen tablecloths. She told me that Bill came to see the gifts one morning when I was out, examined everything, and talked about how wonderful it all was. Mother said he seemed kind of melancholy seeing the girl next door heading to the altar. I think he was probably making a few notes for his own wedding one day, which would be a home wedding like ours.

We invited friends to a reception after our ceremony. The table held a beautiful double-tiered wedding cake, mints, nuts, and punch in our silver punch bowl. We've kept the wedding bells and doves from our cake, and we put them on our Christmas tree each year. Several friends attended, including Virginia and Jeff Dwire, Marge Mitchell, classmate Mary Jo, and Ouachita classmate Al Wetherington. Bill came, too, and it was special to share this time with him. He was wearing a pale blue necktie. Knowing his sentimental nature, I wondered if it might be the one I had given him years before. Bill, Jerry, and Al sported beards, and the photographer got a great picture of the three of them together. Sadly, the picture disappeared from my album after he was elected President, but I still remember the three smiling, bearded men.

Bill asked to see where the ceremony took place, and we walked together into the living room. He looked at the flowers, candles, kneeling bench, and altar and asked, "Is this where it happened?" It sounded like he was investigating a crime scene, and we laughed at the funny comment. We talked about life, our plans, and our friendship. He wondered aloud what our futures might hold and shared some of his own thoughts. He said he had thought I would marry first and he'd marry later. We promised to always stay in close touch.

We returned to enjoy the reception and then moved to the front lawn for the toss of my bouquet and garter. Bill watched my siblings decorate our car with "Just Married" and detach a battery cable to slow our getaway. As friends waved goodbye, Jerry and I left to begin a new life.

The next day, Tom Campbell, Bill's Georgetown roommate, came to Hot Springs. He and Bill toured downtown and walked along Central Avenue. Jerry and I spent our wedding night at the Hill Wheatley Hotel in Hot Springs, a gift from the Wheatley family, before driving back to Bloomington. As Jerry and I were strolling along Central, we ran into Tom and Bill. It was a funny encounter but a joy to see them. They were slightly shocked to see the newlyweds out and about. I felt different now as a married lady with my husband. Adult life and adventures were becoming real.

"You're not going to marry someone we haven't met, are you?"

Our precious daughter, Sarah, arrived in Bloomington, Indiana, in September 1971. We were surprised but excited to learn we were expecting our first baby, a honeymoon gift. Sarah was born on September 2, and we welcomed her with open hearts. We both cried at this newfound joy and miracle of creation. Fathers weren't yet allowed in delivery, but Jerry and I used the childbirth training we learned in Lamaze classes, and he was a big help.

Jerry and I received our graduate diplomas in 1972 and took Sarah with us to commencement. She wore her pink Easter dress and coat and a pink mortar board I made to match. Her picture was on the front page of the next day's paper. What a wonderful life we experienced, filled with new developments. So much had happened so quickly: my first college teaching position, engagement, marriage, moving back to Bloomington, and welcoming our first child. It was a lovely, happy time.

Jerry found the perfect apartment for us with Professor John Stoner and wife Margaret on the Brown County highway surrounded by wooded acreage that burst into color each fall. We had free lodging in exchange for Jerry's lawn care and my light housekeeping. Sarah's birth while we lived there meant she had another family to adore her each day. After Sarah's birth, Bill sent a beautiful letter saying he had learned from his mother that Sarah was here. He said he felt such "exhilarating happiness" for us. He expressed amazement at our whirlwind of life since marriage and the birth of our first child and was so happy for us. We kept up a steady correspondence and shared pictures as Sarah grew.

Jerry's first teaching job was in Chesterton, Indiana. Because the school district was supported by taxes from the regional steel industry, he had funds to build a dream photography program in the high school. His love of photography always tugged at him as a possible full-time job, but the income was not dependable. As an option, he taught full-time but had evening and weekend photo work.

I taught private voice lessons at home and at Valparaiso University. Campus performances in the university's remarkable and renowned chapel kept me busy singing. Our daughter Mary Caroline was born in 1974 after we moved to a big farmhouse there. Mary and Sarah gave us untold joy as the dual centerpiece of our lives.

Sinai Temple in Michigan City asked me to sing for the High Holidays, and I became a soloist for services and director of the holiday choir. Life had gotten busy very quickly. I enjoyed the singing opportunities, and the income was a help to our family. Temple Rabbi Joseph Edelheit became one of our dearest friends. President Clinton appointed him to the HIV/AIDS Commission, and we went together to the White House with our son Will to introduce Joe to the president and to have Will's photo taken with his namesakes, Bill Clinton and Joseph Edelheit.

Hearing from Bill always brought joy. He met Hillary at Yale in the spring of 1971 and their relationship had become serious. He wrote that he was happy and thought he had "been struck by the proverbial bolt." While teaching law at the University of Arkansas, he traveled to Chicago to visit Hillary's family. He called to say he was in the 'neighborhood' and wanted to say hello. We talked a long time, and I asked if marriage was on the horizon. He said we'd just have to wait and see. I teasingly asked, "You're not going to marry someone we haven't met, are you?" He said the relationship was still developing, but it sounded likely to me.

Hillary was a gifted intellect and a real catch. Bill admired her strong mind and excellent legal skills and knew she was deeply respected. She was a champion for children's legal rights even at Yale with her legal work for New Haven Legal Assistance offices. Fresh out of Yale Law School at age 26 after working as a lawyer for the Children's Legal Defense Fund, she joined the Watergate impeachment inquiry staff. Bill marveled at her heart for service and was fascinated by her strength. She fulfilled his dreams for a mate. He told his family that she was the one for him and asked them to please accept her with open hearts.

Virginia also told us about Bill bringing Hillary home to meet the family. She stayed in touch with letters in her beautiful penmanship, sharing news about her life and family in her correspondence. My parents moved to Greenwood, Mississippi, in 1972, so I didn't see my neighbor Virginia on trips home anymore. I missed that closeness a lot.

"Bill Clinton got married, and it's in the NEWS, not the society pages—the NEWS!"

Our family kept up with Bill's foray into politics as he ran for Congress in 1974. We knew several of his campaign staffers and looked forward to news about the race. He talked about the whirlwind of life that we'd jumped into with marriage and Sarah's birth, and I thought the exact same thing about his entry into politics. It seemed he had only started teaching law at the University of Arkansas and now was running for Congress. He narrowly lost the race to popular incumbent John Paul Hammerschmidt, but he did very well and made strong inroads into Arkansas politics.

After a few years of courtship and the launch of her impressive career in law and public service, Hillary gave in to Bill's pleas that she move to Fayetteville. He bought a house she admired as an engagement gift. Bill and Hillary were married there on October 11, 1975, in a home wedding that I hoped was inspired by our wedding five years earlier. A friend from Arkansas sent a letter to me at Valparaiso University about their marriage. She noted in the letter, "Bill Clinton got married, and it's in the *NEWS*, not the society pages—

the NEWS!" He was a public figure now, and making news was their destiny. I was happy for them and pleased that Bill had found a life partner. Hillary seemed to fit the description of the ideal woman Bill told me he thought he'd someday marry.

In 1976, Bill ran for Arkansas Attorney General and won. He reflected later that, while it had been disappointing to lose the Congressional race, it actually worked to his advantage because, living in Arkansas, he established a base for future elections. We called Bill to congratulate him and sent a peace lily plant to his office. We were proud of him and this major political launch. I visited Arkansas on a trip home and stopped by the attorney general's office. He seemed happy to be serving his home state. I arrived with a bushel of peaches from Clarksville as a gift. Bill took a big bite and was thrilled to receive them. As peach juice dripped from his chin, we caught up on families, work, and plans and we savored the moment.

I saw photos of Hillary on his desk and looked forward to meeting her. I met Freddie Nixon whose husband, Vic, had officiated Bill and Hillary's marriage. Vic also later helped my transition from Baptist ministry to serving a Methodist congregation. Freddie and I worked closely on death penalty issues as members of the Arkansas Coalition to Abolish the Death Penalty.

1976 was a busy political year for Bill and Hillary. In addition to his election as Arkansas' Attorney General, Bill chaired the Jimmy Carter presidential campaign in Arkansas. He spent much of the late summer and fall canvassing the state, and Carter carried the state handily. Hillary also campaigned for Carter as state field coordinator for his campaign in Indiana. We hoped our paths would cross as we hadn't yet met. Hillary called us to say she was organizing the "Peanut Brigade," a series of bus tours, and would be in Valparaiso. Her visit fell during a scheduled class, and I couldn't get away. Jerry met her, however, and joined the Peanut Brigade as photographer. Indiana voters gave their electoral votes to Gerald Ford, but Carter did very well and was elected President in November 1976. Hillary and Bill negotiated major dramas in presidential politics that would soon come in handy.

"You have to sever friendships with other men once you're married."

Bill stayed in touch, and we liked hearing how well life was going for Bill and Hillary. Our family continued living in northwest Indiana, enjoying teaching and raising our two daughters (our son, Will, arrived later, in 1981). In one letter exchange, Bill and I discussed whether it would be better to become rich and famous or to live a life of quiet service.

In the summer of 1977, my mother and I took our daughters to Pine Bluff to visit my siblings Walter and Lynda. We stayed at the Holiday Inn Walter managed. Pine Bluff was a major concert venue with artists including Elvis and Tom Jones. Walter gave us the suite where Tom Jones had stayed. While we were there, Sister Sledge was performing in town and staying at the hotel. We shared the pool and respected the group's privacy, but we were star-struck fans.

After two years as attorney general, Bill ran for governor of Arkansas in 1977. He was thirty-one years old. While we were in Pine Bluff, Virginia called to say Bill was speaking in Hot Springs at a campaign event and asked me please to come surprise him.

Mother put her foot down. "Absolutely not, Carolyn. You are married. It would look bad, and Jerry wouldn't understand. You must sever friendships with other men once you're married." It was hard to understand her idea that I couldn't be close to my oldest friend, and I was disappointed not to go. Jerry was confident in our relationship and knew my friendship with Bill was rare and special. I felt sure he would have no misgivings about it. I was always so thankful for Jerry's strong self-esteem that allowed his friendship with Bill to flourish. Bill wrote a note to wish Jerry well and added at the bottom, "I love you." Indeed, Bill and I have continued our friendship through marriages, careers, and children. Some things are worth the effort.

In the 1970s, our personal lives remained full and rewarding with singing, photography, teaching, and more. The beautiful Indiana Dunes State Park at Lake Michigan was in our backyard. We made regular trips with friends to Chicago, just an hour away, for museum visits and plays, but had to budget because it cost about thirty dollars for food and gas each trip. Life was good and we were busy but elated. It was exciting to watch our lives unfold. Our dreams were coming true.

CHAPTER FOUR

Governor Clinton is Elected, Neighbors Again

Bill said, "I always thought if I did something good with my life, maybe you could be a part of it. Will you come back home and be part of my administration? And one more thing, can we be neighbors again?"

In November 1978, Bill was elected Governor of Arkansas. At age 32, he was the youngest governor in the country. Elated, we called from Indiana to celebrate with him and Hillary. Jerry and I visited Little Rock several weeks after the election, and Bill and Hillary invited us to spend the night in their Heights home on L Street. I met Hillary on this visit. She worked at the prestigious Rose Law Firm. Founded in 1820, it was the oldest law firm west of the Mississippi.

We met Hillary for dinner at That Little Restaurant in Hillcrest and enjoyed getting acquainted. She had a business trip, so she couldn't be home with us, but I was happy to finally meet her. Jerry and I slept on the sofa bed in the living room under a beautiful Chinese screen, a wedding gift from Bill's friend, David Edwards. The Clinton's home was comfortable—full of art and mementos from their active early lives—and in the master bedroom, a beautiful brass bed. A small park across the street offered swings and picnic tables for neighbors to enjoy.

While Bill was busy assembling his staff and cabinet, Jerry and I made dinner for Bill, John Danner, and Nancy "Peach" Pietrafesa, who were moving to Little Rock to join his administration. Hillary called as we were finishing dinner, and Bill bragged about my fruit dessert. I was uncomfortable at the compliments but happy he had enjoyed it. After dinner, Bill finished laundry, and I heard him exclaim after folding clothes, "Hooray, all the socks came out even. No singles!"

Bill was recruiting Paul Levy from Massachusetts to direct the Arkansas Department of Energy. Paul's wife, Barbara, a choral conductor, was hesitant to move. Bill asked me to talk with her about the potential for continuing her work in Arkansas. Paul and Barbara moved to Little Rock, and Barbara founded the Arkansas Chamber Singers, an auditioned group that gave excellent performances each year. I enjoyed singing with the group she led so capably.

While visiting Little Rock, Bill invited me to sing at his gubernatorial inauguration in January 1979, which thrilled me. He asked me to sing in the inaugural "Diamonds and Denim" gala. I also sang with the Arkansas Symphony in an inaugural concert in the capitol rotunda. It was wonderful to be a part of his inauguration.

The bigger question came next. Bill said, "I always thought if I did something good with my life, maybe you could be a part of it. Will you come back home and be part of my administration? And one more thing, can we be neighbors again?"

Jerry and I talked about the move. We were doing well in Valparaiso, but we were working multiple jobs. I enjoyed teaching and singing in Chicago and concerts on campus. I was teaching two semesters at Valparaiso University, teaching summer classes at St. Joseph's College in Rensselaer, temple soloist and choir director for Bethlehem Lutheran Church in Chesterton, and was a residence hall director as well. Jerry had started a professional photography business. We had just experienced the worst winter in decades that blew across Lake Michigan and dumped mountains of snow. We couldn't see the car on our parking lot for days. Our daughters loved sledding on the drifts, but it was a difficult winter. We decided that warmer climes would be a welcome change, and the warmth of being with of old friends helped make the decision even easier.

Years later, after Bill was elected President, I was invited back to Valparaiso University to speak about my experiences as a lifelong friend of the president. A few on campus were aware of our friendship when he was elected Governor of Arkansas and heard me predict he would be president someday. Now, the former voice professor and residence hall director had a new and fascinating story to share.

"It was wonderful! Thanks, Bill"

Our family traveled to Little Rock for Bill's inauguration on Tuesday, January 9, 1979. I worked with the Clintons to plan the music for the oath of office and the Rotunda concert. We were eager to be with them for the celebration.

As we neared Little Rock, we felt the car start to slip on the roadway. Tuning into local news on the radio, we quickly discovered that an ice storm had made the interstate impassable. Many cars lost control and skidded into the interstate's median and off the shoulder. I called the Clintons to say I wasn't sure we could get there to perform the following day. Bill alerted the Arkansas State Police, and an officer who located us an hour outside of Little Rock escorted us the rest of the way. We finally reached the Camelot Hotel and were relieved at our safe arrival.

We attended the Inaugural Prayer Service at Immanuel Baptist Church and saw Bill, Hillary, and Virginia there for the first time. We went to the governor's mansion to visit them after the service. The Inaugural Gala, "Diamonds and Denim," was Monday night, January 8. The concert was billed as a "Showcase of Arkansas Talent" and took place at the Convention Center Music Hall. It was a nostalgic evening planned by Bill and co-chairs Rose Crane and Cliff Baker. I sang the opening of *You Light Up My Life* and was joined by Gladys McFadden and the Loving Sisters on the refrain. Bill spent much of the evening backstage, mingling with performers and celebrating. It was good to see high school friend and composer Randy Goodrum, who wrote the Grammy-award-winning song, *You Needed Me,* recorded by Ann Murray. Levon Helm, the Cate Brothers, Colonel Sanders, and Jimmy Driftwood also performed.

The Arkansas Symphony Orchestra conductor, Kurt Klippstatter, invited me to sing for an inauguration day concert in the Capitol Rotunda. I performed *Alleluia* from Mozart's *Exultate Jubulate* and *Tacea la notte placida* from Verid's *Il Trovatore.* The capitol Rotunda, with its domed ceiling, was a marvelous place to sing. The orchestra's soaring sounds filled the space, and the arias resonated wonderfully. At the conclusion, Bill walked to the stage to hug me and say thanks. I cherish a photo of that moment captured by an *Arkansas Gazette* photographer. Bill inscribed my program, "It was wonderful! Thanks, Bill." He hadn't heard me perform arias with an orchestra and enjoyed this introduction to my classical singing. The concert opened opportunities for me to perform with the Arkansas Symphony in later concerts, including Mahler's *Symphony No. 4* and Mozart's *Mass in C*.

Following the rotunda concert, a public reception was held in the ornate, walnut-paneled Governor's Conference Room. Deep blue velvet draperies hung at the windows, and portraits of all former governors were hung at ceiling height around the room. Bill and Hillary invited me to join them in the receiving line beside Virginia. I was still wearing my long ivory concert gown. It was a special honor to be included. Jerry and our daughters, Sarah and Mary, were there to enjoy it all, and my parents also came to Little Rock for the events.

The oath of office and inaugural address took place on the Capitol steps following the reception. I changed into warmer clothes and a heavy coat to sing the National Anthem. The roads were still too iced over for travel, so the University of Arkansas at Pine Bluff choir was unable to travel, so I sang "The Battle Hymn of the Republic," which they had planned to perform.

Later that evening, the inaugural ball at the Ricks National Guard Armory wrapped up the celebrations. Hillary wore a dress in the same style as her wedding dress—this gown designed by Connie Fails in burgundy velvet. We returned early to our hotel to rest before driving back to Indiana. It had been a grueling trip and whirlwind visit, but so worth it—a dream come true.

Bill was on his way to the life of public service, as I, his high school classmate, and others had foreseen. The sky was truly the limit for him. New opportunities were on the horizon for our family to serve alongside our friend, to continue a special friendship, and to witness his continued ascension in a life of public service.

He asked me to sing for them and whispered, "It's good politics."

After the inauguration of Governor Bill Clinton in January 1979, our planning to return to Arkansas moved into high gear. I had always wanted to move back home, and Jerry loved the state and its natural beauty. We were confident he could find a teaching position and I could teach as well at one of the area universities, teach private students at home, and find a church music position. Little Rock would also be near my parents and siblings, giving our children time with them. I still harbored an interest in public service that germinated in high school and wondered if maybe someday I could make a political race.

Jerry hoped to continue his career in photography. We considered buying a photography business that was for sale but ultimately decided that purchasing both a house and a business was too financially risky. We appreciated advice from George Gleason, president at Bank of the Ozarks, to whom Bill introduced us.

Jerry secured a teaching position with the Pulaski County School District, whose paycheck supplemented his photography income. He set up a photo studio in our home off the library. It was spacious and ideal for tabletop photography. Jerry's photography clients included the Arkansas Industrial Development Commission, the Old State House, and local businesses. He also photographed for the Quapaw Quarter Association, our neighborhood historic district organization, as well as general portraiture.

When Bill and I talked about a possible collaboration, the Directorship of the Arkansas Arts Council came up. Rose Crane, a neighbor of Bill's from childhood and a mutual high school classmate, directed the Department of Natural and Cultural Heritage, of which the Arts Council was a division. This felt like a perfect blend of arts and public service, so I happily accepted the job. I awakened later to realize that this was a 12-month job, 8-to-5 daily, and quite a schedule change from being a university professor with semester breaks, summers off, and a class schedule that allowed time with the children. I was confident we could work it out.

We took Bill's suggestion to be neighbors again to heart and looked for a home near the Governor's Mansion. Bill and Hillary invited me to use the guest house at the mansion when I was in Little Rock searching for our new home. I deeply appreciated their hospitality and the opportunity to spend time with them.

On one of my visits, the Clintons were entertaining supporters from El Dorado. Bill invited me to meet Theodosia Murphy Nolan of the Murphy Oil family, her son Bill, his wife, and Diane and Edwin Alderson. Bill asked me to sing for them, whispering, "It's good politics." Theodosia chaired the Arts Council, so it was a welcome introduction. She and I became close friends. We traveled often to Kansas City for meetings of the Mid-America Arts Alliance. We shared a room on overnight trips. She hosted my daughter Sarah and me in her home as we toured the South Arkansas Arts Center in El Dorado and attended a theater performance.

I still chuckle at a funny experience in El Dorado. Theodosia called frantically to ask me to substitute for Donna Axum, a former Miss Arkansas and Miss America, who was ill and unable to sing a concert with the South Arkansas Symphony in her hometown. Theodosia sent her plane to whisk me to town for the concert. I rehearsed mid-flight as the conductor played the score on a small tape recorder for me to hear the arrangement.

After I was dressed for the concert, I went to the hallway for a drink of water. Two women saw me, and we nodded politely. A few moments later, I heard them exclaim to another friend, "Have you seen *Donna?*" It was hysterical that the Miss America beauty queen they expected to see, slim and perfect, had really changed.

Staying at the Governor's mansion allowed me to meet the wonderful staff there, including administrator Carolyn Huber, mansion chef Liza Ashly, and housekeeper Rosie Spann. On Mother's Day weekend, Rosie invited me to sing with her in the Mt. Pleasant Baptist Church choir. I was the only white person there. The pastor invited all mothers to come to the altar to receive a rose, and Rosie nudged me to go with her. It was tough being away from my family, but I felt warmly welcomed. It also began a long friendship with the church's Pastor Willingham and invitations to sing his favorite spiritual, *Deep River*, in worship. After church and house hunting, I returned to the Governor's Mansion for a quiet afternoon. I saw Bill and Hillary relaxing and reading in the sunshine on the balcony that overlooked the mansion's back lawn. They looked settled at home, right where they should be.

We finally found a home with plenty of room for us for only $35,000. It was enormous, with fifteen rooms and ten-foot ceilings. Built in the 1880s, it was one of the earliest houses on record in Little Rock. The two-story farmhouse was charming. Sadly, it was dilapidated and slated for condemnation. The elderly owner of the original Dickinson family told me she hadn't been upstairs in twenty-five years. We found wallpaper weeping off the walls. It had been turned into a rooming house with additions of bathrooms and a kitchenette. I don't know what I was thinking, but the house appealed to me. It was stately, beautiful, and full of potential. And it was just four blocks from the Governor's Mansion.

"Does Bill ever walk past a mirror and not look at himself?"

Jerry was open to the historic home venture. We made a $5,000 deposit that we'd saved by living in the residence hall apartment. Finally, we were homeowners and what an adventure we had begun! The house at 515 West Fifteenth Street made us neighbors with the Clintons again. That made the daunting business of home restoration seem manageable and worth the effort.

I moved to Arkansas a couple of months ahead of the family to begin work at the Arkansas Arts Council. When I was free, I went to our house, often with my sister Lynda, to clean and prepare it for my family's arrival. We mopped every room and polished the wood trim. Just knowing it was clean made the house feel fresh. We knew there would be years of work ahead, but we were excited.

As I worked, Bill and Hillary often stopped by to check on my progress. They walked through to examine the latest project. One Sunday afternoon, as I was pulling up old carpeting, they arrived to find my face black with soot. After they laughed at my appearance, I led them to the kitchen to show off my efforts to remove grease from the green kitchen walls and paint it white. The previous owners were rarely in the kitchen as they had servants who lived in a small house in the back and did all the cooking. The walls were coated with greasy cooking residue. One dim light bulb hung from the ceiling. I was barely making a dent in the project. Bill could see the enormity of the project and my despair and said, "Why don't you just wait and get it painted professionally?" I explained I wanted to brighten things before the family came. We lived with my blotchy, half-painted walls for a good while. We washed dishes in the bathtub while awaiting a new kitchen sink. But we made a comfortable home, step by step.

Thankfully, Jerry was game to use his handyman skills and learn historic preservation along the way. He restored every room and often did it the hard way, refinishing walls with plaster on the old lathe instead of sheet rock. Sometimes, there simply wasn't adequate space to use sheetrock because the door facings weren't deep enough. Step by step, he plowed through the projects. Each room began to sparkle with fresh paint in Victorian colors. We managed the cold winters and hot summers until we could afford to add central heat and air. With safety in mind, we replaced the wiring and plumbing. We hired professionals to paint the exterior and repair the roof.

Our antique furniture was a perfect fit in our historic home. My father enjoyed woodworking and refinishing antiques. He could find a walnut chair in pieces, refinish it, and cane the seat until it resembled a masterpiece. He also made twin beds from cherry wood for us in Clarksville. He found a hundred-year-old walnut dining table and made three walnut leaves to extend it to seat twelve. With rebuilt walnut cane-seated chairs to go with it, this table was the scene of many board games, especially Trivial Pursuit, with the Clintons. Our family enjoyed Thanksgiving dinners and Christmas parties around it as well.

We inherited a large mahogany hall mirror with beveled glass. It had hung in my grandparents' home in their entry hallway and was from the estate of Cousin Cora Lee Webb. My mother gave it to us when my grandmother died. One day, when the Clintons were visiting, Bill walked past the mirror and caught a glimpse of himself. Hillary and I were walking behind him, and I asked her, "Does Bill ever walk past a mirror and not look at himself?"

She replied, "I don't believe I've ever experienced that."

Winters in our old house could be bitterly cold. We kept the original gas space heaters busy, although they proved woefully unable to give much warmth. We kept doors closed to stay comfortable in a few rooms. We read books and watched TV while wrapped in blankets. My mother was terrified of the open flames that flickered from the space heaters. We kept a careful eye on them and made sure the rooms were well-ventilated. One particularly frigid winter, I wasn't sure we could stay in the house. We thought about going to a hotel for a few nights. Bill and Hillary checked on us and suggested we stay in the gardener's house at the mansion. We appreciated it but decided we'd finally gotten the house warm enough to stay.

Our neighborhood was integrated but still socially segregated. We did our best to meet our neighbors. We were advised there were risks to living downtown but hoped we were part of a group trying to make a difference, building bridges of understanding. We made it our goal to shop downtown, attend public schools, and attend the integrated Second Baptist Church. Jerry and I made friends with neighbors, and our children played with Black children across the street. We were burglarized a couple of times, once by our contractor, who we learned had a long arrest history. Jerry tried to break up a gunfight to help a sobbing woman on the corner, only to find that the dispute was between a pimp and a prostitute. Jerry narrowly avoided being shot in the head as he rolled on the ground with the man. Fortunately, he escaped to safety. Otherwise, our memories of living near historic Central High School are good ones.

We had lived in segregated northwest Indiana, where real estate redlining was the unspoken rule. One day, Sarah, age 4, asked me if all people in the world are "peach-colored." I told her that there were people of many races in our world and that she would meet them throughout life. I found some brown fabric and made a baby doll for her as a reminder that God made many colors of people. She still has it.

We lived in our historic home for fifteen years and made lifetime friendships and memories there. Families were restoring historic homes nearby, so we shared what we were learning. We accessed historical records to research the history of our house. Besides learning the construction date and backgrounds of the original owners, we learned that future president Herbert Hoover was a boarder in the house as a budding civil engineer and rented the upstairs room that was now our daughter Mary's. When Bill was elected President, we realized we could say that two future presidents had been in our home.

We belonged to the neighborhood babysitting cooperative. Other parents and friends in the cooperative included Cleve and Susie May, John and Anne Jarrard, Cal and Veeta Biggers, Nick and Jerrilyn Nicholson, and Joel and Caroline Pugh. The spring tour of homes by our historic neighborhood's Quapaw Quarter Association was a weekend of celebrations. The association also sponsored the annual Easter egg hunt. Our children enjoyed friendships with neighborhood kids and joined the downtown Girl Scout troop. Our energetic and creative scout leader, Claretta Cogdell, kept the girls active and learning. We enjoyed being near the Arkansas Arts Center for classes and children's theater.

By the time we moved to DC in 1994, we had restored our home's beauty and comfort. The new owner benefited from our updated wiring and plumbing, plus new central heating and air conditioning. She made upgrades for the future bed and breakfast, the Rosemont Inn. All bedrooms became suites with full baths and walk-in closets. Now, when we drive by our old house, we look at the windows and remember the rooms. Ours was yellow with green shutters but now is painted a pale pink with white trim. Everything else looks the same. Our years there hold many great memories.

Bill said, "It's the best baby gift we've received."

Bill and Hillary's daughter, Chelsea Victoria Clinton, was born at 11:24 PM on February 27, 1980, at Baptist Medical Center in Little Rock. She was the first baby to be born to an incumbent governor and wife since 1949 when Governor Sid McMath's son James was born. Chelsea's birth was a major event. Bill and Hillary wanted a child but waited as they established their careers. Now settled in the Governor's mansion with Bill as governor and Hillary at the Rose Law Firm, parenting became an exciting change of pace for them.

Hillary took good care of herself during the pregnancy. She needed a picture for a publication and asked Jerry to take it. Instead, she decided to use an earlier one, but we thought she looked wonderful, sporting the "glow" of pregnancy. She and Bill took childbirth classes. She had an Indian nurse to help her, and all was ready for the baby's arrival. Bill was in a mild panic when he learned Chelsea was on the way. He alerted the state troopers and dashed to be at Hillary's side. Finally, she was here. They chose the name Chelsea Victoria, which was full of personal meaning and inspired by London visits and Judy Collins' song.

Congratulatory gifts poured in to celebrate her birth. One supporter made a cherry cradle for Chelsea. A young poet working in the Little Rock Schools presented poems by first-graders commemorating Chelsea's birth. Another friend gave them a wicker basket with red, white, and blue ribbons woven through the top. Hillary offered these to us at Will's birth in 1981, and we enjoyed using them.

I wondered what we might give Bill and Hillary to welcome Chelsea. I remembered how much it meant to me when Sarah was born that Jerry came to the hospital with a small bud vase holding three roses. Two long-stemmed red roses represented us as parents, and a small pink one was for our new baby girl. I thought Bill and Hillary would like the same gift, so I asked a florist to create it and took it to the Governor's mansion. I walked into the mansion kitchen and was overwhelmed to see the room filled with enormous vases of roses. Every inch of the ample counter space held arrangements of long-stem red roses sent by governors, friends, agencies, and businesses. It was a breathtaking sight. Reading some of the cards, I noted a few from foreign leaders. There I stood with my little vase. I felt there was no way it would even be seen, but I decided just to leave the vase on the counter and trust it would be discovered. We also gave them the book *The Family of Children*. I later received a lovely thank you note from the Clintons, with a handwritten postscript from Hillary thanking me for the roses and book.

I continued to think about what someone could give a friend on the birth of their first child. I decided I'd give them something of myself. I would write a song. I thought about the song as I drove our girls to Mississippi to visit my parents. 1979 had been the UNESCO "International Year of the Child," and that theme came to mind. Arkansas is known as "the natural state," which might also work. I decided to work with the themes of the specialness of childhood, the natural wonders of our state, and the natural wonder of a newborn. I went to my father's church with the words I'd drafted and began to write. The lyrics came pretty quickly and were a joy to compose. At my parents' home, I sang it for my mother, and she cried because it touched her. Gaining confidence, I hoped Bill and Hillary would love it as well.

I copied the lyrics in my best calligraphy and made a tape recording of the song. This would be our gift. I wanted to sing it for them personally and called to ask if there might be a good time to meet baby Chelsea. One afternoon, we gathered in the living room of the Governor's mansion. Bill and Hillary took turns holding Chelsea while I sang. Hillary was still exhausted from the birth, but both were euphoric and adjusting to parenthood. As we left, Bill told me, "This is the best baby gift we've received." That meant the world to me, and he wrote a note later to echo those words. The lyrics reflected that holding a newborn child evokes a sense of wonder at the miracle of new life and a sense of humility at the majesty of God's creation. (See "Poems and Songs")

Chelsea brought unparalleled joy to Bill and Hillary's lives. They watched in amazement as she grew and developed. Hillary tells the story of how Bill watched her every move as an infant and was stunned that when she started rolling over, she seemed to sense where the edge of the bed was. Or so he thought until she kept rolling, until—thankfully—Bill caught her.

He tried to encourage family and friends. "I'm going to be ok. We'll be back," he said.

Bill's 1980 campaign for re-election as Governor seemed to go well. We did all we could to support him. I volunteered at the headquarters and made calls. Sometimes, I baked treats for his road trips. Everything pointed to re-election victory. The two big issues that threatened votes were "Cubans and car tags." Bill was criticized for raising the price of license plates. While the cost increase was meager, it was a tax increase and raised the ire of many. President Jimmy

Carter had also asked our state to take Cuban refugee interns at Fort Chaffee near Fort Smith. Irate residents in the area bought guns for protection against a feared outbreak. It made the news for weeks. Still, we thought Bill would win reelection.

We went to bed election night thinking Bill had won but woke up to the shocking news that Frank White had defeated him. Bill had been the youngest governor in America and now was the youngest former governor. It seemed unbelievable. As soon as I got the children to school, I walked to the mansion to check on the Clintons. Bill stood in the kitchen taking phone calls from supporters, casually dressed in a plaid shirt and jeans. He appeared stunned but always looked on the bright side. He tried to encourage family and friends. "I'm going to be ok. We'll be back," he said.

A few days later, Bill held a press conference on the mansion's back lawn to respond to his election defeat. Hillary and nine-month-old Chelsea stood beside him. His mother, Virginia, and many friends and staff members were there. Bill promised to continue to serve and work for the people of Arkansas.

Christmas 1980, after the election loss, was particularly somber, but we did our best to celebrate with all our old traditions. Bill asked me to accompany him to play *What Child is This* at Immanuel Baptist Church's Christmas Eve service. I played for many Christmas parties at the mansion. For the last one, I asked a group of friends from high school to come caroling as a surprise for our friend Bill. I remember cueing them to sing *O Come, All Ye Faithful* as I played, and told Bill, "Listen, I think I hear carolers outside!" He looked out the window and was stunned to see old high school friends singing. He invited everyone in for a visit and lots of hugs. It brought a tear to his eye. It was a sad time, and friends always made things better.

After Bill lost the 1980 governor's race, Bill and Hillary found a wonderful house in Hillcrest on Midland Avenue. It was an historic home with a porch and swing. The wood frame home was painted a soft yellow with white trim. The house was sunny and full of light. A detached carport was at the side of the porch. The backyard was fenced.

I stopped by often to check on them. Hillary continued her work at Rose Law Firm, and Bill joined the Wright Lindsey Jennings Law Firm. He told me he thought it was obscene that he was making $100 an hour for legal work. The job kept him occupied, but the defeat was a blow. Before he took the law firm job, Hillary suggested he work at several short-term jobs to better understand the lives of working people and what it's like to draw a forty-hour week paycheck and try to make ends meet. "Get out there, Bill, and see what real people are facing and feeling." But he decided to take the law firm job instead. He knew he'd be running for reelection. He had to endure these months until he could start campaigning again.

Governors served two-year terms when Bill lost in 1980, so he was barely defeated before it was time to plan his comeback. I went by his office at the Wright Lindsey Jennings one day to share advice from friend Skip Rutherford and found Bill plugging away but seeming a little down. This was not what he wanted to be doing. I was pregnant and due in just a few weeks. Bill looked at me and said, "You're HUGE!" We laughed at his lack of diplomacy. Skip told me to tell him to create a "kitchen cabinet" of regular people to talk with for advice. He needed to know what was on voters' minds to stay engaged and ready to run again in a few short months. Bill listened and made notes.

The Clintons undertook a big project to build wall-to-wall bookcases for a library in their front sunroom. They are voracious readers and own a vast library of books. Bill organized the books by subject and author so he could quickly locate one. The shelves stretched from the floor to the ceiling. Bill liked antiques and sometimes brought something he couldn't resist home. One favorite purchase was a massive German dark wood hutch with ornate carving. Hillary wasn't sure about it, but they found a place for it in the dining room.

When I visited Hillary in the spring of 1981, she was in the backyard working in their iris bed. Enjoying the fresh spring air, she was planning the furnishings for their deck and asked my choice of color. A talented decorator, Hillary selected high-quality fabrics for draperies and upholstery. She'd learned about fabrics as her father worked in that business in Chicago. She used her father's lessons, plus her native skills, to beautify their home.

Bill loved playing with Chelsea. During one visit, I found him lying on a quilt, juggling her overhead. She wasn't yet a year old. They were raising campaign funds, and Hillary suggested names of people he could call for help. But that morning, Bill seemed to want to forget about it for a while and spend time being Chelsea's dad. Stress was always present, and problems were rarely resolved.

The Clintons enjoyed entertaining. On Christmas Eve, 1980, Hillary invited a few friends for a chili supper. She made a big pot of chili and side toppings of cheese, onions, peppers, salsa, rice, and homemade cornbread. It was a delicious meal and fun to be together. In February, Hillary gave a party for Chelsea's first birthday. The guests were Virginia or "Ginger," as Chelsea called her, Carolyn Huber, the Governor's mansion staff, including mansion cook Liza Ashley, and our family. Zeke, their blonde cocker spaniel, romped with Chelsea. Hillary hung streamers and balloons and served cake and ice cream. We found two swimsuits for baby gifts. One was a two-piece silver lame suit we thought was fun. I think Hillary preferred the pink one, but we enjoyed laughing at the styles available for baby girls.

"I don't trust politicians. I think they all ought to be strung up by their thumbs."

Our family was growing. William Joseph Staley was born on April 13, 1981, the day after Palm Sunday. We named him after two strong men in our lives, Bill Clinton and Rabbi Joseph Edelheit. Because our daughter Sarah was being baptized on Easter Sunday, we took Will straight to church from the hospital. A preacher friend, Paul Cain, called him "the Will of God," and indeed, he has always sought to make a difference.

After Will was born, Jerry's mother, Mary, came to stay with us for a while. She was very strict about my going up and down the stairs after the Cesarean delivery. I felt good, but she warned me that complications could result if I didn't rest. One day after we got home from the hospital, Bill came to visit. I was upstairs resting, and Will was sleeping in the cradle the Clintons loaned us. Mrs. Staley answered the door and met Bill for the first time. She showed him upstairs to my room. Jerry was teaching school. Mom Mary Staley chaperoned our visit, sitting at the foot of the bed as Bill admired Will and we visited. Mary was not a fan of politicians. She said to him with characteristic bluntness, "I don't trust politicians. I think they all ought to be strung up by their thumbs." I was horrified, but Bill just chuckled and took it in good stride.

After completing graduate school in 2009, our son Will founded Thrive, Inc., a nonprofit in Helena, Arkansas, to help revitalize the Delta economy and provide job training and design education. He earned a master's degree at Pratt Institute, NYC, and his thesis presentation about Thrive brought the faculty and students to their feet in an unprecedented standing ovation. Thrive continues to serve today. Will has been grateful for support from the Clinton Foundation. Bill and Hillary have taken a personal interest in Thrive.

A few months after Will's birth in 1981, Bill brought Chelsea over to visit as they ran errands. She was a toddler, 14 months older than Will. We marveled at the life-changing effect of parenting and how amazing it is to watch our children grow and develop. Bill told me Chelsea was doing new things every day. As we sat in our library to visit, Bill and Chelsea got comfy in the big gold velvet chair across from us. It was nice to talk with an old friend who dropped by to see the new baby with his child in tow. I knew Bill was in a time of transition since his defeat and needed company and friends. I was happy we were neighbors.

Hillary and I also talked about parenting. She asked once about how often I thought children should take a bath. I told her our children took baths every day during the summer but less often in winter because their skin quickly became dry. We enjoyed raising our children together as friends and neighbors. Always offering fun opportunities for Chelsea and her friends, Hillary invited our girls to go with Chelsea to a performance of *Annie* at Murray's Dinner Theater. When she came to pick up our daughters for a play, I had my hair in a ponytail, which I didn't wear often. She remarked that she liked my hairdo, and I laughingly said, "I have to pull my hair back sometimes to keep men from chasing me so I can get some work done." Slightly taken aback as a more seasoned feminist than I'd yet become, she was not amused and advised that I should wear my hair as I pleased *anytime*.

"Be not afraid, I go before you always."

History was made when Bill was re-elected Governor in 1982. He had learned a valuable lesson when he lost in 1980 for raising car tag fees. He apologized to voters for the misstep and for losing touch with voters' concerns. When Bill ran for re-election, a man told him, "I voted against you last time. You raised my car tags. I'll vote for you now because you ain't dumb, and you're the least likely one to raise our car tags again, so I'm for you."[i]

During his tenure, the Arkansas General Assembly changed the constitution to make the position of Governor a four-year term. He was re-elected in 1984, 1986, and 1990. We worked in all of Bill's campaigns and celebrated how he was helping improve Arkansas' quality of life.

The Clintons asked me to help plan the inaugural prayer services. The 1983 prayer service was the first one I participated in. I introduced Bill to "Be Not Afraid" by St. Louis Jesuit priest Bob Dufford. He loved it and asked me to sing it for his dedication service. I learned it teaching at St. Joseph's College in Indiana, where priests and nuns from across the US and Canada earned a church music diploma. I hoped the words would speak to Bill's heart and encourage him. He subsequently asked me to sing it at every future inaugural prayer service, including both of his presidential inaugural prayer services. After I sang at the 1993 Presidential Inaugural Prayer Service, I received requests for copies of the words from around the world. Scriptures from Isaiah 42 and Luke 6 form the lyrics:

"Do not fear, for I have redeemed you;
I have summoned you by name; you are mine.
2 When you pass through the waters,
I will be with you;
and when you pass through the rivers,
they will not sweep over you.
When you walk through the fire,
you will not be burned;
the flames will not set you ablaze. (Isaiah 43:1-2)
"Blessed are you who are poor,
for yours is the kingdom of God.
21 Blessed are you who hunger now,
for you will be satisfied.
Blessed are you who weep now,
for you will laugh.
22 Blessed are you when people hate you,
when they exclude you and insult you. (Luke 6:22-23)

from Isaiah 43, Luke 6 (King James Version)

Bill asked me to come by their home after his 1982 re-election. He asked if I had ideas for someone to head the Department of Arkansas Heritage. I told him I would like the job, but if he didn't give it to me, he should keep the current director, Tom Dillard, because he was doing well. Though a Republican appointee, Bill kept him on in a show of bipartisanship. I'm also not sure if he knew my governing skills or saw me as a department director, but maybe he wanted to protect me from state politics.

Bill tackled his campaign commitment to improve education in Arkansas right away. He appointed Hillary to lead the new Education Standards Committee to address shortfalls in Arkansas's educational needs and the concerns outlined in the US Department of Education's 1983 report, *A Nation at Risk*. Hillary and her committee conducted hearings in every county. As director of the Arkansas Arts Council and concerned parent of two children in public schools, I addressed one of the hearings in Pulaski County and urged the committee to make arts a requirement because of its proven benefits in boosting problem-solving skills and creative thinking.

Hillary completed the hearing and put recommendations together in a report to the Governor that became the centerpiece of a special session of the Arkansas Legislature in September. I was delighted that the arts were included as an essential requirement in every grade. The biggest challenge the recommendations faced was the teacher testing requirement. The legislature passed the recommendations and increased state sales tax to help pay for teacher salary raises. It was a banner day for our state. The Clintons celebrated in their kitchen with a glass of champagne. I looked on and cheered this historic success.

Bill said, "She's going to sing that at my funeral.

Many visits with the Clintons at the Governor's mansion were times I played piano for parties. These were wonderful experiences and memories. I enjoyed seeing old friends and meeting visitors from all over the world. The parties usually ended with Bill and Hillary singing along at the piano.

I sometimes sang new songs for them, and it was at a party that I introduced them to *Be Not Afraid,* which became an inaugural prayer service mainstay. I sang *Going up Yonder* for them—a gospel song I first heard on the televised funeral for Vice President Hubert Humphrey in January 1978. Bill decided on the spot that I would sing that at his funeral. Every party after that, for a long time, he'd asked me to play and sing *Going Up Yonder*. Then he'd again declare, "She's going to sing that at my funeral." I always just smiled and said something like, "Oh no, I'll go way before you!" And we'd leave it at that.

Bill loved Ray Charles' version of *I'll Be Seeing You* and *Love Walked In*. Sometimes, when I played at special events, I included those pieces. He would look toward the piano and smile when he heard them. It was a kind of communication we had through music.

One evening, Bill was chatting with a guest from out of state about my piano playing. "She could've had a major music career. She is one of the most talented musicians I have ever known. She can play anything," he said. I was happy he was proud of me.

Hillary exclaimed, "Look, Bill recycles the plastic dinnerware!"

Bill and Hillary hosted an annual Valentine's party for neighbors in the Quapaw Quarter, our historic neighborhood that included the Governor's mansion. I played the piano, and friends gathered around to sing, Hillary included. She laughed uproariously as I encouraged her to belt out a tune. Everyone was dressed in red and pink, and the décor and food were festive. When she was 8, Chelsea played the piano for a few people at the end of the party. Bill gleamed with pride.

In 1984, Bill and Hillary hosted a July Fourth backyard cookout for staff and friends. When guests left, Bill began pulling red plastic Solo cups out of the trash. Hillary thought that was hilarious and exclaimed, "Look, Bill recycles the plastic dinnerware!" He was a guy after my own heart because I did the same thing.

The Clintons hosted a Halloween cookout on the back lawn for friends and neighbors in 1986. After our picnic, the children were told to go trick-or-treating at Chelsea's playhouse. When Will and their friends arrived, a witch was inside handing out candy bars. They cautiously approached for their treat and found the witch was Bill dressed in a costume.

In the summer of 1989, Tom and Jude Campbell and family, Tom Jr, Patrick, and Ciara, came to visit the Clintons. Tom was Bill's roommate at Georgetown. Bill and Hillary invited us for a picnic supper. We were joined by Dorothy and Hugh Rodham, Tony Rodham, Virginia and Dick Kelley, Marie Bruno, Carolyn and Joe Huber, and Sarah's friend, Beth Buffalo. We played softball before supper and cheered when Bill pitched the ball to young Ciara in her wheelchair, and she popped it into the air. Jerry captured a picture as Bill and Ciara gleamed. We let Jerry capture a group picture before we left the party. We knew it was a very special time.

Bill played the roles of Santa and Rudolph.

For the fifteen years we lived in Little Rock, the Christmas season at the Governor's Mansion was a month-long celebration. Bill and Hillary entertained the Arkansas Legislature and spouses, the Governor's office staff, state troopers, and a host of other agencies. There were also parties for family members who came from around the state and out-of-state for a reunion. The Blythe and Clinton families came from Texas and elsewhere, and the Rodham family and cousins near and far were invited.

As Christmas neared, the mansion administrator called me with dates for parties. I was delighted to help. I had carol song sheets we'd enjoy for singalongs at the piano. I hoped the music helped make the parties fun and memorable.

I searched for ideas for simple props. Sarah and Mary brought home reindeer antler headbands they had made in school, so I made a dozen for guests to wear as we sang *Rudolph the Red-Nosed Reindeer*. The antlers were made by drawing around two hands on brown construction paper, cutting, and stapling onto a cardboard headband. With the thumbs turned inward, the hands looked just like antlers. My collection of red noses for Rudolph included a foam rubber ball with a slit halfway through that pinched open to fit on the bridge of the nose. Another had an elastic band to hold it on the head, and one was illuminated by battery power. A collection of "reindeer" bells added to the merriment on *Jingle Bells*. It was also fun to ask people to jingle their car keys as we sang. We had a couple of red Santa hats with white fur trim.

Wondering about props I could use for *The Twelve Days of Christmas*, I stopped by a neighborhood variety store before a party to find the props. In the pet section, I found a silicon aquarium fern, tied a plastic bird on it, and made a headband for a partridge. I found turtle beanie toys for two turtle doves. A French beret was perfect for three French hens. In the sporting goods section, I found a duck call for calling birds. A group of gold-glittered bells worked for five golden rings. Six geese a-laying was the blue plastic egg used for Legg's hosiery packaging. Seven swans a-swimming required swim goggles and a red feather boa. Eight maids a-milking was a galvanized pail. Nine ladies dancing was a tiara and a star-tipped wand. Ten lords a-leaping was a red sash with a costume jewelry medallion pin worn diagonally across the chest. Eleven pipers piping and Twelve drummers drumming were from the kids' toy rhythm band instruments. I packed them all into a bag and raced to the mansion to prepare for the fun.

I played background music for the party as guests arrived for supper. Sometimes, guests came by the piano and picked up song sheets. At the party for family members, Virginia and Roger, Jr. always joined me at the piano to sing "O Holy Night." Before the party ended, Bill would also join the singing. He and Roger sang beautifully together, and their cousin from Forrest City liked to join them on *Do You Hear What I Hear?*

After supper, we started the entertainment. Chelsea's job was to tap "volunteers" for the *Twelve Days of Christmas* and *Rudolph the Red-Nosed Reindeer*. Who could turn her down? We started with *Jingle Bells,* and *Rudolph* usually followed. Guests played the eight reindeer: Dasher, Dancer, Prancer, Vixen, Comet, Cupid, Donner, and Blitzen. Lastly came the starring roles of Rudolph and Santa Claus. Each reindeer put on an antler headband. As we sang the reindeer names, each did something to act out their name. Rudolph led the way with antlers and a red nose, and Santa brought up the rear. The reindeer sometimes stood at the piano but usually pranced through the crowd. It was loads of fun. Bill played the roles of Santa and Rudolph for many years.

For the *Twelve Days of Christmas,* ballet student Chelsea took the role of nine ladies dancing. Each participant stepped forward, holding a prop, and pantomimed their character as guests sang along. The funniest one was always six geese a-laying as the big blue egg appeared. A close second was eight maids milking. Guests loved seeing their friends holding props and acting out their characters.

Years later, I added props for the song Up on the Housetop, including a Santa hat and "little Nell's" stocking with a bow for her hair and a small doll that "could open and shut its eyes." "Little Will" had a baseball cap, a baseball, and a small tack hammer. It gave us three more spots to involve guests.

One year when Chelsea was about age ten, I got an idea for a skit to add. Our church had recently performed a musical entitled *Celebrate Life.* One of the songs, *The Three Kings,* had camels cut from large mattress-size foam rubber glued together with a space in the middle for the kings to step into it, pull up to the waist, and look like they were riding camels. I borrowed the camels and took them to the mansion for one of the parties. Chelsea rode into the living room wearing the camel costume. To the horror of the mansion administrator, Chelsea tried to walk through the room, but there wasn't enough space with all the guests. She quickly turned around and walked out the front door. It was not a good plan, but everyone who saw the camel was entertained.

The staff Christmas parties included a time for their gift presentation to the Clintons. One year, they received a video camera—perfect for recording family time with Chelsea as she grew. After the staff party, the Clintons had a gift exchange with the mansion staff who enjoyed a party with the Clintons. We were making great memories.

Bill told Hillary, "We really should go to the Staley's to help them eat all the party food."

The Christmas season was also a time of celebrating in our home with the Clintons and friends. We hosted a party every year for old friends and new including Joe, Glenda, David and Linda, Danny Thomason, Janice and Keith Sjostrand, Mary Jo and Gene Fraley, Horst and Linda Fischer from the Arlington Hotel in Hot Springs, and Rabbi Gene and Bobbye Levy. I made pots of Creole gumbo and French onion soup. Chelsea helped our children bake dozens of cookies. We also made eggnog, boiled custard, pound cakes, bread pudding, and trifle. Mary Jo brought a huge tray of cookies. Glenda made a healthy kale salad, and Linda Leopolous brought her famous Greek dolmades. David spoiled us with his decadent chocolate crème brulee.

We filled our plates with food and gathered in the dining room at a long table my parents gave us. My Dad refinished the hundred-year-old walnut drop-leaf table and made four walnut leaves to extend it with wood from the Baldwin piano factory in Greenwood, Mississippi. The table had walnut chairs that he also refinished and caned. It seated twelve easily, and there were more seats around the room. The table centerpiece was an antique white stoneware soup tureen filled with fresh apples, oranges, lemons, and a pomegranate on top. Fresh holly and greenery were tucked around candles on the mantle.

After we ate, we started music and games. Janice and I played piano. We played rhythm band instruments, including tambourines, maracas, and lots of sleigh bells. We wore props for *The Twelve Days of Christmas, Rudolph the Red-Nose Reindeer,* and *Up on the Housetop*. Everyone joined in, and we laughed like kids. Christmas worksheet games added fun. A favorite was decoding the titles of Christmas songs that had been rewritten using fancy synonyms. I found one in my files with Bill's handwritten responses. We played Pictionary with a flip chart over a door and markers. Players selected words to draw from a box so their team could guess correctly. We were a competitive, creative bunch.

One year, I planned a Christmas party and had everything ready. We scheduled it around Bill's availability so he could attend. Just before the party, an ice storm hit. There was nothing we could do as the sky darkened and sleet descended, making the streets impassable. Bill called to ask if the party was still on. He called Danny Thomason, offering to send a trooper to pick him up. Bill wanted the party to go on as planned. I called a neighbor friend and asked if he would like to walk over with his wife, and he came. We had all the food ready—French onion soup and gumbo, breads, tabbouleh, crackers/cheese, and tons of sweets. We chatted in the living room for a long time before saying goodnight and venturing out into the treacherous night.

On Christmas Eve, Bill told Hillary, "We really should go to the Staley's to help them eat all the party food left over from the ice storm." The family agreed, and Dorothy Rodham, Hillary's mother, joined them. We had a great meal together. Bill had to deliver some gifts to a needy family and was running late, so we went ahead with dinner. When he joined us, we listened to his tale about the gift delivery that had made him late. He described an apartment house with a tall staircase and a long, narrow, dark hallway. He had a difficult time finding it but delivering the gift box was worth it. Hillary and Dorothy were accustomed to his schedule and delays. All was well and we chatted as he had a bite to eat.

One Christmas Eve, the Clintons invited us to meet them for dinner at the Capital Hotel after our church candlelight service. Carolyn and Joe Huber and Liza Ashley joined us. A women's group at Second Baptist Church made ceramic ornaments of Mary and baby Jesus. I remember Dorothy really liked this gift. I took one for each of the families. I also took English Christmas "crackers," and we enjoyed popping them and wearing the paper crowns inside. I also took some word puzzle games we enjoyed. It was always a party when we were together.

Chelsea liked to come to our house to bake Christmas cookies with Sarah, Mary, and Will. She especially liked making "stained-glass" cookies. They were made from dough shaped into outlines of bells, candles, angels, and trees. They were baked on tinfoil for a few minutes then removed from the oven. Crushed Lifesaver candies were sprinkled in the spaces, and the cookies were returned to the oven to finish baking. The heat melted the candy, and they hardened to form stained-glass "panes." They were beautiful.

Many years later, when Chelsea introduced us to her fiancé, Marc Mezvinsky, she told him about our cookie baking. She reminisced that she thought Christmas would always be like it was when we baked cookies and sang *The Twelve Days of Christmas* and *Rudolph the Red-Nosed Reindeer* with friends when she was younger. As she moved to the White House, she realized how unique our Little Rock Christmas traditions were. That touched me deeply, and I was happy for these memories we all treasured.

He always did his own gift-wrapping and wrote messages on gift tags.

The Clintons usually adopted a needy family for gifts at Christmas. A local television station sponsored the program, and participants received a family's information and wish-list. One Christmas, Bill and Chelsea—about 10 at the time—stopped by our house and said they had a dilemma. Chelsea was troubled and needed to talk. They shopped for their adopted family, and everything was wrapped and ready to deliver. They drove to the address to surprise the family. As they arrived, they saw several luxury cars in the driveway. What did this mean? Were they a needy family, after all? How could they afford these cars if they needed help with Christmas gifts? Bill and Chelsea decided to drive around for a while and talk about the situation. Could the cars belong to visiting relatives or friends? Maybe the family shared the house with others, and the cars belonged to them. Maybe they needed help with Christmas gifts because the expensive cars left no money for presents for the children. We decided they should go ahead and deliver the gifts. We had to trust that the station had done a thorough job of screening applicants. We can't always know what others are going through and should never judge. We hoped we were right.

Bill had his Christmas Eve shopping tradition with his friend Webb Hubbell in the Heights area. He normally wore blue jeans, cowboy boots, and a leather jacket. Jim Bell's Publishers Bookshop was a favorite of Bill's. He also liked unusual jewelry and crafts made by Arkansas artists. He found a pottery cheese keeper shaped like a helmeted opera singer to give us one year. After moving to DC, he continued the tradition with Chelsea—and sometimes Bruce Lindsey—at a Georgetown shopping center or shops on M Street. Bill's mother, Virginia, was always the first to have her Christmas gifts wrapped and under the tree. But she always told Bill and Roger that Christmas Eve was the smartest time to shop. "Everything's marked down!"

Bill also shopped for Christmas gifts when he traveled. Some of our gifts came from his travels. Over the years, his gifts included Chinese silk tapestries and embroidered silk squares, interesting shirts for the children, and always books. The girls received crystal ring dishes. Bill gave Jerry and Will beautiful neckties. I enjoy wearing a necklace of African trade beads and an original brooch made by an Arkansas artist from pocket watch parts. He gave me several beautiful silk scarves. He selected some hand-carved wooden spoons one year and a ceramic wall hanging of an antique store inscribed, "Old Friends are Best Friends." Other gifts came from places the Clinton Foundation supported like Haiti and Rwanda. The Clintons were extremely thoughtful.

We discovered that the gifts they liked to receive were books and music CDs, so we shopped accordingly. We shopped estate sales for antique books that Bill collected, particularly by Arkansas authors. One year, I spotted a painting by Arkansas artist Beverly McClarty of a young ballerina. Looking closely at the face, I saw Chelsea. Beverly saw a photo of Chelsea's Nutcracker performance in the newspaper and had been inspired to paint her. At another estate sale, I found a framed antique silk embroidered map of New York State and gave it to the Clintons for their New York home. One of the things I loved about receiving gifts from Bill was that he always wrapped his own gifts and wrote personal messages on gift tags. Official Clinton Foundation gifts had a card wishing us *Happy Holidays* from Bill and Hillary. But when his personal gifts arrived, it was always a treat to see how he wrapped them, lots of tissue and all.

In an agitated voice, he called, "There's one over there, Chelsea! Go, go!

Easter was another season we loved to celebrate with the Clintons. Sometimes, we met for lunch after church on Easter Sunday. One year, we had brunch at the Excelsior Hotel. Hillary wore a wide-brimmed hat. Not many women were wearing hats, and she looked regal. Easter egg hunts for Quapaw Quarter residents were held at the Villa Marre, the historic home featured in Harry and Linda Bloodworth-Thomason's television series *Designing Women*. The neighborhood children came in their Easter finery to enjoy egg hunts with the Easter bunny in costume.

The Clintons arrived with seven-year-old Chelsea. A volunteer explained the egg hunt rules. The younger children looked for eggs at the Villa Marre, and the older kids at the Quapaw Quarter neighborhood association office next door. The younger children's eggs were in plain sight in the grass. Will searched there. Chelsea was in the older group, and hers were well-hidden. A prize awaited those who found the most eggs. Everyone lined up for the cue to start. Chelsea raced to search for eggs. Parents stood along the fence to watch. We suddenly heard Bill yelling at Chelsea to tell her she'd overlooked an egg that he'd spotted. In an agitated voice, he called, "There's one over there, Chelsea! Go, go! Look by that flower! Come this way. Look over here!" Hillary couldn't believe his coaching. She glanced at the other parents standing around, and they all burst out laughing. She reminded him that this was a *children's* egg hunt and that he should relax and have fun.

Hillary asked me to come to the Governor's Mansion to talk about the issue.

I returned to the Arkansas Arts Council after Will's birth in 1981 and was fortunate our church had a good daycare. The first drop-off was tough. I needed to return to work because grant season was upon us, and we had received a decrease in federal funding. We had to plan the grants very carefully. A large percentage of the funds went to major institutions, including the Arkansas Arts Center, Arkansas Symphony, and Arkansas Repertory Theater. No one questioned their value and the high-quality touring they provided statewide. But if we increased their funding, the local arts agencies would suffer. This created a widely publicized conflict about quality versus quantity. The major arts institutions argued their touring provided high-quality arts access. The local arts groups wanted support for local arts organizations. My experience as a young musician in Clarksville, West Memphis, and Hot Springs had shown me the importance of touring groups and local arts organizations' full-time presence. The conflict between major arts organizations and local arts groups made it into the headlines. State arts funding depended on legislative support, and elected official wanted funds to go to their counties. We felt pressure on all sides.

Hillary asked me to talk about the arts issue at the Governor's Mansion. I was grateful for her interest in learning the facts. The Clintons' supporters in Little Rock wanted them to tell the Arts Council to increase funding for major arts organizations. I was sorry for the pressure they received. It eventually was sorted out, but being the subject of unfavorable editorials in our state newspaper was no picnic.

Two years later, in 1983, I resigned from the Arkansas Arts Council. Bill told me he was stunned to receive my resignation. The stress about grant funding wasn't the issue. I wanted to explore a singing career, and I needed to do it before I aged further. I had performed with the Tulsa Opera in Strauss's *Der Rosenkavalier* and in concerts with our state orchestras. Jerry was teaching, and I had income as a private voice teacher and as a church and temple musician. We felt we could manage for a short time on those incomes. At least we were willing to try.

Since I was no longer employed, our financial situation worsened. Jerry started his own photography business, hoping to earn more as a freelance photographer, so he resigned from his teaching job. But even his excellent photographic skills (plus free office and studio space at home) couldn't guarantee success. Some months, he did well, but others were very slow. We began to spiral into debt. Eventually, he returned to teaching for its financial stability.

Bill told the press, "Drugs are a curse ..."

There were other struggles we would soon need to deal with as friends. We were heartbroken to learn that Bill's brother Roger was using drugs. We later learned Roger was struggling with toxic anger over his dad's drinking bouts, rage, and endangering his mother. In 1983, his problem became severe. Bill received a call from the director of the State Police at the Governor's office. Roger had been videotaped selling cocaine. He had been arrested. Roger had an addiction. He wasn't dealing big-time but was selling drugs to support his habit. Bill was distraught but told the state police to do their job. Bill told the press, "Drugs are a curse which has reached epidemic proportions and has plagued the lives of millions of families in our nation, including many in our state."

Roger was arrested and went to trial. The judge was Oren Harris, whom I knew through his family. Carolyn McLeod and Jim Harris were our fellow church members. I wrote to Judge Harris and asked him for mercy and leniency. I hoped he viewed drug addiction as a matter best addressed by rehabilitation and treatment. Still, Roger was sentenced to fourteen months in a Texas prison for his drug dealing.

After Roger was released early for good behavior, he lived in a drug treatment home on South Broadway Street blocks from the Governor's mansion during his probation. I visited him a couple of times to encourage him. I also wrote a song for him while he was in prison, "I Believe in You." I mailed a tape of it to him at the prison. (See "Poems and Songs")

Not hearing an answer, he asked, "Carolyn? Carolyn, are you ok?"

The Clintons knew we weren't making much money. One night, I was distraught reviewing the bills when Bill called. He said, "I'm sitting on the floor coloring pictures with Chelsea and wanted to see how you're doing." I couldn't find the words to answer right away and grew quietly teary. I managed to say yes. He asked, "What's the matter? Is it money?" I told him things were tough. "Hillary and I can help you." He said he'd be over later with a check. The following morning, Bill came over with a check for a $1,000 loan to help a bit. Their caring was more than I could imagine. Jerry and I were deeply grateful. After he left, however, we thought more about it and decided we'd like to try to make it without the loan. It wasn't pride as much as we knew money could create problems between friends. Nothing was worth that. So, we returned the check with enormous gratitude and love. Just knowing they wanted to help was a gift that buoyed our spirits. Jerry resumed teaching, and we returned to sound financial footing. My earnings helped our family, too. We weren't financially wealthy, but we felt rich in our lives and experiences. And we certainly felt rich in our friendships.

---

[i] Clinton, Bill, *My Life*, p. 300-1, Alfred A. Knopf, New York. 2004

The author's senior portrait, Hot Springs High School Old Gold Book yearbook, 1963.

Carolyn meets JFK in the White House rose garden during Girls Nation, 1963.

Carolyn Staley plays the piano at a Christmas party for the Clinton family. Virginia Clinton Kelley, Roger Clinton, Jr., Bill Clinton, Carolyn, and two young cousins. (Photo by Jerry Staley)

Gov. Bill Clinton and friends enjoy a game of USA Trivia at the Staley home after his announcement he would not run for president, July 1987. Janice Sjostrand, Carolyn Huber, Paul Leopoulos, Bill Clinton, Carolyn Staley, and Joe Newman. (Photo by Jerry Staley)

President Clinton and Chelsea with Carolyn and family at Easter egg hunt, 1988.

President-elect Clinton visits with high school friends Jim French, Phil Jamison, and Carolyn Staley outside Culpeper Baptist Church on the final leg of his campaign tour across America, Sunday, January 18, 1993. (Photo by Jerry Staley)

Hot Springs High School friends Randy Goodrum, Phil Jamison, and Jim French chat with President-elect Clinton at a post-election day brunch on November 4, 1993, at the Staley home. (Photo Jerry Staley)

Friends from Hot Springs High School and Georgetown University gathered at the Staley home for a post-election brunch on November 4, 1992, joined by president-elect Clinton, Hillary, and Virginia and Dick Kelley. (Photo by Jerry Staley)

Carolyn Staley visits with Norman Mailer and Hillary Clinton at Gov. Clinton's Inauguration Day, 1987 lunch. (Photo Jerry Staley)

Carolyn greets President Clinton and Hillary on her first visit to the White House for a Prayer Breakfast, September 1993.

President Clinton joins soloist Carolyn Staley and conductor Sarah Caldwell with the Sverdlovsk Chamber Orchestra in Moscow, January 1994.

To Carolyn — This was a grand night for us — You were great Bill

President Clinton and Carolyn Staley chatting at the White House.

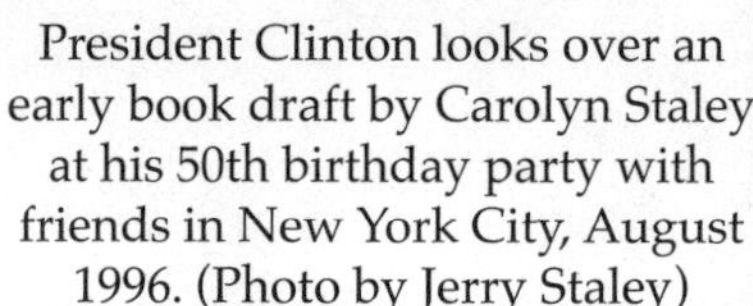

President Clinton looks over an early book draft by Carolyn Staley at his 50th birthday party with friends in New York City, August 1996. (Photo by Jerry Staley)

Carolyn visits the White House for the first time in March 1993 and chats with the Chief of Staff, Mack McLarty, and President Clinton. (White House photo)

President Clinton and Carolyn Staley at a THEA Foundation fundraiser in Washington, D.C.

Carolyn and Jerry Staley visit with President Clinton at a White House Christmas party. (White House photo)

Bill and Georgetown University housemates at a reunion in December 2023. Tom Caplan, Tom Campbell, Ambassador Christopher Ashby, Bill Clinton, and Jim Moore.

CHAPTER FIVE

Open Doors, Fresh Starts, New Horizons

He whispered, "There's something else in the envelope I hope you will pay attention to."

After I resigned as Director of the Arkansas Arts Council, I continued working with my vocal coach. In 1985, I performed a concert to celebrate the 300th birthdays of Bach and Handel and sang several Handel arias with a string quartet. I hoped to use this period between full-time jobs to explore a singing career.

In 1984, celebrated mezzo-soprano Marilyn Horne came to Little Rock to perform with the Arkansas Symphony Orchestra. We didn't have tickets, but Bill and Hillary were going and asked Mary to babysit for Chelsea. They said they'd be home late because there was a reception for Ms. Horne afterward. My thoughts started spinning about how I could connect with Ms. Horne about a singing career. When Bill and Hillary brought Chelsea to our house for babysitting, I handed Bill a tape recording of the recent recital Bach-Handel concert and asked if he would give it to Ms. Horne after the concert. When they came to pick up Chelsea, Bill told me that he had presented Ms. Horne with an Arkansas Traveler certificate, and when he handed it to her, he whispered, "There's something else in the envelope I hope you will pay attention to." He put my tape and resume in the same package he gave her. I couldn't have asked for more.

The next day Bill called to say Ms. Horne called him after midnight to say she had listened to my tape and wanted me to call her. She was interested in helping me. I was in disbelief. I got a babysitter for Will so I could make the phone call to her without distractions. Ms. Horne told me that she liked my voice, thought I had great promise, and wanted to help me. I told her I was thrilled and that "maybe, finally, my ship has come in!" She replied, "Well, it's not coming down the Arkansas River!" and we both laughed. I told her I'd prayed long about this direction, and she said, "You're not one of those born-again believers, are you?" I assured her I was simply a person of faith. She offered to arrange a Carnegie Hall audition for agents to hear me sing. We agreed on spring 1985 and she asked me to stay in touch with her as I felt ready. She suggested some arias I should learn for the audition.

I embarked on a whirlwind of preparation for Carnegie Hall. I added the new repertoire. As spring approached, Ms. Horne set the date for Carnegie Hall and arranged rehearsals with her accompanist, Martin Katz. I sang a recital at church of the audition repertoire and friends gave generously to help defray travel costs. The Clintons hosted a reception following the recital. Bill said the party food brought by church friends was the most beautiful he'd seen. People were very supportive.

The audition went well. It was a dream to sing at Carnegie Hall, in the "big hall," as my NYC singer friend calls it. St. Joseph College sent flowers to the stage. Afterward, Ms. Horne took me to the Russian Tea Room for some helpful advice ahead of the next audition in San Francisco. The next day, Bill called the hotel asking how the audition went. I was grateful for his enthusiasm and support.

Bill told me that Dr. Ralph Wynn, an opera enthusiast, wrote that he wanted to help my career. Bill urged me to meet with him. Dr. Wynn invited me to his office and told me he wanted me to observe a Caesarian delivery. He believed it would help me understand the effect of my surprise Caesarean delivery with Will and the muscles that were severed. He said that a return to my former singing strength might be compromised. I was astounded. Dr. Wynn was a taskmaster, and when the nurses heard he was attending, they flipped a coin to determine who would assist. He had me stand on a stool over the table. Because I was too close to the hot lamp, I grew weak and nearly fainted as I watched muscles being reattached. I had to step down and leave, but I'd seen enough. Bill couldn't believe Dr. Wynn wanted to help me in that way.

My rehearsals continued until I would see Ms. Horne in San Francisco. During the summer, I struggled with seasonal allergies. My allergist recommended shots. We discussed my upcoming audition, and he prescribed a beta blocker for anxiety. I knew singers who found them beneficial for calming nerves.

I went to San Francisco in the fall to sing again for Ms. Horne at the San Francisco Opera. I found a quaint hotel nearby and a church where I could practice before the audition. I never questioned the wisdom of my allergist, and on the morning of my audition, I took the beta blocker and went to warm up my voice. As I started to sing, I knew something was wrong. I felt well and happy. But something was wrong with my vocal production. My singing felt labored, and I had trouble reaching my high notes. I was genuinely concerned but didn't know what was happening or how to overcome it. I met the accompanist to run through an aria from Verdi's *Masked Ball*, which was being produced that season, and they had an emergency opening for the lead soprano role. Ms. Horne said maybe I would be cast. I was soon on stage, singing my heart out, but I struggled. My high notes were heavy, and my voice sluggish. I was unable to correct it.

Afterward, Ms. Horne took me to lunch, and she was concerned but said I was a strong singer to have pushed through. I knew the only explanation for the problem was the beta blocker. I didn't have the heart to tell her what I'd done. I felt so naïve that I blindly trusted. Why hadn't I tried the pill beforehand to see the effect it might have on me? How could I have taken this chance with my hard work and dreams? Ms. Horne wasn't disappointed in me. She was glad she'd given me this opportunity. She said, "Carolyn, you have the voice, and if you really want to do this, you can. But why would you leave your family? There's so much more to life than singing." She had met our family and children in NYC and told me, "I would trade places with you in a minute. You have such a beautiful family and a wonderful husband." She shared the sadness she felt about her failed marriage and how infrequently she could see her children because of her busy performance schedule and global travels.

Ms. Horne called one day when she was home in NYC, packing for her opera season tour. "I'm sitting here on my bed and looking at three trunks I have just packed for the three seasons that I'll be away from home. Today I hired a car, went shopping for a few things and went to the bank. I won't be home for nine months." She thought my life was ideal. She said I should accept a future without a major opera career as my "*La Forza del Destino*—the title of a Verdi opera meaning "the force of destiny." It simply wasn't my destiny to have an opera career. I would continue singing but the travels away from family wouldn't be required.

A few weeks later, Bill, David Leopolous, Joe Newman, and I went to lunch. I told Bill I'd decided not to continue pursuing an opera career. He was shocked, looked at me in a pained way, and simply asked, "Carolyn?" He was concerned that it was a decision I'd later regret. Until then, I never explained what led to my decision. I was embarrassed I'd taken the beta blocker. I felt I'd blown the opportunity of a lifetime. At the same time, I felt at peace.

I was never totally sure I had the heart for the opera stage. That's why I needed this experience. While the music was glorious, many operas didn't have a meaningful message, in my view. I wasn't sure singing them was the life I wanted. I'd been taught that a life of service was the best goal. I had many friends with opera careers and knew they would keep the art form alive. I recalled asking myself as I took my curtain calls at the close of the final performance of *Der Rosenkavalier* with Tulsa Opera in 1983, "What difference did that make in anyone's life?" I had seen the glazed-over faces of the audience in the orchestra section. What difference had the three months I'd spent memorizing the German role and difficult music made in my life or anyone else's? Divas don't ask that question.

"Can you take a child?"

Singing in Strauss' *Der Rosenkavalier* with the Tulsa Opera in 1982 had provided another remarkable experience that helped me understand what an opera career could mean for our family. Jerry called before the last performance and told me they had to cancel plans to attend because he'd been hospitalized with blood poisoning. I listened in amazement and concern. While taking aircraft photos, he had wiped off the plane's exterior. Chemicals had entered a small opening in his skin and traveled through his bloodstream. The doctor showed Jerry's arm to the medical students at UAMS and said, "If the poisoning had traveled just an inch higher and reached his heart, he would have died." Not only could the family not come to the opera, I couldn't be home to care for Jerry or comfort the children. I had no understudy for my role and had to sing the final two performances before I could go home.

Friends told me how twelve-year-old Sarah, our first child, called neighbors to find places for our three children to stay while Jerry was hospitalized. My sister Lynda kept Will, who was just two years old. Sarah called friends and neighbors, asking, "Can you take a child?" What a plaintive request! Sarah and Mary stayed with friends for a couple of days, but it was a difficult time that brought home to me how an opera career could impact our family.

I remained incredibly grateful for the experience of a lifetime. I was grateful to Bill for giving my concert tape to Marilyn Horne. I was grateful to Ms. Horne for taking me under her wing to see if this was the life I wanted. I also saw the hand of Providence in this. I had been allowed to get close enough to see the realities of a concert and opera career, and I didn't have to wonder, "What if"?

Thanks to Bill Clinton's introduction, Marilyn Horne and I have remained friends. We reunited at the 1992 Democratic Convention hall before she sang the *National Anthem* for the opening session. Seeing her and sharing the joy of Bill's election was wonderful. She was a strong Democrat and very proud of Bill. She sang at the 1993 presidential inauguration. I had hoped I might be asked to sing the *National Anthem* because I had sung it for many events. But I understood it was now time to invite the stars. She was a star indeed and had provided a starring chapter in my life. And Bill had made it all happen.

Chelsea exclaimed, "He eats the core and seeds, too!"

Bill was Governor, and Hillary practiced law; their lives were full. But Chelsea's life was the top priority. One morning, I stopped by the mansion as Hillary and Chelsea walked through the kitchen to their car. Chelsea was due for immunizations, but Hillary also had another appointment and was gleaming. "Can you believe it? I'm going to meet Bill, and we're getting life insurance. He finally talked with me about it and decided we should take this step. I am in shock!" Being a parent can end procrastination on such decisions. It was a big day.

Bill and Hillary were always present for Chelsea's school events, including countless performances of the Nutcracker ballet, piano recitals, soccer games, softball games, and anything else she was doing. Once, Bill was scheduled to play a duet with her at her piano recital, but storms delayed his arrival. At the last minute, I stepped in. When he finally arrived, they played the duet together. Every moment with Chelsea was a priority.

As Chelsea started to talk, her vocabulary quickly became prodigious. Bill and Hillary never used "baby talk" with her, and she developed a rich vocabulary. Bill took her to school many mornings on his way to work. They helped with homework when she needed it. Bill famously called once from the presidential campaign trail to help with a tricky algebra problem. Her mind was strong, and she excelled in all her academic life.

When Bill and Hillary came home from an event, and our daughters or I had been babysitting for Chelsea, and she was awake, Bill always went to her room and knelt by the bedside for prayers. They read together and introduced her to new books. She loved visiting the library and bookstores. They spent hours riding bikes through the neighborhood, always wearing helmets. She enjoyed making discoveries about her parents, too. One day, when she was about 8, she and her dad dropped by our house. Bill was eating an apple. When we commented that it looked tasty, Chelsea exclaimed, "He eats the core and seeds too!" Bill just smiled at her disclosure.

Bill and Hillary had a moment of angst when sixth-grader Chelsea went to a German language camp in Michigan. The sendoff was emotional. Bill and Hillary couldn't wait for her to return. They knew, however, that educational camps were necessary for her growth. Chelsea was also encouraged to think for herself and to make wise decisions. Once, as a pre-teen, she asked Hillary for permission to shave part of her head and dye her hair green. Without missing a beat, Hillary replied, "It's *your* head." That seemed to take all the fun out of the threat. The hair changes never happened.

The nurses were astonished that he called, but that was just the kind of friend he was.

Being neighbors gave us many opportunities to see the Clintons, just as we'd hoped. Bill, Hillary, and Chelsea were often in our home. Bill came by some mornings on his jogs to say hello, get a cup of water, and be on his way. Being nearby meant our girls were quickly available to babysit for Chelsea. We could also drop by the mansion to see them, run into them as I walked my loop around Spring Street and Arch Street, see the Clintons' cocker spaniel Zeke wandering outside the fence and help him get back home, see Bill riding his new mountain bike, and know we were just a stone's throw from our friends. They were in our home for parties, board games around our dining table, Christmas and Easter celebrations, or just to chat.

The Clintons came by many times, bringing gifts. They brought a bath powder and lotion set after Will was born in 1981. They came by for my 40th birthday party in September 1986, even though Bill was campaigning for reelection as Governor and the family had been traveling all day. Hillary and Chelsea were exhausted and retreated to our library to just sit a bit while Bill interacted with guests. They brought a fun gift—a zippered pouch labeled an "Emergency Kit for Turning 40." We laughed as we examined the contents: a magnifying glass, antacid, denture polish, and a black balloon. When I broke my collar bone in a fall at the Arkansas Arts Center in 1990, they visited and brought a decorative dried garlic braid we hung in our kitchen.

Snowfalls were a rare treat in Arkansas. One snowy Saturday morning, Bill and Chelsea stopped by while walking through the neighborhood. I had made a pot of potato soup, and we shared a bowl. Bill said the hot soup was perfect for the snowy day. Chelsea also often came to play with Will and our daughters, Sarah and Mary. Our daughters babysat for Chelsea, mainly at the mansion but sometimes in our home. Being neighbors and having drop-in visits to cheer any day was a joy.

Bill and Hillary were proud of our children's accomplishments. I created a "brag wall" and hung their framed certificates. Bill and Hillary examined the wall when they came to visit. It was a reminder of how proud we were of our youngsters' progress in life. Sarah and Mary got fabric autograph hounds for Christmas one year. Bill and Hillary signed their names on the fabric toy dachshunds I have kept. The Clintons watched our children's antics and comedy routines, listened to piano recital pieces, and watched ballet pirouettes.

Bill helped Mary with a research project during her senior year at Little Rock Central High School in 1990-91. Her Gifted and Talented English class at Central High School had assigned the topic "Arkansas's Negative Self-Image: An Obstacle to Progress?" She needed to interview someone for their perspective on the question. Mary asked Governor Clinton if he would be interviewed for the project. He agreed and returned his hand-written answers:

1. Do you believe Arkansas has a negative self-image? If so, what evidence has led you to this conclusion? If not, what evidence supports your response?
Gov. Clinton: Many Arkansans have a negative image of our state and of themselves

as Arkansans. I have seen evidence of this in public opinion polls and in specific comments people have made to me, putting themselves or the state down. On the other hand, most Arkansans also feel a lot of pride for the state, its beauty, the old-fashioned values, and the friendliness of its people.

2. If Arkansas has a negative self-image, what has happened historically to create this?

Gov. Clinton: The historical basis of our self-image problem is 150 years of being one of the poorest, most rural, least educated states, aggravated in the last 33 years by the Little Rock Central High crisis.

3. Has there ever been a time that Arkansas had a positive self-image? (i.e Sesquicentennial, inaugural events, visits by the President and other U.S. leaders, visits by foreign dignitaries, special recognitions for the state?)

Gov. Clinton: Yes, the state often has a positive self-image, especially when an Arkansan or group of Arkansans achieves something outstanding in sports, the arts, politics, business, or another area, especially education.

4. What can Arkansas do to overcome a negative self-image for the state? Can it best be overcome at the local, county, or state level? What can students and schools do to help boost Arkansas' state image?

Gov. Clinton: The best things we can do are: 1. Publicize our strengths among ourselves and to others; 2. Attack our weaknesses openly, especially in education; Arkansas has received great publicity nationwide for education reform, but we have so much more to do; 3. THINK BIGGER, in terms of investment to achieve excellence in education, economic development, and other areas; 4. Protect and promote both our natural and cultural resources.

Bill and Hillary were always with us in times of sickness. When Jerry was hospitalized with pancreatitis after a family wedding in Ohio, Bill called the hospital to check on him. The nurses were astonished that he called, but that was just the kind of friend he was. Other friends have commented that after the President calls the hospital room, the staff seems more attentive. Hillary called after my miscarriage to express concern. While working at the Arkansas Arts Center, I had a near-tragic accident when I fell backward down a flight of stairs in an enclosed stairwell. I stepped back on a top landing to allow a coworker to pass, lost my footing and slid headfirst into a concrete wall. Thankfully, I only broke my clavicle, but it was a scary experience. Bill and

Hillary were soon at our home to check on me. Anytime there was a celebration or concern, Bill and Hillary were there.

"To Carolyn, who stamped me a long time ago."

Bill's campaigns for governor were always a priority. We were relieved when he was re-elected in 1981 and 1984. Frank White was back as his opponent in 1986, and we got in high gear. We called voters to tell them what a good personal friend Bill Clinton was. Our kids volunteered as well. We never assumed victory after Bill's 1980 defeat.

The Garland County Democratic Party asked me to entertain for their 1986 fundraiser that also celebrated Bill's 40th birthday. I recreated memories of our life in Hot Springs High School and recruited former teachers, classmates, cheerleaders, and T-Steppers to be on the program. I made sure Virginia, Roger, and Dick could attend. I contacted their former housekeeper, Earlene White, who agreed to bring fried pies. I asked David Leopoulos to co-emcee the program with me. We wore sequined top hats for our opening number. High school teachers, including Burma Bryan (Geometry), Jane Beasley (English), and Lonnie Lueben Warneke (English), came to the podium to share memories of student Bill. Guidance counselor Edith Irons recalled her stress as Bill delayed applying to college and made her a nervous wreck by only applying to Georgetown. Rodney McWilliams represented Arkansas teachers, sporting an arm sling and crutches to symbolize the toll Bill's teacher testing requirement had taken on teachers as part of his new education reforms. The cheerleaders cheered in their uniforms, and the T-Steppers walked out holding a "HELLO" sign, but the O was on the front end, so it spelled "O Hell." Carolyn Wilson, as Principal Johnnie Mae Mackey, led us in our rousing cheer, "Hullabaloo." Virginia and Roger spoke. Earlene carried a platter of her famous fried pies to the stage and Bill grabbed one on the spot. Bill and Hillary seemed to enjoy every minute of the event.

The 1986 campaign had some tough days, and we did all we could to help. As Election Day approached, I baked something every morning to deliver to the mansion for car trips around the state. Bill called to say, "Thanks for taking care of me."

On election night in 1986, we gathered outside the campaign headquarters at an old paint store on 7th Street. Friends and campaign workers gathered for a victory rally. After his victory was announced, Bill joined the cheering crowd to thank supporters. Then he looked at our little group of friends that met him earlier when he voted and said, "There's a group here who would support me even if I were next door making pizza." He pointed to Vino's pizzeria next door. We applauded to let him know he was right, and it warmed our hearts on that November night.

1986 was a memorable year also because it was Arkansas's sesquicentennial year of statehood. Arkansas was admitted to the Union on June 15, 1836. Major events were planned to mark the state's 150th birthday. In June, the US Postal Service introduced a commemorative Sesquicentennial stamp. A dedication program at Robinson Auditorium featured all living former governors on stage. I sang the *National Anthem*, and Sarah and Mary joined me to sing the folksong *Down in the Arkansas* as Sarah accompanied on her dulcimer. After the ceremony, I joined the dignitaries to autograph First Day covers of the stamp. I also have another First Day cover of the commemorative stamp marking Bill Clinton as the first Arkansan elected President of the United States on November 3, 1992. I have it framed with Bill's inscription, "To Carolyn, who stamped me a long time ago, Bill Clinton."

Our family enjoyed many of the Sesquicentennial activities throughout the year, but none more than the closing celebration at War Memorial Stadium on June thirteenth. We dressed in old-fashioned garb and enjoyed the celebrity-studded showcase. Afterward, we went with the Clintons to Arkansas River Park for fireworks that filled the summer sky over the river with the Arkansas Symphony in the background. Bill is a true patriot, and I watched him take it all in, speechless, moved, and filled with reverence. He was honored to lead our state during this historic time.

In 1986, after a few years of exploring a singing career and working with Hands Across America, Townsend Wolfe, director of the Arkansas Arts Center, asked me to direct the State Services touring programs. He remembered my interest in getting the arts to rural parts of the state when I directed the Arkansas Arts Council and knew I had a passion for the job. The Clintons were frequent visitors to the Arts Center. When Bill served as chairman of the National Governor's Association in 1987, the governors came to Little Rock for their annual meeting. The Arts Center was exhibiting the Anschutz Collection of American Western art. It included panoramic western landscapes by Thomas

Moran and Albert Bierstadt and portraits of Native Americans by George Catlin. The meeting included dinner at the Arts Center, and I suggested that Bill lead a brief tour of the Anschutz exhibit. I prepared notes about how the paintings played a major role in initiating government funding for the arts and westward expansion. The landscapes introduced Congress to the natural beauty of the West and led to the establishment of our national parks. Replicas of the paintings hung in post offices and train depots in the early Twentieth Century and encouraged Western travel, leading to the completion of the railways, roads, and Western development. Paintings of ceremonial meetings between Native American and US military leaders depicted diplomatic gift exchanges. I listened as Bill did a masterful job showcasing the arts and the importance of government support.

"Please pray for me," the President asked me.

Planning for inaugural prayer services with the Clintons as both Governor and President was always an honor, and the 1987 service was no exception. They wanted the time to be uplifting and worshipful, dignified yet exuberant. Bill wanted the worship and music to touch the heart.

The Inaugural Prayer Services were important to the Clintons because faith was important in their lives. As a boy, Bill lived within walking distance of Park Place Baptist Church. He regularly attended Sunday morning worship. His childhood friend, Patty Howe Criner, remembers him walking along Park Avenue, holding his Bible as he went to church. During a revival service when he was about 8, Bill accepted Christ as his personal savior and was baptized. He remembers his baptism vividly. As he and classmate Bert Jeffries waited their turn, the woman ahead of them lost her balance as she was immersed, and her foot flew up and caught on the glass splash panel. The pastor was able to help her regain balance, but not before laughter rippled through the church. Years later, Bert was killed in Vietnam. Bill has remained close to Bert's family. After the Clintons moved next door to us, Virginia often had to be at the hospital early and wasn't available to take Bill to church, so he stopped attending for a while. He came to our church on special occasions for youth revivals and at Christmas when I sang *O Holy Night*.

Bill and I didn't talk much about our faith as young people. We simply weren't comfortable having these discussions yet. Later, however, we began to share more about the importance of our faith journeys. He often said to me during our years growing up, "Please pray for me." I have always prayed for him. When he was governor, I wrote letters of encouragement to him and included a scriptural verse. Once I copied an entire Psalm that I hoped would bring him strength when I knew he was going through a difficult time.

Bill's faith has always been intensely personal and private. He believed that was the way it should be, following the Bible's teachings about displays of piety. Virginia told me that when he began seeking political office, a news outlet asked to use a photograph of him praying in church. Bill was uncomfortable with this because he believed the Bible taught that prayer should be private and not for public display. He thought it was wrong to use one's faith to garner votes.

Bill and Hillary were active church members in Arkansas. They attended different churches because of their upbringing. Bill had been a Baptist since childhood, and Hillary was an active member of her Methodist church youth group in Park Ridge, Illinois. They enjoyed having two sermons to discuss each week. Chelsea attended church with Bill at Immanuel Baptist Church for a while. In the summer, she started Vacation Bible School at First United Methodist Church, where Hillary was a member and her mansion nanny was a teacher. Soon, Chelsea and Hillary were regulars at First United Methodist. Chelsea was active in children's programs and the Christmas Eve nativity plays. When she was eleven, she was proud to be assigned the role of Joseph. It made no difference to her to play a male role.

It was a special day in Little Rock in 1988 when Billy Graham came to town for an evangelistic crusade held at War Memorial Stadium. I signed up to sing with the volunteer choir each evening. As Governor, Bill was invited to sit with Dr. Graham on the stage at the crusade and welcome him to our state. Bill had long been a fan of Dr. Graham's and, at age twelve, attended Graham's 1958 crusade in Little Rock with a teacher who invited a few to go along. Bill was impressed by Dr. Graham's insistence that the crusade be open to people of all races instead of limited to whites only, as had been suggested by local organizers. Bill was touched to see all races gathered at the altar at the close of the service as they came to commit to Jesus. Because of Graham's stance on integration, Bill sent a part of his weekly allowance to the Billy Graham offices and kept his donation a secret.

Bill was an active member of the choir at Immanuel Baptist Church. His baritone section sat in the center of the back row on Sunday mornings. Because his schedule didn't allow him to attend rehearsals and he was a good musician, the director told him to come on Sunday mornings before worship to rehearse. Bill sang with gusto and enjoyed the choir experience. Some critics said he sang on the televised service just to be seen by voters. This bothered him but didn't deter his participation. He sang with the choir until he became President. Dr. Danny Thomason was also in the choir, and they sat side-by-side. As the scripture was read, they opened their Bibles to follow along. One Sunday morning Bill looked over at Danny's Bible and saw it had a great deal of commentary that his Bible didn't include. Bill was amazed at the detailed study notes." Hey, where'd you get that Bible?" he asked. Danny bought a Bible like his and gave it to Bill to help his friend study.

One of the reasons Bill attended Immanuel Baptist Church was because of its pastor, Dr. W.O. Vaught, known for his strong Biblical scholarship. Bill frequently sought advice from Dr. Vaught, a conservative, on issues popular with the religious right, including abortion and the death penalty. Bill appreciated Dr. Vaught's help to see these issues from a Biblical perspective, the translations of passages from Greek and Hebrew, plus the historical and social context. Billy Graham was a friend to Dr. Vaught. Bill went with Dr. Graham to visit Vaught in the hospital as he neared death. It was a meaningful time for the three to share.

Bill thought that euthanasia would become an even bigger issue than abortion as the baby-boomer generation aged. Religious views on euthanasia varied widely, particularly among Christians, Jews, and Hindus. As physician-assisted dying gained legal support, some Protestant and Catholic groups supported it with limitations. The death penalty was also an ethical and legal issue that Bill confronted as governor. He believed it was his duty to uphold the laws of the state, regardless of his personal view. This put him at odds with many, including his staff member, Ms. Freddie Nixon, who was for the abolition of the death penalty and a regular visitor to death row. The execution in 1992 of convicted murderer Ricky Ray Rector, who was mentally unsound, was particularly difficult. Many appealed to the governor for clemency. Bill knew I was opposed to the death penalty, but he believed it was his duty to uphold the law.

In 1981, Bill and Hillary accompanied Dr. Vaught on a tour of the Holy Lands. As soloist at Temple B'nai Israel, I had read the *Gates of the Home* prayer book, and I bought a copy for them to enjoy. They became good friends with Rabbi Gene Levy when he served as rabbi at the temple and enjoyed Jewish services and the "people of the book." Dr. Vaught was a good friend during the political ups and downs of Bill's life. He stood by him during elections and attended victory celebrations. Bill often singled him out for thanks. During Bill's 1982 campaign, when he sought to make a comeback as governor, the Immanuel Baptist Church choir came as a group to watch the election returns and cheer his reelection. The church choir enjoyed having its annual Christmas party at the Governor's mansion.

A memorable time the Clintons visited our home was Sunday, January 1991, following President George Bush's announcement that US troops were going to Iraq as part of an international coalition. Hillary asked, "Did your pastor speak today about the Gulf War and our troop deployment?" Bill said, "Yes, we asked God to bless our troops and our country."

Hillary said, "Our pastor also prayed but asked that God bless our world and all those going into harm's way to fight for freedom." Later that year, at the end of Operation Desert Storm, our state welcomed home troops who served in Iraq. Bill and Hillary invited friends to join them on the rooftop of the Legacy Hotel to view the parade and celebrate. As the troops marched past us, Bill was enormously proud and acknowledged their contributions.

Some Sundays, the Clintons would drop by to say hello on the way home from church. Our family tried new dishes on Sundays for "international cuisine days," and we enjoyed having the Clintons join us. One Sunday, when they dropped by, we talked about how people came to accept Jesus as their savior and become Christians. I commented, "I think Baptists really have that process right. We don't have infant baptism; instead, we encourage people to make a personal decision to follow Christ when they feel led to do so and to follow with a believer's baptism. We don't have a "conveyor belt" process (my inelegant choice of words) with confirmation classes at about age twelve. A personal decision is made when the individual is ready."

Hillary quickly spoke up. She disagreed with my understanding of how Methodists choose to become followers of Christ. She said her confirmation day, when she stood before her congregation and spoke about what it meant to her, was probably *the most important day* of her life. She said her confirmation was a profound experience that continued to guide her life.

I apologized if I had offended her and told Hillary how meaningful her testimony was. I realized God uses other denominational traditions to guide people to follow Jesus. Baptists, Methodists, and other churches have differing processes for affirming faith in Christ. Some come to believe through fiery revival services, and others through high liturgical worship. God uses any way possible to touch the heart. I knew that, but Hillary affirmed it, and I appreciated her strong testimony. She has frequently quoted the John Wesley motto, "Do all the good you can, by all the means you can, in all the ways you can, in all the places you can, at all the times you can, to all the people you can, as long as you ever can." More importantly, she lives by those words.

Bill and Hillary's faith continues to be central to their lives. Bill and Hillary are both students of Bible history and theology. I've witnessed their personal relationships with God, which have led them to explore faith as not only a mental search but also a matter of the heart. I recall a conversation in 1988 with Bill and Danny Thomason in our home. We talked of personal spiritual growth. Bill volunteered that a spiritual turning point for him was reading C.S. Lewis' *Mere Christianity*. He said, "It's one of the most important books I've ever read." The book helped him sort through aspects of faith that he had not been clear about before. He found a kindred spirit in Lewis, whose book he read several times. Our conversation motivated me to pull the book from my shelf and re-read it. It occurred to me that what C. S. Lewis did so splendidly in *Mere Christianity* was to narrate his personal struggle with faith and the difficulty of surrendering to the truest test of faith—that a relationship with God is not intellectual. Only through faith can it be discovered. In C.S. Lewis, Bill found an intellectual comrade who could boldly state that he had accepted God's existence and love on faith. Faith alone made belief possible. It was a fascinating conversation and a look into Bill's heart.

"Have you ever heard anything more beautiful in your life?"

Governor Clinton was frequently invited to visit churches, particularly for special anniversaries. He formed lasting relationships with pastors of all denominations. His relationship with Pentecostals became a special friendship. Early in his tenure, Bill met Pentecostals, including Rev. Anthony and Mickey

Mangun and Mickey's father, Rev. Lumpkin, superintendent of the United Pentecostals of Arkansas. He also became good friends with Rev. Keith Sjostrand and his wife Janice of the Apostolic Church in Lonoke, Arkansas, and countless others. Governor Clinton was invited by the Manguns to attend the Pentecostal's summer camp meeting at Redfield, AR. His first invitation was during a campaign year. The Pentecostals were a considerable voting bloc, but he always attended, election year or not. He loved the camp meeting and found solace in the spirit-filled worship and music. He also appreciated their support in addressing Arkansas's statewide need for foster homes for dependent children.

One spring day, I saw Bill and Hillary at the Toggery children's clothing store. Bill asked me if I had a minute to come to his car to hear a song by a singer named Mickey Mangun, whom he'd just met at the Pentecostal camp meeting. We fairly ran to the car; he was so excited to share the song. He had just received the tape recording of *In the Presence of Jehovah* and wanted me to hear it. We listened, and he watched for my reaction. Bill asked, "Have you ever heard anything more beautiful in your life?" I agreed it was phenomenal.

Music has always been a great love of Bill's, and the experience of hearing powerful, spirit-filled presentations of Christian music was a revelation for him. It touched his heart in a profound way, so much so that he had to share the experience with others. This was a new shared experience for us. I was impressed that the beauty of the song for him lay both in the voice and song, which were gorgeous, but also in the messages of God's love, power, and personal presence. I was interested and excited to see how Bill was open to God's presence through the Holy Spirit. Watching Bill's courage and vulnerability amazed me.

The new music Bill introduced me to helped me grow spiritually, as well. I learned to play *In the Presence of Jehovah*, and Bill and I sang it sometimes after events at the mansion. The lyrics are deeply meaningful:

In and out of situations that tug of war at me,
All day long I struggle for the answers that I need,
Then I come into his presence and all my questions become clear,
And for a sacred moment no doubts can interfere.
In the presence of Jehovah, God Almighty, Prince of Peace,
Troubles vanish, hearts are mended in the presence of the King
(Geron and Becky Davis, 1985)

Years later, when Bill produced a CD of some of his favorite musical selections, he included *In the Presence of Jehovah*—a tribute to the power of the music in his life and possibly an introduction to others so they could have a similar experience.

Bill invited me to the Pentecostal camp meeting at Redfield a couple of times. The first time, we rode in a state trooper's car. Arkansas movie star Gil Gerard (best known as Captain Buck Rogers) was a guest at the mansion, as were Harry and Danny Thomason and Bill's secretary, Lynda Dixon.

The Pentecostals deeply admired Bill. They found him to be a Christian friend and brother. Though a conservative bloc of voters, they respected his leadership. The pastors never hesitated to express concerns about policies because they knew he would listen. Mostly, they discovered his open heart for worship and loved him for it.

Arriving at Redfield, we found the Pentecostal campground filled with campers and dotted by several small cabins. The worship tabernacle was a huge metal building with 5 or 6 air conditioners on the roof. It was enormous, the size of a football field or larger. At the doorway, folks were waiting to greet the Governor. I sensed an overwhelming spiritual presence in the sanctuary where worship music was playing. The campers had been praying and singing and were already "fired up" for worship. The pastors invited the Governor into a room where they prayed before worship. Seats on the pulpit area were reserved for Bill and the guests. When Bill was introduced, he was greeted with warm, extended applause. They loved him.

Worship for Pentecostals takes on a new meaning for those accustomed to traditional worship. The full-throated gospel singing was robust and thrilling, accompanied by piano, organ, guitar, trumpet, drums, and a small orchestra. Worshippers also brought their own tambourines. Having the governor with them didn't mean anything should change about worship, and they knew their governor loved worshipping with them. They danced, lifted their hands, and remained on their feet as they sang. When they prayed, everyone prayed aloud. The presence of the Holy Spirit was so real that it nearly took my breath away.

Bill invited me to go again another summer. After the sermon, the pastor called for a special time of prayer for families. He asked families to stand together for prayer. I was standing alone on the pulpit. Bill was on the floor of the sanctuary, and Janice was with her family. I became aware of a small group standing, praying with me, and realized Bill had joined me because he didn't have any family present either. Then Janice and Keith joined us to pray. It was a touching moment.

The Pentecostals became dear friends and supporters of Bill Clinton in both political ups and downs. When he was defeated as governor in 1980 after serving two years, a group of Pentecostal pastors was among the first to visit him. They prayed with him for peace and comfort through this dark time. They showered him with unconditional love, which he never forgot. They told Bill that prayer would strengthen his leadership, and that prayer was the greatest power available to humankind. They were never hesitant to ask Bill to kneel with them to pray.

Bill told us about a trip his family made to Alexandria, Louisiana, in 1989 for a performance of the Pentecostals' original production of *Messiah,* a dramatic musical work they performed every other year during the Easter season. Bill talked about it in an interview with *Rolling Stone* magazine, saying, "*Messiah* is better than *CATS* on Broadway."[1] Bill begged us to go. We fulfilled that goal in 1994.

One of the songs from *Messiah* that was particularly poignant for Bill was *The Darker the Night*. When we planned the 1991 Governor's Inaugural Dedication Service, he specifically asked that the choir sing this song. I listened to the *Messiah* tape, wrote out the parts and accompaniment for the choir, and went to the Immanuel Choir rehearsal to teach it. They decided it was outside their traditional repertoire style, so Janice Sjostrand and a trio from her Lonoke Pentecostal church performed it for the service. The refrain's lyrics are powerful:

> *The darker the night, the brighter the light is gonna shine,*
> *The harder the fight, the greater the victory,*
> *So hold on tight. The sun'll come shining through you'll see,*
> *The darker the night, the brighter the light is gonna be.*
> (Geron Davis, *Messiah*, 1985)

The lyrics' autobiographical nature was unmistakable. It was clear that the song meant so much because its lyrics told the story of his life.

The Pentecostal campground visits had more than a political value. The friendships spawned there felt rich. It was a spiritual time for Bill. He discovered a new way of worship, and he loved their music. He found a relationship with the Holy Spirit that took him deeper in his faith. His friendship with the Pentecostals continues.

A bolt of fire shot through my head

My own life was touched by my friendship with a Pentecostal friend, Janice Sjostrand. She lived in Lonoke, Arkansas, taught high school Spanish, and led the music at Lonoke Apostolic Church. Her husband Keith was the church's co-pastor, serving alongside his father. I heard Janice's opening act at a Ray Charles concert in Little Rock. Her voice and piano playing were powerful, and I thought what an honor it was to be invited to open for such a legend. Janice and I met later through the Redfield campground visits. She asked me to have lunch at the Arkansas Arts Center, where I worked as director of State Touring Services. She wondered if I would begin a Bible study with her, and I gladly accepted. We met in my home at our dining table every Saturday afternoon at 3 p.m. for four years.

A most remarkable spiritual experience for me occurred during one of our studies. I was reading aloud from Hebrews chapter 11 and came to verse 6, "Without faith, it's impossible to please God." As I read those words, I felt a sudden bolt of fire rush through my head and body. I was startled, and tears welled in my eyes.

Janice knew something had happened, so she said, "Carolyn, read it again." I did and was transported by the experience. I didn't know such a thing was possible. I knew that the New Testament scriptures in Acts 2 described how tongues of fire appeared on the heads of those gathered in Jerusalem on the day of Pentecost about 29-33 AD. But I'd not heard of any contemporary bolt of fire experience. Janice and I prayed together. I had been very troubled about our family's finances. I'd recently begun work at the Arkansas Arts Center after exploring singing under the tutelage of Marilyn Horne. Jerry was back to teaching, but we were still recovering financially. My faith had been tested during this period. I prayed that my faith would increase and that my life might please God. It was an experience I will never forget.

"It's time for us to have lunch. See if you can get everyone together."

Being in touch with old friends was important to Bill. Many of our high school friends lived in Little Rock and others in nearby Hot Springs. When Bill was governor, we tried to have lunch every few months. Birthdays were always a good excuse to get together, but sometimes we just agreed that it was time. Sometimes, Bill would tell me, "It's time for us to have lunch. See if you can get everyone together." The usual group was David Leopoulos, Joe Newman, Glenda Cooper, and when they could come over from Hot Springs, Mary Jo Rogers, and Mauria and Bob Aspell. Others from Hot Springs would sometimes come, too. We enjoyed Juanita's, a Mexican restaurant in our neighborhood, now closed. We liked the Dixie Café, Whole Hog Barbeque, and Doe's Eat Place. Any place with barbecue was a favorite. In recent years, birthday lunches with David, Joe and Glenda have continued, and we tell Bill we miss him. Our lunches with Bill gave us valuable time to catch up on news about family and friends, but we also loved hearing Bill talk about what was going on in his life, campaigns, issues, and plans. He appreciated our points of view.

Bill has never missed our Hot Springs High School class of 1964 reunions. The first was the tenth reunion in 1974. Our daughter Mary had just been born, so I couldn't attend, but Bill gave me a full report. Classmates have been thrilled to see Bill at reunions as a friend, Arkansas Governor, and US President.

Bill's Georgetown University roommates also visited Little Rock for inaugural events or just time together. Sometimes, if events were happening at the mansion, they would gather at our home to visit. Bill would come over when he was free and join them.

Friends were always at our home for Christmas parties and other celebrations. We were a tight-knit group in high school, and that continues today. Many went on to major achievements. Phil Jamison became a US Navy commander and a member of the Strategic Arms Limitations negotiating team. Dr. Jim French was a plastic surgeon in DC who did pro bono trips to Africa and Haiti for cleft palate surgeries. Dr. Barney Bond became a highly respected physician in Hot Springs. Fredrick Silverman, Jim Moshinske, Jack Ridgeway and Peggy Woodall became university professors. David Dunham practiced law, and Joe was an accountant for UAMS. Glenda, Kenny, and Anne became teachers, and Mary Jo and Claire became successful businesswomen. David Leopoulos founded the Thea Foundation in honor of his daughter, Thea, who died at age sixteen. The foundation has raised and awarded millions of dollars in scholarships to students who win annual visual and performing arts competitions.

Bill is a thoughtful, caring friend. He calls at times of illness and on birthdays. He calls family to express his condolences on a friend's death. One friend who recently heard from him said they had a long chat that felt like they were sitting together in the kitchen. He asked me for a phone number so he could call a friend for his birthday. I texted back the phone number and then double-checked to find that I'd been off by one digit. Bill responded, "Well, I just sent birthday wishes to a total stranger. Hope they enjoyed it!"

"What key would Summertime be in if the first note is an F#?

In July 1988, Bill was invited to give the nominating speech for Michael Dukakis at the Democratic National Convention. The event turned out to be a major debacle. The Dukakis campaign gave Bill a long speech to read and did nothing to bring order to the unruly crowd. Friends watching his speech grew concerned when it seemed to go so long, and people weren't listening. When Bill received bad press afterward, we were crushed. Some thought maybe the Dukakis campaign had done this intentionally to dim Bill's star. It didn't matter, though, because Bill was widely respected for his speaking ability. We knew this uncharacteristic experience would soon pass.

After the speech, Johnny Carson invited Bill to be his guest on The Tonight Show on July 28, 1988. Harry and Linda Bloodworth Thomason made the arrangements to ensure maximum exposure for Bill. Johnny had made a few jokes about Bill's speech a couple of nights earlier, and his appearance would be an opportunity for Bill to make a comeback. Bill was a bit concerned about playing his saxophone on the show (Harry's idea), but Carson wanted him to play. Bill called and asked, "What key would *Summertime* be in if the first note is an F#?" I was sound asleep when he called very late at night, but we worked it out. We decided it would be a good idea for us to practice before the show. We rehearsed at the Governor's mansion. Chelsea was with us and took a turn at trying to play the sax. Mostly, she entertained by tap-dancing on the hardwood living room floor. Bill and I decided the best selections would be *Summertime, A Taste of Honey,* and *My Funny Valentine*. Bill added *Delta Dawn* in honor of Joe Cocker's appearance on the show. I wished I had a video camera at our rehearsal to record Bill's imitation of Joe Cocker singing *You Are So Beautiful to Me*. It was hilarious. We practiced until midnight, and he was in terrific spirits—relaxed, excited to go, and feeling confident.

Bill's appearance on the *Tonight Show* was amazing. He was at his best, both conversing with Johnny and playing his sax on *Summertime*. Any setback he might have experienced as a result of the convention speech was erased. He was fantastic, and the viewers loved him.

They just didn't have the "fire in the belly" to make the race.

The last years of Bill's service as governor after the 1986 election were marked by a game of trying to guess what he would do next. He had considered running for President in 1988 after Senator Dale Bumpers announced he would not run. Senator Gary Hart of Colorado, the front-runner, quit the race. In January 1987, Bill began a new term as governor. He said he wasn't sure he wanted to run for President. He was thinking of Hillary and Chelsea. Chelsea, aged seven, would be in the second grade in public school in the fall. Bill told friends at a recent visit that Chelsea can count on one hand the few times he missed a special event in her life.

One day, I caught up with Bill jogging in the neighborhood, and I asked him what he planned to do. He wouldn't tell me, and I wondered if he knew. Later, I saw him at the mansion and asked how he was leaning, and he smiled and said I'd know soon. Suspense had been growing. A press conference was held on July 15, 1987, at the Excelsior Hotel. A loud cheer erupted as Bill and Hillary entered. We could sense, however, as they walked to the podium that they had decided not to run for president in 1988. There were no smiles on their faces, just recognition and gratitude for old friends present. Bill said that after much discussion and thought, he and Hillary decided this was not the right time for a presidential race. He cited Chelsea's young age. He spoke of his love for serving as governor, and the work left to do. Hillary took the podium and said that running for president requires a laser-like mental readiness and sharpness about the decision, and they didn't have it. They weren't ready to run. Bill said he wanted to continue to serve the people of Arkansas. He said he'd been involved in many presidential campaigns as a campaign worker and had seen the toll it could take on families. He didn't want to do that to his family, especially as Chelsea was so young. They just didn't have the "fire in the belly" to make the race.

On the way to the press conference, I passed an *Arkansas Gazette* newspaper coin box and saw a placard on the front that read "Clinton Will Run for President." I reached in for it as a souvenir. I called the newspaper because Bill's brother Roger wanted one of the placards, too. The staff told me they actually printed two versions of the card, one that read "Clinton Will Run" and the other "Clinton Will Not Run." I asked if they would give me a couple of the alternate ones. I kept one and gave a set of them to Bill and Hillary framed in double-sided glass with a chain at the top to face either way, depending on his future decision. Bill autographed mine at a party in 1987 and wrote, "Yes, we will, later." After he was elected president in 1992, I asked him to sign it again. He wrote, "And we did!"

We had a party for friends to "welcome" Bill home rather than leaving on the presidential campaign trail. We hung a big "Welcome Home Bill!" banner in red, white, and blue at the front door. We invited Harry and Linda Thomason, Janice and Keith Sjostrand, David and Linda Leopoulos, Joe Newman, and Carolyn Huber to be there to greet Bill and Hillary.

We sang 60s favorites at the piano and Chelsea and our children joined us for board games after we ate. We played Trivial Pursuit for hours, and we were competitive. David Leopoulos kept us laughing as he tried to answer questions. His jokes made Bill laugh so hard he could hardly breathe. He had a lot of one-liners, such as, "She was only a farmer's daughter, but she had trouble keeping her calves together." It was a relief to have this decision behind them, it was relaxing to be with friends, and we were aware this was, indeed, a "homecoming" party. We were happy he'd be home with us a while longer and could sense his relief in having made this difficult decision. We knew he would run when the time was right.

"If I could sing like that, I would never do anything else!"

Family has always been important to the Clintons. Virginia, or "Ginger," as Chelsea called her, often came to the mansion to watch Chelsea on weekends when Bill and Hillary were away. In 1987, Dorothy and Hugh Rodham, Hillary's parents, moved to Little Rock from Park Ridge, Illinois. They wanted to be near Chelsea as she grew, spend time with Hillary and Bill, and enjoy their time as governor and first lady.

Dorothy turned age 70 in 1989. To celebrate her beloved mother's new decade, Hillary planned a surprise party at Marlsgate Plantation in Scott, Arkansas. The party on a sunny afternoon was attended by about thirty guests. Jerry was asked to take pictures of the party. The Rodham's sons, Tony and Hugh Jr., joined the Clintons as hosts. Guests included Ann and Grady McCoy, Carolyn and Joe Huber, Danny Thomason, Patty Howe Criner, and Marie Clinton Bruno. Dorothy, who thought she was going to a family dinner party, was surprised as friends greeted her. We enjoyed a beautiful dinner buffet followed by cake, ice cream, and singing.

Dorothy was always Hillary's hero. She overcame many obstacles in her life. Dorothy was a lifelong learner, enrolled in courses even while living in Little Rock. She adored being close to Chelsea as she grew, and their bond was a gift.

Dorothy was very encouraging and supportive of me, as well. She told me at after I sang at an inaugural event, "If I could sing like that, I would never do anything else!" It was high praise. We had an interesting exchange after a Christmas Eve party at the governor's mansion. Hillary wondered how to recycle all the beautiful poinsettias that decorated the mansion. She insisted that her friends take some home with them. I bent down and spotted one that looked forlorn and like it could use some extra care. Dorothy was standing nearby and heard me say, "I'll adopt this sad one." She said, "Why wouldn't you choose the prettiest one? Here, take this one instead!" We laughed. I knew the others would find happy homes.

I was pleased when Hillary became a friend. She is thoughtful and caring. She has always wanted the best for our family and has done anything she could to open doors for our children.

Hillary was with me in tough times. I had a miscarriage a few years after Will's birth. When I arrived home from the hospital, she called to check on me. "Carolyn, how are you doing?" I didn't know she was aware I'd had a miscarriage, but I deeply appreciated her caring.

Hillary took an interest in my singing and encouraged me to pursue a career in it. After she heard me sing, she wrote notes and told me how much she loved it. She told me she wanted me to become a star. She said, "I want you to become so famous that when I come backstage and someone tells you, "Hillary is here to see you," you'll ask, "Hillary *who?*"

Hillary's faith is genuine and personal. She is an ardent Christian with a deep, anchoring knowledge of what it means to be a disciple of Christ. I was proud of her during the 1992 presidential campaign when a member of the press spotted her looking at some scriptures in her wallet. She said she draws great strength from scripture and prays throughout the day.

When our daughter Sarah entered high school, Hillary, an advisor for Choate Rosemary Hall in Connecticut, called to ask what we thought of a private boarding school experience for her. Our family discussed the idea, but Sarah wanted to go to Central High School in Little Rock, with its high academic standards and national historical significance. We appreciated Hillary's good wishes for our children's education and were honored she thought of Sarah.

Hillary cheered as Sarah embarked on a modeling career in 1988. Earlier, Sarah modeled for the *Arkansas Gazette* fashion section. People often commented about what a beauty Sarah was. But I remember the time Hillary looked at Bill, Jerry, and me and said, "I think Mary is one to look out for. I think she's going to be a real beauty!" And indeed, she was right. As Mary grew into her teenage years, she proved Hillary right. Our daughters are gems.

I deeply admired Hillary. She was a brilliant lawyer, nationally recognized for her advocacy for families and children and her educational reform work in Arkansas. She had a strong network of professional women friends. Before Chelsea was born, she had a party at the mansion to entertain her women friends, and Jerry took photos at the event. They were happy to be celebrating their work in Arkansas.

I reflect with gratitude on the time when Hillary and Bill offered a financial loan when we were having a tough time, the happy times singing together around the piano, the ups and downs of political wins and losses, and watching our children grow. Our families have shared many love-filled memories. Hillary and I talked about our lives back in the early 1980s, and she asked me poignantly, "I wonder how history will remember us?" We can reflect decades later on her accomplishments. She has been named "The Most Admired Woman in the World" fourteen consecutive times and twenty times overall—a Gallup poll record.

She invited friends to visit

Hillary's father died on April 7, 1993, just three months after the Clintons moved to the White House. He had a stroke on March 19th and was hospitalized at St. Vincent Infirmary in Little Rock. Hillary spent the first sixteen days at his bedside. She was with him even as her healthcare task force was working to reshape our healthcare system.

Mr. Rodham's service was on April 9th at First United Methodist Church in Little Rock. The Rev. Ed Matthews and Rev. Vic Nixon presided. President Clinton spoke about Mr. Rodham's life. Burial followed the next day in his hometown of Scranton, Pennsylvania. Though distraught, Hillary was strengthened to be with friends at the service. She invited friends to visit after the service.

Dorothy and Hugh's home in Little Rock continued to be home for the Clintons in Little Rock. After Hugh's death, Dorothy remained in Little Rock until Hillary's election in 2000 to the U.S. Senate. Then Dorothy moved to Washington, D.C. She was a vital speaker at Hillary's campaign events. She and Hillary shared dear times in D.C. Dorothy was close to Chelsea and cherished celebrating her wedding to Marc Mezvinsky in 2010. Dorothy passed away in 2011 in Washington, D.C., after an illness. She is still keenly missed by her family.

As we walked, he said, "Let's just see how it plays out."

Bill was reelected as governor in 1990, and his last term was going well. Hanging over the minds of voters in 1991 was the question of whether he would run for president. Would he fill his term as governor as he said he would when he ran in 1990? Bill was torn and didn't want to go back on his word. But he also knew his supporters would support his decision to run for president if it's what he felt he should do. He had come close to running in 1987, but it wasn't the right time. Most everyone, however, expected he would eventually make the race.

Bill and I discussed a job decision before me, as well. In the spring of 1991, the Governor's Commission on Adult Literacy was created as a liaison between the state Office of Adult Education and the Arkansas Literacy Council. I was encouraged to apply to be executive director. As a former state agency director with a background in education, I had the heart and skills for the work. The agency would encourage adult high-school dropouts to finish school through tutoring help at literacy councils or adult education centers. Family literacy programs provided adult education plus Head Start for children. First Lady Barbara Bush championed family literacy, and the White House created the National Institute for Literacy in 1991.

I saw Bill jogging outside our home one morning and caught up with him to ask again about how he was leaning about a presidential race. We chatted a bit, and I also asked him if he would put in a good word for me with the search committee for the director of the Governor's Commission on Adult Literacy. As we walked, he said, "Let's just see how it plays out." I was disappointed he wouldn't help, but after I was selected, he was elated. He expected I'd be chosen on my own merits and was proud of me. Neither of us knew that this position would lead to my work in DC during the Clinton presidency.

Bill's 1990 race for reelection as Governor had been a particularly bitter one. Many felt he'd soon be on his way to announcing a bid for the presidency and wouldn't serve out his full term. His opponents lobbed endless attacks on him for a variety of false claims. To help boost his spirits on Election Day, November 4, 1990, I planned some extra fun. Some friends and I decided to surprise Bill and Hillary when they went to vote. David Leopoulos Joe Newman, Glenda Cooper, and I drove to Dunbar Community Center at Chester and 17th Street, the Clintons' polling location. We took campaign signs with us. I asked to borrow a candy store's Valentine's Day costume—an enormous pair of red satin lips worn for candy and balloon deliveries. I pulled it on when we saw them arrive with Chelsea, and we began cheering and whistling, carrying signs. They laughed uproariously. Chelsea waited as her parents voted, and we shared hugs after they came back outside. We tried to do anything we could to brighten the campaign trail.

Big decisions and major life changes were closer than we realized. We could feel the energy and did our best to buckle down for the ride.

[1] Wenner, Jann, "Bill Clinton: The Rolling Stone Interview," *Rolling Stone*, December 2000

CHAPTER SIX

Road to the White House

"We gathered around the piano... Carolyn played just as she had done since we were fifteen."

As the weeks passed, the signals became clear that Bill was planning to run for President of the United States. October 3, 1991, was set as Announcement Day, and excitement built throughout the state and nation.

The announcement setting was the Old State House. Its tree-covered lawn provided a picturesque location. The Old State House is the oldest surviving state capitol west of the Mississippi River and held the 1861 secession convention and the fourth constitutional convention when delegates ensured voting rights for freedmen. It served as the Arkansas capitol until a new one was constructed in 1912. It also was a medical school, an Arkansas war memorial, and an office for federal and state agencies. In 1947, the General Assembly designated the Old State House as a museum.[1]

I spent much of the announcement day assisting staff and ensuring the US flags at the back of the stage were straight. Sound checks were underway, and the campaign song *Don't Stop Thinking About Tomorrow* played loudly. Bev Lindsey, campaign staff, contacted me earlier about campaign song ideas, and I suggested Diana Ross's *Ain't No Mountain High Enough*. However, the Clintons liked the hit by Stevie Nicks and Fleetwood Mac, and after obtaining legal permission, it was selected. Our son Will was excused from school to help with the setup and to be part of the historic day. Our girls were home and had passes to attend the announcement. Jerry had a press pass to be close for pictures.

The city was bustling with excitement. Press risers stood on the lawn and outside the fence. The podium for the master of ceremonies was in place. Vendors with newly minted "Clinton for President" merchandise lined the sidewalks and volunteers distributed posters. It was a sunny day, and we were ready to go.

As the event began, I took the podium to welcome everyone before Jimmie Lou Fisher introduced the Clintons and felt honored to have a role on this historic day. Seeing our children Sarah, Mary, and Will at the stage front was thrilling, with Virginia, Roger, Dorothy Rodham, and Jerry taking pictures. We had dreamt of this day for years.

Finally, the doors opened, and Bill, Hillary, and Chelsea walked to the stage. As they were introduced, shouts erupted from the capacity crowd, waving posters in a frenzy. Bill spoke about his vision for America and why he wanted to serve as president. It was a stirring speech, and we felt confident we were on our way to seeing our friend elected. Yes! Bill Clinton would run for President of the United States! The Clinton Road to the White House had begun.

After the announcement, friends went to the governor's mansion to celebrate. In his autobiography *My Life*, Bill writes, "That night, we gathered around the piano with old friends. Carolyn Staley played just as she had done since we were fifteen. We sang *Amazing Grace* and other hymns, many songs from the sixties, including *Abraham, Martin, and John*, a tribute to the fallen heroes of our generation. I went to bed believing we could cut through the cynicism and despair and rekindle the fire those men had lit in my heart."[2]

After the announcement, campaigning began in earnest. The best political pros in the country joined the campaign. The first headquarters was a former paint store on 7th Street that had served as campaign offices for his last race for governor, then moved to the Department of Higher Education building on 3rd Street. The campaign quickly outgrew the space and relocated to the old *Arkansas Gazette* building, two blocks from the Old State House where it all began.[3]

Our family actively campaigned. Sarah, president of the Young Democrats at William Jewell College, led the campus campaign, Mary and Will volunteered locally, and I gave interviews and traveled. The press called nonstop as world news outlets clamored for information about Bill Clinton, especially from friends.

There was always excitement at campaign headquarters, and the energy was electrifying. My high school friend David Leopoulos and I started a newsletter for Bill to encourage him, and George Stephanopoulos delivered it. The campaign staff depended on old friends for background information, and they knew that Bill loved hearing from us and seeing us at events.

High school friends campaigned for Bill in both presidential campaigns, traveling around the country to talk about friendship with Bill and his heart for public service. Sheila Galbraith Bronfman organized "The Arkansas Travelers" to hit the road and talk to voters. I went with the Travelers to New Hampshire for the February 18, 1992, primary. David Leopoulos created a leaflet about his friendship with Bill since childhood and brought copies to New Hampshire.[4] We followed Bill's itinerary each day, driving ahead of him to go into shops and get people out. When Bill arrived, we directed him to people with questions. A woman carrying a child caught my eye. I introduced Bill to her. She asked about healthcare and the high cost of her daughter's treatments. Bill outlined his plans for a better healthcare system. Her story touched his heart, and he gave her hope.

After campaigning, we gathered for supper with the Clintons. We talked about the people we'd met, hoping we had made a difference. Hillary and Bill were grateful for our help and for the brochure David had created. We got a little rest and were up early at the polls to hand out materials and ask for votes. I had to fly home that afternoon, but I worked the polls first.

I hosted an election night party with friends to celebrate what we hoped would be a victory. Paul Tsongas from neighboring Massachusetts was expected to win as "favorite son," but we hoped Bill could make a good showing. As votes were tallied, Bill was second with nearly 25 percent to Tsongas' 33 percent. Bill was euphoric and said that New Hampshire made him "The Comeback Kid." He told voters, "I'll be with you 'til the last dog dies."

The New Hampshire primary kicked off a long year of campaigning. Bill won most primaries, losing only to Tom Harkin in Iowa and Connecticut, and to Jerry Brown in Colorado. Bill was known primarily as the young governor from Arkansas when he entered the race. Interestingly, the Flowers story may have helped with name recognition. People were drawn to his energy and impressed by his showing in New Hampshire. Voters liked the "Comeback Kid" a lot.

Because of my work as director of the Governor's Commission on Adult and Family Needs, I couldn't do much out-of-state campaigning, but I made calls to tell voters of my friendship with Bill. I also continued press interviews, many during my lunch hour. Jim Pledger, the Governor's Chief of Staff, called and asked to see me. I couldn't imagine the purpose. He came to my office and told me he received two calls saying I'd had lunch with reporters and overstayed the lunchtime allotted to state employees. He said I had to be careful about campaigning on the taxpayer's dime. I apologized for my mistake and vowed to watch the time from now on. It was a reminder that not everyone supported Bill's candidacy.

"Everything you say is on the record and likely will be seen in print."

Of the interviews I did with the press, many were with international reporters. I spoke with French, Norwegian, Swedish, Japanese, African, Hispanic, and German journalists. They all asked the same thing: who is Bill Clinton? What was he like as a teen? Did you think he would be president? Why? What is he like? I came to realize more than ever that the President of the United States impacts the world.

One of the interviews I gave was to biographer David Maraniss, who was writing a book about Bill Clinton. Bill wasn't pleased with the project, thinking it was premature since the presidential election hadn't happened. Maraniss interviewed me in our home. He was respectful and warm. I believed I could trust him, which proved a terrible mistake.

At the end of the interview, Maraniss asked me if I could share any other stories with him to help him better understand Bill and Hillary. He promised that anything I said would not be for publication but was on "deep background" to understand them better. I wish someone had pulled me aside and said, "Everything you say is on the record and likely will be seen in print. You should expect to read anything you say." That advice should be shared with candidates' friends. Unfortunately, I was trusting and believed David's reputation was above reproach. I learned that the profit motive often takes priority over an author's commitment. This may not always be true, but David's use of an anecdote I'd agreed to share as unattributed background was painful to me.

Thinking I was 'off the record,' I told him about singing the song I wrote for Chelsea for the Clintons as a baby gift. I shared my conversation with

Hillary after I sang it for them. I told him she asked me about the line in the song about not feeling "worthy." I had meant nothing personal but was reflecting on the wonder of holding a baby.

When Maraniss' book *First in His Class* was published, I read the quotes he attributed to me and was devastated that he included the incident about the song. I wrote apologies to Bill and Hillary, and Bill thanked me and said he'd suspected something like this had happened. He told me not to worry about it. But I feared it would be hurtful to my relationship with Hillary. Hillary and I have stayed in touch through the years since, but I know my quote hurt.

At a 1996 campaign event, when President Clinton was arriving in Chicago by helicopter to attend the Democratic National Convention, I saw Maraniss standing nearby. I asked him why he had printed a quote he promised was for his background only. He explained that his publishers told him to go back through his notes and find material to make the book juicier. I told him I'd trusted him and that the book hurt my relationship with Hillary. He said he was sorry. This remains a painful experience and one I wish I could relive, to do differently. Solomon 8:6 says, "Love is stronger than death, even stronger than hell." For that promise, I am most thankful.

We felt a tap on our shoulders and a staffer told us to hurry and follow her.

Sarah and I attended the 1992 Democratic National Convention in New York City from July 13 to 16 at Madison Square Garden. We shared a room with Patty Howe Criner, another of Bill's oldest Hot Springs friends. We stayed in the same hotel as the Clintons and spent time with them daily.

Before the convention, the campaign asked David Leopoulos and me to give press interviews about our friendship with Bill while there. We wrote a press release with contact information and held interviews around the clock. Each day of the convention we met just after breakfast in the press area to speak with reporters and give interviews. We must have given a dozen or more each day. It was a small way we hoped we could make a difference.

Convention credential lanyards were distributed at the hotel each day with seating locations. Special events each day included city tours and visits with state delegations. We were treated royally and met Michael Dukakis, Vernon Jordan, Rev. Jesse Jackson, and New York Mayor David Dinkins. I went by the Kentucky state delegation to say hello to my family friend,

Senator Wendell Ford. Dad performed his wedding, and he was the best man for my parents' wedding.

The evening sessions at Madison Square Garden were celebrations. Rock stars and performing artists took the stage. Barbara Jordan gave the keynote address. DNC chair Ron Brown and New York Governor Mario Cuomo spoke. Governor Ann Richards of Texas brought the house down. The Arkansas delegation sat front and center on the convention floor, and Bill's mother, Virginia, was on a cloud, celebrating every moment.

Friends of the Bill (FOBs) had box seats and a VIP suite at the convention. We shared supper one night with Aretha Franklin, Roger Clinton, Mary Steenburgen, and Ted Danson sat with us. We visited with Norman Mailer, actors Markie Post and Michael Ross, and Harry Thomason. Clinton's family, Georgetown, and high school friends shared the historic time. When we returned to the hotel each night, we found an invitation for a party with the Clintons under our door. They loved knowing what was going on and the feedback we were hearing. Bill always wanted to know what we'd done that day, who we'd met, and to hear about the many experiences we were having, both at the convention and visiting NYC sites. We especially enjoyed telling him about the many press interviews we were giving each day. He was deeply appreciative.

Bill was nominated on the third night of the convention. As states cast their votes, the cameras showed Bill, Hillary, and Chelsea watching at a nearby shopping center. Ohio's vote put Bill over the top for nomination, and Chelsea jumped for joy. We watched the Clintons walk with an entourage to Madison Square Garden, and when they arrived, the crowd cheered thunderously. Friends were crying and euphoric. It was more exciting than we ever imagined.

On the final convention night, July 16, Bill gave his masterful acceptance speech. He ended with the now-famous words, "I still believe in a place called Hope." The crowd roared, and he acknowledged his deep appreciation. There was no question that this remarkable young man possessed the skills, heart, and mind to lead our nation.

The campaign theme song *Don't Stop Thinking About Tomorrow* began pulsing as everyone danced. Bill took the stage first, and then Hillary and Chelsea joined him. Vice Presidential nominee Al Gore followed. He and Bill held arms high in victory. Tipper Gore and Hillary shared a hug and spontaneous dance, and the Gore children came onstage as the balloon drop began. Roger Clinton sang a song, *"Circle of Friends,"* by friend Randy Goodrum. Thousands of blue balloons filled the stage as the Clinton and Rodham families joined the fun. A multicolored downpour of balloons fell from the ceiling and bounced atop the heads of the dancing crowd.

We felt a tap on our shoulders and a staffer told us to hurry and follow her. Bill's friends were invited onstage for the balloon drop and confetti shower. This was amazing! We never dreamed we'd be invited onstage. Members of Congress, Mac McLarty, Ron Brown, Ann Richardson, and Geraldine Ferraro joined us. C-Span captured it all on tape, and it's lovely to re-watch.

I took a breath and tried to realize this moment had come. Yes, the boy-next-door who I'd thought would be president someday had won the Democratic nomination. I thanked God and asked for strength and safety for Bill and his family through the campaign.

The next morning, we joined the Clintons in the hotel penthouse for brunch. He was officially our Democratic nominee! We told him how much we loved being invited to the stage after his nomination. A photo of Bill with our high school friends taken that morning hangs in my home. I've never seen bigger smiles on the faces of friends David Leopoulos, Jim French, Phil and Susan Jamison, and Mauria and Bob Aspell.

Sarah and I had the experience of a lifetime at the convention. She was a political science major and led the campus movement for Clinton. I had traveled to New Hampshire, done interviews, and campaigned tirelessly and now we savored the outcome. The only sad note was that I left my jewelry case with the gold Omega watch Jerry gave me when Sarah was born in the hotel, and it was never found.

Lunch with candidate Bill and friends

During the campaign, Bill returned home as often as possible and always called to have lunch. He wanted to catch up on our lives and learn what we were hearing about the campaign. We encouraged him about how well things were going. One day, we met at the Dixie Café for lunch, and he shared stories of people he'd met on the trail. He recounted healthcare needs and other concerns. Tears welled in his eyes as he talked about a woman trying to raise her family as a single parent on a low income. The pain he had seen in the faces of real people was etched in his mind and heart, and he wanted the opportunity to improve their lives.

Jerry and I wanted to help with fundraising, so we invited the 1964 Hot Springs High School class to our home in October. Bill was enthusiastic about attending. He thought the press would be interested in hearing about his high school classmates' support. The party drew over eighty classmates, and everyone was happy to see Bill, now the Democratic nominee for President of the United States. A group gathered in the living room to talk with Bill about issues at the forefront of their minds, and Bill outlined his vision. One asked, "Bill, how will you do it all?"

Bill replied, "I can't. Only when every American begins to care about one another's lives will we begin to solve the really difficult problems in our country."

He told us about the inner-city school principal who determined she wanted to make a difference in her students' lives, so she met each one of them at the front door every morning with a personal word of encouragement, a smile, and a pat on the back. He said each one of us can be a peacemaker and bridge builder. It doesn't matter how insignificant our role may seem; we each can make a difference. Bill encouraged us to remember and share this vision that he still talks about today.

Election Day, November 3, 1992

Election Day, November 3, 1992, began early. Bill, Hillary, and Chelsea were flying to Little Rock to vote and await election results. Friends greeted them at midnight at Central Flying Service. The night before, November 2, I went to the Old State House for the choirs' election night sound check. Crowds shouted, "One more day! One more day!" Later we met Georgetown friends at Doe's Eat Place, a favorite for Bill and campaign staff.

When the Clintons' plane landed at midnight, about forty staff and friends welcomed them home. They had been campaigning for seventy-two hours straight at rallies day and night. News accounts said 10,000 people were at a rally at 4 AM in Colorado. Bill Clinton gave people hope again.

As Election Day morning dawned, the excitement was almost unbearable. We expected to work from dawn until the wee hours of the next morning. Before sunrise, I drove downtown to see what was happening and to sense the energy. An eerie excitement filled the air. The press risers were surrounded by enormous satellite dishes in front of the Old State House. Police barricades surrounded the perimeter, and people were already mingling.

I got Will off to school and met with British Channel 4 which planned to follow a friend of Bill on Election Day. We met at the Old State House with staff Redmond Walsh and Robyn Dickey to talk about the music. I was honored to be singing the *National Anthem* at the celebration. The evening music would also feature two choirs. Janice Sjostrand, a friend with whom I'd held Bible study for years, was bringing her Lonoke Pentecostal choir. The Philander Smith College choir, directed by Stephen Hayes, would also sing.

By 8 a.m., I was at my voting location, Dunbar Community Center, at Chester and 16th Streets. It was also the Clintons' voting place. The line already stretched outside the doors, and the estimated wait time to vote was two hours. Reporters from three networks stopped me for interviews. The British film crew arrived, and we got in line to vote.

The streets were barricaded in preparation for the Clintons to arrive to vote. When it was my turn to vote, the film crew followed me inside. Poll coordinator Vaughn McQuary, a friend and former state Democratic Party executive director, rushed up to me and was furious. "Get these people out of here!" he screamed. I explained that they were with the news. He said he didn't care and repeated, "Get them out!"

The news crew left and waited for an hour and a half as I voted. I made my way around the cavernous gymnasium as lines snaked to the voting booths. I understood that security was tight, the Clintons were coming, lines were long, and the film crew was just an annoyance.

The crowd was growing as I came outside. I spotted my son, Will, standing with classmates nearby. Will was a fifth grader at Gibbs International Magnet School adjacent to the polling place. Principal Donna Davis took the Student Council outside to experience history. She knew Bill, Hillary, and Chelsea were coming to vote. As Student Council president, Will had a speech prepared for Bill to say, "This was my lucky year to be elected president of the Gibbs student council, and I hope it will be YOUR lucky year too!"

Soon we heard the shouts, "He's here! He's here!" I waited with the students as the Clintons' van arrived. Secret Service members guarded every step. Chelsea saw Will and walked over to him. I shouted, "Hey, Bill!" and he walked toward us to give Will a long squeeze, turned to me for a hug, and we embraced Hillary and Chelsea. The press was capturing every moment. High school friend Claire Callahan called from Chicago to say she'd seen us on the news.

After voting and greeting the Clintons, Will and I went to the Old State House to help decorate for the victory celebration. We ordered pizza for the choirs and campaign friend Dave Anderson gave us press credentials for access to the Old State House and lawn. Will helped me check the flags and the holding rooms for the choirs. We saw the throngs swarming the streets. Staff raced around with clipboards and checklists. The press was staking out places to wait through the day. We also had a final interview with the BBC and a German film crew.

We ran home to freshen up, planning to be back at 5:00 p.m. for a long evening. When we stopped by the Camelot Hotel for tickets to the after-party, we ran into Georgetown friends.[5] We shared a joyful hug before dashing away to prepare for the historic evening.

I let go a couple of times, but he kept clinging.

Arriving back at the Old State House, Jerry's press credentials gave him access to the stage and grounds. Will and I also had passes so we could come and go throughout the evening. Surveying the risers filled with photographers, the satellite dishes, and the crowds jammed into the streets, we marveled at the excitement. The choirs arrived in dark suits and dresses and rehearsed. I wore a red wool blazer for warmth on the chilly November night.

As night fell and anticipation mounted, I walked around to see the crowds. Bianca Jagger, wife of the Rolling Stones' Mick Jagger, was seated in front. Bill's friends, Mickey and Anthony Mangun, from the Pentecostals of Alexandria, Louisiana, were nearby. Campaign staff stood nearby with our high school and Georgetown friends.[6] The moment for celebration was quickly approaching.

The choirs were asked to remain in the holding room until 10 p.m. We had water and room to stretch, but it was a long wait. A courier gave us election results since we didn't have a TV. I was sent onstage to announce that Clinton had 254 electoral votes and Bush 33, and the crowd went wild. At 9:30 p.m., the choirs were sent to the risers by the stage. Several program changes kept us on our toes, but we worked out the last-minute requests. We had rehearsed and were ready.

The Clintons arrived at the Old State House, and we expected an announcement to be imminent. I was to sing the *National Anthem* at 10:05, and choirs were set to sing immediately following. The color guard was in place. Senator David Pryor introduced me to sing the anthem. I performed a Capella. As the throng sang along, we filled the clear night with joy. The mercury dropped to a chilly 50 degrees. I was deeply honored to sing and happy that CNN covered it.

Columnist John Brummett, speaking on NBC's Arkansas affiliate, Channel 4, said, "Bill Clinton's childhood friend Carolyn Staley just sang the national anthem, and it was a spine-chilling and beautiful rendition. She is a loyal friend and tolerates no detractors of Bill Clinton." Paul Greenburg, editor of the *Arkansas Gazette*, wrote glowingly about my singing in the next day's edition, and I thanked him for the tribute.[7] Not a Clinton fan, Paul was my friend from Temple B'nai Israel, where I was the soloist. Linda Bloodworth Thomason called to say she'd loved my singing. She said, "I've never heard you really sing! You sounded like someone from the Metropolitan Opera!"

The choirs began to perform. As they ended their program, the staff kept telling us, "Lengthen everything! Stretch!" The crowd was upbeat and ready for the news of victory, but the waiting continued. Janice led the singers in a medley of *God Bless America, America the Beautiful,* and *the Battle Hymn of the Republic,* plus *Together* and *We Will Stand*. The choirs were prepared to sing for 15-20 minutes, but the staff kept coming back to say, "Keep going." The choirs repeated their program again and again. Janice led the choirs in a rousing song, "You're My Brother, You're My Sister":

> *You're my brother, you're my sister, So take me by the hand*
> *Together we will work for the world, There's no foe that can defeat us*
> *We're walking side by side, As long as there is love we will stand.*[8]

They sang on and on for over an hour as we waited for what seemed like an eternity for the victory announcement. I went inside the Old State House and saw Bill and Al Gore huddled in a back room. I learned they were awaiting a call from President Bush to concede the election. This was the holdup.

Finally, the moment arrived. The choirs brought *America the Beautiful* to a rousing finale. Emcee Skip Rutherford announced, "Ladies and gentlemen, welcome to the stage Chelsea Clinton, Hillary Clinton, and the next President of the United States, Bill Clinton!" A deafening roar rose from the crowd.

The Clintons walked through the front doors and onto the stage. I stepped to the edge of the stage and snapped a picture of Bill, Hillary, and Chelsea as they walked through the Old State House's double doors. They waved and hugged each other and looked at their friends with elation and gratitude. Next came Al and Tipper Gore and their three young adult children. The rest of the family followed: Virginia and Dick Kelley, Roger Clinton, Dorothy, Hugh Jr., and Tony Rodham. We had a new president, our friend Bill.

Bill gave a powerful speech filled with gratitude, hope, and confidence about the days ahead. Afterward, he moved to greet Janice and the Philander Smith Choir, still on the risers. Bill thanked the choirs profusely. Janice struggled to reach Bill with a book she wanted him to sign. Hillary saw Janice was having trouble reaching him and asked her to hang on a bit longer. Later, Janice showed me his inscription, "Please pray for us."

As the president-elect moved through the crowd, I waited for him as if I'd never seen him before. He moved toward me, and we embraced. I told him I was so proud and so grateful to God for this moment. I said, "I've known since I was fifteen years old that this day would come, that one day you would be President of the United States. I will keep praying for you. I hate for you to go and don't want to lose touch." He didn't say anything. I let go a couple of times, but he kept hugging me. I began feeling uncomfortable because I knew the television cameras were recording every minute. Still, I felt honored. Indeed, it was remarkable to congratulate my dear friend. He may have been thinking that this moment would mark the hour that changed our lives forever. He knew that time with friends would be limited. There were no words to express our feelings adequately. Whatever his thoughts, that hug was a gift and memory. I still become emotional when I watch it on tape.[9]

We had a few loose ends to tie up before we could leave but finally got to the Excelsior Hotel next door for "Virginia's Election Night Party." Upon arrival, we were told the ballroom was at capacity. Bill was already mingling with guests, and no one else could enter. Thankfully, someone nearby saw our plight and arranged to get us in. The Stephen Stills band was playing, Roger was performing, and the crowd was on fire. Bill walked to each table to thank everyone.

Our high school and Georgetown friends were dancing euphorically. We formed a large circle, held arms, and danced to *Jailhouse Rock* while balancing champagne glasses. I remember Tom Campbell stunned us with his old party trick of somehow chewing a broken champagne glass. How in the world? But we saw it firsthand. We felt invincible. Our friend Bill was the next President of the United States.

Rabbis Gene Levy and Matt Friedman wondered if it was appropriate to be dancing while President Bush was making his concession speech. They placed their hands on my head and said the *Yevarechacha,* a priestly benediction from Numbers 6:24-26:

The Lord bless you and keep you;
the Lord make his face to shine upon you,
and be gracious to you;
the Lord lift up his countenance upon you,
and give you peace.

I almost cried. Lazar Palnick, son of retired Rabbi Zeke Palnick, told me he saw them saying the blessing. God's peace felt near and real.

Around midnight, our friends closed in on me. Jim Moore, group representative, spoke, "We think a brunch at your house at 10 a.m. tomorrow is a great idea!" I agreed that would be wonderful, then became frantic at how we would manage on short notice. I knew the goal was simply to be together and to make this memory last as long as possible. Will, Jerry, and I stopped on the way home for brunch items. This was before the advent of 24-hour grocery stores, but we found a 7-11 open and bought eggs, bacon, sausage, and cheese. Already exhausted from the long day in front of the public, I assembled breakfast casseroles to bake the next morning. We also prepared a biscuit mix to bake in the morning. After that, we straightened up the house a bit, made sure we were ready for a party, then got a little rest.

The President asked, "Why not? Why should anything change?"

Everyone arrived at our house the next morning with bells on, still jubilant. David and Linda Leopoulos and kids Thaddeus, Nick and Thea, Joe Newman, Glenda Cooper, Mary Jo Rogers, Mauria and Bob Aspell, Randy and

Gail Goodrum, Jim French, and Phil Jamison—all Hot Springs High School chums—came. The Georgetown friends were there too—Kit and Amy Ashby, Tom Campbell with sons Patrick and Tom, Tom Caplan and friend Vanessa Brown, Jim and Jane Moore, and Bob and Denise Hyland Dangremond. Claire Callahan Johannesen, in town from Chicago, joined us.

A buffet of egg-sausage-cheese casseroles, bacon, baskets of homemade biscuits, and dishes of fruit was accented by tabbouleh I had on hand. Guests brought champagne and juice for mimosas. Amy kept the biscuits baking, and everyone seemed to have plenty to eat. I wondered later why I hadn't just scrambled lots of eggs. We weren't hungry, just elated and eager to continue the celebration. We gathered in the kitchen for a champagne toast. David Leoupoulos called Bill so he could hear us cheering. We didn't consider inviting Bill and Hillary because we knew they would be exhausted, but we wanted them to know we were still on a cloud.

A few minutes later, we were thrilled to see the Clintons walk in to join us. Bill said they tried to drive over but couldn't get through the barricades, so they walked. Moments later, Virginia and Dick Kelley arrived, and our group was complete. We cheered, sat around the dining room table, and stood hugging for over an hour. We were honored that our home could host the post-election celebration. Back in 1979, Bill had asked if we could be neighbors again. Because of that, we lived a few blocks from the mansion, and the Clintons could easily join us. What a gift.

Kit Ashby proposed a toast to the newly elected President, saying, "We know things will never be the same now."

The President asked, "Why not? Why should anything change?" We hoped he was right but felt a little surprised that he didn't expect change. We knew that our access to him would not be the same for a while, if ever.

We took endless photographs, asked him to autograph our souvenir newspapers with the election headlines, and exchanged a few gifts. Vanessa Brown, Tom Caplan's friend from London, brought Bill a beautiful framed original work. I'm sure Bill wished we'd stop handing him things to autograph, but we were with the new President-elect of the United States! We were partly stunned by what we had just witnessed but so happy for Bill and hopeful for our nation. We cherished the time.

Someone asked, "Carolyn, have you looked out your living room window?" I had been busy in the kitchen and hadn't thought to look outside. When I did, I saw the vacant lot across the street filled with at least a hundred journalists and photographers. The Secret Service had barricaded our block. Neighbors were standing in the street, awaiting the Clintons' departure. It was an unbelievable sight.

As our celebration drew to a close, we moved to the front porch to say goodbyes. Jerry suggested we take a group picture. Bill and Hillary stood on the steps in the center, as we formed three rows around them and along the porch railing with Will at the end by the swing. I stood next to our American flag. Virginia was in front of Bill, and Dick was just behind him. We didn't bother with the lineup, just wanting a quick memory of the day. Jerry took a wonderful picture that is now on display at the Clinton Presidential Center. Photographers across the street were snapping, too. Jerry couldn't be in the picture, but other photographers captured him in the shot that appeared the next day in newspapers around the world. There we were, front page above the fold, gathered as friends with our new president-elect. The picture also ran in all major news magazines and was *Newsweek*'s centerfold. A friend from Pittsburgh called me to say how much the picture on our porch meant to him. "When I saw that picture, I understood that Bill is like me, like my friends. Standing in jeans, a casual shirt, and a jacket, gathered with lifelong friends, that picture helped me understand my new president more fully. Thank you!"

We waved goodbye to the Clintons and exchanged last hugs. Neighbors rushed over to congratulate Bill, who took time to greet everyone. The same guy who jogged this street uninterrupted many previous mornings now attracted throngs.

You shall be called the repairer of the breach, the restorer of streets to live in.

Following Bill Clinton's election as our 42nd president, inaugural planning moved into high gear. With only two months until January 20, 1993, we worked at a furious pace. Thanksgiving, Christmas, and New Year's holidays called for celebrations, as well. At an Arkansas Advocates for Children and Families gala at the Excelsior Hotel to honor Hillary, she asked Rodney Slater and me if we would co-chair the Presidential Inaugural Prayer Service at Metropolitan AME Church on inauguration morning. What an honor it was to be asked to organize this event!

The Clintons took an active role in helping plan the inaugural prayer service. They wanted a variety of musical styles and suggested favorite hymns. I was honored the President asked me to sing *Be Not Afraid* at the service. To allow for all the music the President wanted, we added an hour of pre-service music to play while guests arrived. Three gospel choirs—the Pentecostals of Alexandria, Louisiana, the Lonoke Apostolic Church of Lonoke, Arkansas, and the choir of Metropolitan AME Church were asked to provide the pre-service music. The Clintons invited their pastors, Dr. Rex Horne of Immanuel Baptist Church Little Rock, and Dr. Ed Matthews of First United Methodist Church, Little Rock, and friend Rabbi Gene Levy of Temple B'nai Israel, to speak. George Stephanopolous's father, Rev. Robert Stephanopolous, represented the Greek Orthodox Church. Dr. Gardner C. Taylor, renowned African American pastor and author, would give the sermon.

Rodney helped contact the clergy of all faith traditions, and I contacted musicians that the Clintons favored. I called to ask composer John Hilliard, Bill's high school band friend and composer in residence at James Madison University, to compose a brass fanfare to be played as the Clintons entered the sanctuary. I reached Phil Driscoll, trumpeter, to play, and Mickey Mangun and Janice Sjostrand to enlist their choirs.

It was exciting to see arrangements come together for the Inaugural Prayer Service. Metropolitan AME Church, located on M Street in the downtown of the District of Columbia, had been founded in 1886, and had a prominent history. We worked with the Clintons and clergy friends on a theme for the service and for scriptures that would speak to God's inspiration and protection of our new president. We chose Isaiah 58:12: "Your ancient streets shall be rebuilt; you shall raise up the foundations of many generations; you shall be called the repairer of the breach, the restorer of streets to live in."

Another prayer service was also planned for inauguration eve, January 19th, at First Baptist Church, Washington, D.C.—after the Inaugural Gala. I assisted the planners, who were led by Dr. James Dunn, director of the Baptist Joint Committee and friend of Bill and Hillary. We met in our home to discuss the service. I coordinated with staff to be sure the service was part of the official schedule. It would be late, but the hope was that the service would both highlight Bill's Baptist life and add a faith dimension to pre-inaugural events. Christian composer Ken Medema agreed to perform, and several clerics signed on to participate. Inauguration Eve would end with prayer.

The President took the gift and ... with tears in his eyes. "That's what I want to be,"

In addition to the inaugural planning, we had other pressures. The press interviews in our home continued non-stop. Journalists from many states and countries sought insight into our new president. They poured through photo albums and high school yearbooks. ABC's Channel 7 News in Washington, D.C., arranged to follow us during the inauguration. Our home was the interview site for countless book and magazine authors. Stories and pictures of our life with President Clinton appeared in books and magazines around the globe.

We reserved flights and reservations at the Holiday Inn Dupont Circle, where our neighbors were David Leopoulos and family. After securing tickets for the Arkansas Ball (and MTV Ball for the kids), we organized our wardrobes. The entire inaugural week was a mammoth but happy undertaking. During the inauguration, military agencies provided a car and driver for all events.

In addition to the prayer service planning, I also became the unofficial contact for Bill's friends who wanted to attend the inauguration. Collecting correct personal data was tedious, but I submitted it all and kept a copy with me for any unscheduled events. Bill and Hillary were hosting a tour of the White House on Wednesday, January 21, and information needed to be in the White House database. It was a joy to help Bill stay connected with his old friends.

Harry and Linda Thomason asked to use our home as the interview site with the Clintons' friends for the film *The Man From Hope*. We had no idea what a film location looked like, but soon learned as equipment trucks lined the street outside our home. Cameras and miles of cables filled the front yard and hallways. Lights and cameras occupied every interior space. People were coming and going all day and evening, and meals were catered for the crew. Our family was excited to watch from the next room as friends, teachers, colleagues, and political leaders gave interviews about Bill. The two-week project provided footage to be shown at the Presidential Inaugural Gala and countless other times, as well.

We had a poignant moment at our home just before the Clintons left for DC. The President was gathered with several friends, many of them from faith-based backgrounds, in our living room for a send-off. Our friend, Lyda Holt Samuels, called her mother to connect her with the President for a sweet chat. Some were from the prophetic tradition of Bill's friend, pastor Dick King. Bill believed in the prophetic word. A pastor seated next to him once at a Prayer Breakfast told him, "I have a word for you from God." Without hesitating, Bill looked at him and responded, "What is it? I believe in the prophets and in prophetic gifts today." The doorbell rang and I greeted an African American pastor I didn't know who had a gift for the President. He showed me a framed verse of scripture, Psalm 78:70-72. Bill came to the door to accept the gift. The verses read,

"He chose David his servant
and took him from the sheep pens;
71 from tending the sheep he brought him
to be the shepherd of his people Jacob,
of Israel his inheritance.
72 And David shepherded them with integrity of heart;
with skillful hands he led them."

The President-elect looked at the pastor with tears in his eyes. "That's what I want to be," he said. The Inaugural Prayer Service program cover included this scripture, and Bill said the words embodied his hope to lead our nation.

Preparing for the Prayer Breakfast was a massive undertaking. I saw the sometimes unflattering nexus of politics, religion, and competing church personalities jostling to contribute and for recognition. When the press proclaimed the service a highlight of the inauguration, we felt rewarded.

Chelsea looked at him and exclaimed, "DAD! It's only a GAME!"

The Clintons lived in the governor's mansion until they moved to the White House. Packing was an enormous project. They had to store much of their furniture because the White House was fully furnished. One day, I went by the governor's mansion to see how things were going. Bill was admiring gifts being cataloged for storage. He generously shared some with us, including an ivory knitted afghan, a quilted table runner with the Democratic donkey and GOP elephant, several Arkansas baskets, and more. My favorite gift was a huge wooden bowl with a beautiful burl design crafted from an Arkansas tree. He said both Virginia and Dorothy had spotted it and said they'd love to have it, but he thought I could use it for entertaining, so he gave it to me to break the tie. We treasure this keepsake.

One of the joys of campaigning was meeting new people who became friends, as was the case with Harry Thomason and Linda Bloodworth-Thomason. An Arkansas filmmaker in Hollywood and brother of Bill's friend, Danny, Harry assisted Bill's communication team. Harry and Linda produced *The Man from Hope* film about Bill's background as a young boy growing up in Hope who eventually became President of the United States. It is shown today at the Clinton Presidential Center as the visitors' tour introduction.

After the 1992 election, Linda planned a lavish birthday party for Harry's birthday on November 28 in Los Angeles. Bill, Hillary, and Chelsea would attend, making this his first major appearance as President-elect. Stars filled the guest list; Dionne Warwick performed; a big band entertained. Harry and Linda wanted Arkansas friends there, so a plane was chartered to fly us to California. Traveling with us were Harry's family members and friends since childhood, Nancy Hernreich, Susan Thomases, and Ann and Grady McCoy. Diane Mitchell, Mary Lynn Lanning, Scottie Shively—Linda's childhood friends—and their spouses came. We had a joyous time on the flight. Linda predicted we'd be friends, and she was right. Mary Lynn and I later took a Zumba class at Little Rock Athletic Club.

When we landed at Burbank airport, a coach was waiting to take us to the Pasadena Ritz Carlton, where our family luxuriated in three rooms. It was a party like no other. Linda recorded me singing *I'm Just Wild About Harry* on a video shown at the party. I sat next to John Ritter and his date and had a delightful visit. Stars Robert Wagner, Jill St. John, Dionne Warwick, and Gil Gerard attended.

At the Thomason party, Chelsea also planned special events for her friends. She took Will and pals to a Cirque du Soleil performance on the beach before the gala. It was a spectacular outing, and they returned to the hotel in time to change into party clothes, with Will in his rental tuxedo.

Linda asked Jerry to take the event photos. Sterling 4" x 6" frames served as place cards for keepsake photos afterward. Looking back through the photos brings back remarkable memories of a true "Hollywood" evening with the stars. Best of all, the party served as a double celebration for Harry's birthday and Bill's election.

We continued the party the next day at a picnic at the Thomason's home overlooking the ocean. There were birthday cakes to top off a delicious cook-out feast. We loved being with the Clintons, Virginia, and Dick Kelley, and Roger Clinton. The Thomasons truly made this a star-studded event.

Our friendship with Harry and Linda deepened in the years that followed. Our daughter Sarah worked on the Thomason's television show, *Hearts of Fire* (1992-95). Their first big hit was *Designing Women,* in which Danny Thomason was cast in an episode and got to sing. They later produced *Evening Shade,* another TV comedy. Linda wrote my name into several *Designing Women* scripts to say "hello." In one episode, Annie Potts told friends she needed to return a potluck dish to Carolyn Staley. In another show, a newlywed discovers her husband's former girlfriend was Carolyn Staley and finds a stash of her letters he'd kept. He assured her it was "over," but when he died, she noticed his burial vault was located under Carolyn Staley's. Not only was the new wife shocked, but I was as well because I'd never seen my name on a tombstone.

For Christmas, Harry and Linda gave us a karaoke player with sing-along tapes and lyrics, plus a volleyball and badminton set, gifts we've enjoyed for years. They also came to parties at our home in Little Rock. We played a competitive game of Trivial Pursuit once with Bill and friends and struggled to get the answers correct. As tension mounted, Chelsea looked at her dad and exclaimed, *"Dad!* It's only a *game!"*

We broke down laughing. "Out of the mouths of babes," indeed!

Hillary called on Thanksgiving Day 1992 to invite our family to the mansion to share dessert with them and other friends that evening. We had 15 family members with us for Thanksgiving. I realized Hillary probably wasn't aware of our large group and I called back. She made sure I knew everyone was welcome. Vince and Lisa Foster and Vince's mother greeted us at the mansion when we arrived. Webb Hubbell and family were leaving. Clinton staff Ann Walker, Capriccia Marshall, Loretta Avant, and Maggie Williams attended. We embraced Bill and Hillary and took pictures. My brother Walter took the recent *Life* magazine with a story on the election. Walter's family also gave him an afghan with a Razorback hog design. My sister, Deborah, took a poster of the White House floor plan. Bill was fascinated as they discussed it.

Mother and Hillary enjoyed a long visit, and we loved talking with the Clintons about the exciting days ahead. Hillary said to Bill, "Just think! We can invite anyone we want to for dinner, and they'll come! Musicians, stars, authors, anyone!" I remembered that later when I saw the president during his second term and told him an Elton John one-liner joke. He laughed and said, "That's funny! I'll call and tell him."

"I have never seen him like this."

After his presidential election, Bill resigned from his governorship on December 12, 1992, as the Presidential transition required his full attention. He was only twenty-four days short of surpassing Gov. Orval Faubus' tenure.

The Clintons savored every moment of their last Christmas in Little Rock. They attended parties at the homes of friends in the Quapaw Quarter neighborhood around the mansion. One was a party at the home of Joel and Caroline Pugh for the neighborhood babysitting co-op. Joel was the Dean of Trinity Episcopal Cathedral. About sixty parents and children visited with Santa. Joel lit real candles on the ceiling-high fir tree, a tradition from Caroline's UK childhood. We sang *Silent Night* before extinguishing the tapers. The Clintons also went to beautiful parties at the homes of Carl Miller and Dr. Dan and Sandra Cook.

The last Christmas at the governor's mansion was joyous. The traditional parties for staff, family, and friends rounded Bill's years in the mansion. We sang around the piano, played games with props, and knew we would miss these times together. At the last Christmas party, mansion administrator Robyn Dickey sat by me at the piano and reminisced. I asked her what she thought Christmas would be like at the White House. "Just like this," she answered. We soon learned that the White House had its own traditions.

Bill and Hillary invited friends to the mansion on Christmas Eve for one last hurrah. They asked me to bring some games and songs. I took our Pictionary game, a paper flipchart, and red and green markers. We set the easel on the living room hearth, and teams sat across from each other on long sofas. The team guessing the most drawings would win. At one point, Bill began jumping up and down in panic that his team was taking too long to answer. Bruce Lindsey looked at me incredulously and said, "I have never seen him like this." Bill was competitive even outside politics.

In January 1993, former Congressman Beryl Anthony and I were guests on CNN's *Evans and Novak* to talk about our friend Bill Clinton, who was about to be sworn in as our 42nd president. Beryl and I talked about how we thought he would serve in the White House. We knew him from different contexts, so we were able to talk about him both politically and personally. In closing, Rowland Evans said, "I hope Ms. Staley is correct in her analysis, in her answer to the big question: What's it going to look like a year from now? What's going to be surprising? And I must say it was elevating, lofty. Families, parents, parties, politicians, people, religions, and children are all going to come together. I hope she's right."[10]

---

[1] The Old State House, *Wikipedia*, May, 2022

[2] Clinton, Bill, *My Life*, Alfred Knopf Publishers, New York, 2004

[3] Early presidential campaign staff included David Wilhelm, campaign manager and wife Degee; George Stephanopoulos, communications; James Carville and Paul Begala, advisors; and Stan Greenburg and Mandy Grunwald, pollsters. David Leopolous serviced the copy machines. Sarge Lozano, Clinton's neighbor in Midland, was the sign manager. Bev Lindsey, Gloria Cabe, and many Little Rock friends worked full-time.

[4] Other Arkansas friends traveling to New Hampshire were Mauria and Bob Aspell, Randy and Gail Goodrum, and Glenda Cooper.

[5] In Little Rock for election night were friends Tom and Jude Campbell and sons Tom and Patrick, Denise and Bob Dangremond, Kit and Amy Ashby, and Tom Caplan with friend Vanessa from London. We saw Bob and Mauria Aspell, Randy and Gail Goodrum, the Leopoulos family, Mary Jo Rogers, Glenda Cooper and sons.

[6] Campaign staff Paul Begala, James Carville, Mandy Grunwald, Bruce Lindsey, and George Stephanopoulos sat at the front. Georgetown friends Tom and Jude Campbell, Tommy Caplan, Kit and Amy Ashby, Denise and Bob Dangremond joined our high school friends.

[7] Greenburg, Paul, editorial, *Arkansas Democrat Gazette*, November 3, 1992

[8] Taff, Russ, *We Will Stand*, Word Music, 1983

[9] We greeted campaign staff George Stephanopoulos, James Carville, Paul Begala, Mandy Gruenwald. We saw the Georgetown and high school friends. Roger Clinton and family were nearby and other Arkansas Governor's office friends including Carol Rasco, Susie Whitaker, Mike Gauldin, Lynda Dixon, and Jim Guy Tucker, our new governor.

[10] CNN television, *Evans and Novak*, December 1992

CHAPTER SEVEN

The Clinton Presidency Begins

Bill jumped for joy and started our way.

The day for our trip to the inauguration finally arrived: Saturday, January 16, 1993. Television crews from WJLA Channel 7 and ABC News Washington were waiting outside our home in Little Rock to film us as we left. Our daughter Mary saw the trucks from her bedroom window, and since Sarah wasn't ready, she went downstairs to greet the crew. They commended her for her natural knack for television, a prophecy that would come true as she became a news anchor. My sister Deborah drove us to the airport. We left a house-sitter for our home and dog, Tess, a six-year-old brown Cairn terrier. Television crews filmed us leaving home and boarding the flight.

We flew to Dulles Airport, where local high school friends Jim French and Phil Jamison met us. Jim brought shopping bags filled with pastries from a friend's bakery in Reston. The guys loaded our bags in their cars and drove us to our hotel. Adrienne and her husband, Mike Feldman, who gave us the pastries, became great friends in the years ahead.

Phil suggested we drive to Culpeper, VA, on Sunday morning, January 17, to meet the Clintons on the last leg of their bus tour across America from Monticello to Washington, D.C. The Clintons and Gores planned to stop at Culpeper Baptist Church for worship, a historic church that still has the jail key used to lock up pastors who preached in colonial America despite warnings from King George that colonists must support the Church of England. I contacted Clinton's staff to let them know we'd like to attend. On Sunday morning, we drove to Culpeper, an hour from DC. Dr. James Dunn, head of the Baptist Joint

Committee for Church and State and Bill and Hillary's friend, joined us there. Clinton's staff ushered us to a front pew so we would be in Bill and Hillary's sightline. As the Clintons entered, we leaned forward a bit and caught Bill's attention. He jumped for joy and started coming our way, but the service was beginning. He was elated to see old friends, and it was fun to surprise him.

After the service, the staff took us outside to meet Bill on the bus. We hadn't seen him since he left Little Rock, and Jim and Phil hadn't seen him since the post-election brunch at our house. He invited our group onto the bus to greet Hillary and the Gores. Al and Tipper Gore treated us like old friends. Bill and Hillary introduced us to them and told them about our long friendship. The bus had banquette booth seating and a table at the back where they had meals and played cards, checked their mail, and kept up with the schedule. They seemed to be having a great time together.

The church visit was an historic opportunity, and I was happy our kids were with us. We joined the motorcade to follow the Clinton bus back to D.C. and saw well-wishers lining the highway with posters as they waved to the Clintons and Gores, a phenomenal outpouring of American spirit.

The Inaugural "Call for Reunion" on Sunday night, January 18, began with a candlelight walk led by the Clintons and Gores to the Lincoln Memorial for a concert. Thousands walked with them. When we reached the Lincoln Memorial, we enjoyed a two-hour outdoor inaugural concert featuring Aretha Franklin, Michael Bolton, Kenny G, Tony Bennett, Bob Dylan, Diana Ross, and rapper L-L Cool J. President Clinton addressed the crowd about our nation's need for renewal and reunion.

The Clintons and the Gores led a procession of thousands across the Arlington Memorial Bridge from the Lincoln Memorial to Arlington, Virginia, for the bell ceremony. The event included a videotaped statement from the crew of the space shuttle Endeavor, plus live video scenes from cities across the nation where crowds gathered to ring bells in a display of national unity. At 6 p.m., Clinton, Gore, and their children held the red rope attached to the bell and led the nation in a bell-ringing ceremony. Spectacular fireworks closed the event, a display historians called D.C.'s largest ever.

"Of course, Mr. President. Thank you."

On Monday morning, January 19, we had a full day of events, including rehearsal for the Inaugural Prayer Service at Metropolitan AME Church. I welcomed everyone, and Rev. Anthony Mangun said what an honor it was to be a part of this service and led us in prayer. We rehearsed, did sound checks, and reviewed details about the program. We hoped the service would be a thrilling and prayerful way to start Inauguration Day early the following morning.

Chelsea invited Will and a group of friends for a Smithsonian tour on Monday. They met at Blair House, where the Clintons were staying. Will enjoyed exploring exhibits with friends from Little Rock. The Smithsonian staff provided an up-close view of museum treasures and provided lunch. It was thoughtful of the Clintons to plan time for Chelsea and friends.

The Monday night Inaugural Gala was at the Capital Centre in Landover, Maryland. The gala stage was in the center of the arena. Seating encircled it. The orchestra pit was in the center of the stage floor. Since there was no "backstage" area, the artists walked up the aisle through the audience to the stage. The cast included Michael Jackson, Barbra Streisand, Elton John, Alvin Ailey Dance Troupe, Chevy Chase, Bill Cosby, Jack Lemmon, and James Earl Jones.

Michael Jackson talked about his young friend, Ryan White, a hemophiliac who contracted AIDS at age 11 and died at age 18. He asked the President to continue research into a cure for HIV/AIDS, then sang *Gone Too Soon*. He dedicated *Heal the World* to all the children of tomorrow as a chorus of young people filled the stage, joining hands with him.

Annette Benning and Warren Beatty introduced Barbra Streisand, who reminisced about meeting the president at a California fundraiser. She said Bill told her he loved her song *Evergreen*, and she had told him then, "I'm not singing it tonight, but I tell you what. I'll sing it at your inauguration when you're elected president." Then she added, "And that is a promise I am happy to keep tonight." Bill and Hillary held hands as she sang. She closed with *Children Will Listen* from the musical *Into the Woods* by Stephen Sondheim. She thanked Bill and Hillary for their advocacy for children and knew it would continue.

Aretha Franklin entered wearing a yellow gown under a full-length red fox cape. She recited the opening words of Martin Luther King's *I Have a Dream* Speech. Then she sang *I Dreamed a Dream* from *Les Misérables*. It was a powerful performance, and she filled the hall with her magnificent presence.

Noted photographer Annie Liebowitz's staff contacted me earlier to arrange a time during the gala for a photo of Clinton's friends for *Vanity Fair*. Her assistant found us during the concert and took us to the studio upstairs at the concert hall. David Leopoulos, Joe Newman, and I posed standing on a paper sweep as a fan blew my hair. Joe spontaneously put my pearls between his teeth, and she snapped that picture, which became the magazine centerfold. When the magazine later hit the newsstand, Nancy Hernreich, the President's assistant, took the picture into the Oval Office to show the president. He loved it and beamed happily. Annie sent us a large-format print of the signed photograph, and we framed it to hang in our home as a special memory.

After the gala, the Clintons suggested we ride in their motorcade to the last event of the day, to a special prayer service I had helped to plan at First Baptist Church to close the day. As we waited for the motorcade, we stood in a small holding room with Aretha Franklin (in her huge fox coat) along with Jack Nicholson and other stars. Michael Jackson crawled on the floor through people's legs to get to his waiting limo. It was a scene. As we stood packed together, our son Will, age 12, got claustrophobic and started to get teary. Jack Nicholson saw what was happening and said, "Hey, everybody spread out a little bit. Let's give this guy some breathing room. Just take a step back, thanks." It was very thoughtful and helped Will feel better.

The Clintons got in their van, and we followed. I commented on how deserted the 495 D.C. Beltway was. Then we laughed as we realized the police had stopped traffic for the presidential motorcade to pass by. Ah, the perks of traveling with the president!

The First Baptist Church of Washington, D.C., at Sixteenth and O Streets, was filled for the midnight service. My mother's inaugural tour group attended. It was my first time seeing her at the inauguration. We hugged with tears of excitement. The Clintons and Gores arrived to warm applause. Our family doctor and wife, Dr. Bruce and Sally Sanderson, were seated in front of the pew reserved for the Clintons and Gores. Bruce later told me they were horrified to be seated in front of the president. Bill, was happy to see them, smiled and said, "Hi, Sally and Bruce!"

Recording artist Ken Medema sang, and several gave prayers and comments. Instead of ending with stars and politicians, the day ended with prayer. It was a poignant close to the day and a fitting tribute to the faith of President Clinton, Vice President Gore, and their families.

We were in bed by 2 a.m. and had only three hours to rest before we were due at church at 6:00 a.m. for the 8 o'clock service. How our family of five managed to stay in one double room with an extra cot, two luggage carts, and hanging garments still amazes me. It was possible only because we were running on adrenaline and were so excited about the historic inaugural festivities that nothing else mattered.

President Clinton decided to televise the prayer service, a change in inaugural protocol, and an addition to programming for news coverage. C-SPAN sent a camera pool to tape the service as countless reporters stood outside.

In planning the service, the president and Hillary gave me a list of clerics and musicians they hoped could be on the program. I spent the months of November and December contacting all of them and clarifying their roles in the service. The president also asked if I would sing *Be Not Afraid,* which I'd sung at his inaugural dedications as governor. I was honored and hoped I could direct the service and manage to sing as well. I said, "Of course, Mr. President. Thank you."

"Where did you find white people who can sing like that?"

As Inauguration Day dawned, I knew my instincts had been correct about trying to both direct the service and sing. I had a *Today Show* interview before the service. The crew positioned me on 15 ft. scaffolding outside the front of Metropolitan AME Church to show the church's exterior as the crowds were pouring in. As the interview ended, I lost my footing and nearly fell to the ground but somehow recovered. Relieved but rattled, I caught my breath, thanked God, and went inside to greet the arriving musicians and clergy.

Another tense moment came after the service started. We couldn't locate the Muslim imam who was on the program. I raced up and down the back staircase looking for him, and a Secret Service agent stopped me and took me to a security office for clearance. I must have looked unhinged for him to pull me aside, and I tried to explain the circumstances. Finally freed to go, I didn't think I'd have time to get back upstairs to the sanctuary to catch my breath and sing.

Regaining my composure, I walked to the pulpit and sang *Be Not Afraid*: "You shall cross the barren desert, but you shall not die of thirst; you shall wander far in safety though you do not know the way. Be not afraid, I go before you always. Come, follow me, and I will give you rest." Looking into the faces of the president and first lady, I prayed the words would be uplifting. I saw the president sing along, his eyes welling with tears. I was deeply thankful.

I'd always heard it said that the devil works to thwart the efforts of those 'trying to do good.' I could tell he'd been busy that morning, nearly causing a fall from the exterior scaffold, having to race through the church to locate the imam, and to go through Secret Service clearance minutes before I needed to return to the sanctuary in time to sing "Be Not Afraid," but by God's grace, we made it through.

The president invited Mickey Mangun of the Pentecostals of Alexandria, Louisiana, and Janice Sjostrand of the Apostolic Church of Lonoke, Arkansas, and choirs to participate. They sang as guests arrived at Metropolitan AME Church. The American Boy Choir stood at the communion railing to sing *Jesu Joy of Man's Desiring* by J. S. Bach before the Clintons entered.

A brass ensemble performed *Fanfare for a New Beginning* by our high school friend John Hillard as the Clintons and Gores walked to the front pew. John was in the Hot Springs High School band with President Clinton and is now a composer in residence at James Madison University, Harrisonburg, Virginia. John offered to compose the fanfare, and the president was elated. It was a regal, thrilling piece that perfectly prepared the service to begin just before the Clintons processed to the front row.

Mickey Mangun sang *In the Presence of Jehovah* and Janice sang *Holy Ground*, both favorites of the president. C-SPAN showed the faces of General Colin Powell, Rev. Jesse Jackson, and Secretary of Commerce Ron Brown as they listened to Mickey and Janice sing. Bill told me that after the service, General Powell approached and asked, "Where did you find white people who can sing like that?" I still enjoy going to YouTube's Inaugural Interfaith Prayer Service and watching the service on C-SPAN. It always lifts my spirits.

Trumpeter Phil Driscoll was scheduled to play *Amazing Grace* at the service closing, but during the service, he was eager to improvise as Mickey and Janice sang. Sitting next to him, I saw him fidgeting restlessly with his horn, wanting so badly to join in. I whispered to him, "Just go ahead and play, Phil. It'll be ok." The spontaneous result was powerful, and the president loved it and smiled approvingly.

Baritone soloist Earl Taylor sang *Precious Lord, Take My Hand,* and *My Living Shall not be in Vain*. The congregation sang *How Great Thou Art*. Rabbi Gene Levy, Dr. Rex Horne, and Imam Wallace Mohamed read scriptures and led prayers. Rev. Robert Stephanopoulos' reading of Isaiah 58: 6-12 was especially fitting for the service:

"Is not this the fast that I have chosen?
To loosen the bands of wickedness,
to undo the heavy burdens
and to let the oppressed go free
and that ye break every yoke?
… thou shalt raise up the foundations of many generations,
and thou shalt be called the Repairer of the Breach,
the Restorer of Paths to dwell in." (King James version)

Dr. Gardner C. Taylor's sermon was powerful and prophetic. Both President Clinton and Vice President Gore were riveted. Dr. Ed Matthews, Hillary's pastor, pronounced the benediction. We left uplifted and honored to have participated. Television hosts Peter Jennings and Bryant Gumbel commented that the prayer service was particularly touching and showed a side of the president that was rarely seen. We hoped America had caught a glimpse of our new president's faith.

"That's Carolyn Staley and David Leopoulos!"

Following the service, a bus took our family and Vince Foster's family to the U.S. Capitol for the swearing-in ceremony. We didn't know tickets were required and quickly realized no seats were available. People who arrived before dawn to get good seats yelled at us to get down and stop blocking the view, so we knelt in the sawdust.

Judy Woodruff of PBS News saw our predicament and whispered to the person seated next to her, "That's Carolyn Staley and David Leopoulos!" I guess she thought that, as friends of the president, we would have seats. David and I finally found a spot to stand with our families under a tree, far away from the swearing-in, almost as though we were in a nearby field. The Joint Congressional Committee plans seating for the swearing-in. Senator

Wendell H. Ford of Kentucky chaired the committee and distributed the tickets. I was delighted my mother was seated on the platform, thanks to her lifelong friendship with Senator Ford.

At the swearing-in, Marilyn Horne sang the *National Anthem*, the Rev. Billy Graham gave the invocation, and Maya Angelou recited her poem, *On the Pulse of Morning*, which she wrote for the occasion. Hillary held Bill's grandmother's Bible as he repeated the oath spoken by Chief Justice Rehnquist. The Bible was open to a favorite passage of the president's, Galatians 6:9, "Let us not grow weary in well doing: or in due season we shall reap a harvest, if we don't faint." David and I hugged and wept as Bill took the oath of office. It didn't matter that we were so far away. It only mattered that it was official now. Our childhood friend was the President of the United States.

Following the swearing-in, the Clintons and Gores attended the Congressional luncheon in Statuary Hall of the US Capitol. Friends had lunch in the ornate Indian Treaty Room of the Old Executive Office Building, where White House staff had an office. We celebrated with friends and remembered our friendships that led to this day.

After lunch, we went to the president's box in the viewing stand for the Inaugural Parade and watched Bill, Hillary, and Chelsea walk past us down Pennsylvania Avenue. Crowds cheered as they passed by. It was thrilling to be with family, members of Congress, cabinet nominees, and stars. We shared the stand with Barbara Walters and Senator John Warner, Madeline Albright and many other dignitaries. Friends with us included Dr. Rex Horne and family, the president's minister at Immanuel Baptist Church in Little Rock, and several Georgetown and Hot Springs High School friends. The Clintons returned to watch the parade, which the president relished. He smiled and saluted as bands, floats, and military groups passed.

We had only a few hours after the parade to dress before the Inaugural Balls were to begin. Jerry and I attended the Arkansas Ball. Sarah and Mary attended the MTV Ball and Will the Youth Ball, all held in the Washington Convention Center. The president and vice president attended *eleven* official inaugural balls. The excitement of the day must have kept them going. Hillary said they practiced their dance before going onstage at the first ball.

At the Arkansas Ball, several friends joined us onstage to await the arrival of the president and Hillary. Also with us were Barbra Streisand, singers Judy

Collins and Dionne Warwick, and Clinton family members. A roar went up when the Clintons and Gores entered the ballroom and stepped to the stage for their first dance. The president thanked the crowd for working hard for the election and helping to get them there.

Bill pulled me aside as he left the ball and asked me to organize a White House reception for high school and Georgetown friends the next afternoon. He felt he hadn't had time with them during the inauguration. I sat with staff on the floor near the stage to plan. Fortunately, I had names and security information with me, so we sent it to White House Security to prepare for a smooth check-in. Our family would have to miss it because of our early flight home, but I was happy to help plan this spontaneous event and knew friends would be overjoyed to attend.

"You're going to see my office before I do!"

We flew back home Wednesday afternoon, January 21. We hated to miss the bonus party for friends but were happy we had time to go to the White House to see the Clintons at the public open house they hosted to close the inaugural week. We joined the receiving line, and the press quickly converged on us for comments and photos. We told the Clintons what a thrilling experience we had and thanked them for the opportunity to be part of it. They thanked me for the Inaugural Prayer Service and other planning help. When I told them about the girls' night out with Jack Nicholson, Bill's jaw dropped. He was incredulous and glad they had a great time.

Bill signaled for his aide, Reta Lewis, and asked her to give us a tour of the Oval Office and White House West Wing. "You're going to see my office before I do!" he said. It was amazing to walk through the White House and to the Oval Office. We stood in quiet awe as we looked around. President Bush had been there only hours earlier. We took pictures behind the HMS Resolute desk that President Kennedy used, and our children sat in the president's chair. Staff told us later that the public isn't generally allowed to sit in the president's chair, but they made an exception for us. As we walked through the West Wing, we spied a large photo of Bill with Will and school friends taken when the Clintons voted on Election Day. We took Will's picture next to it to share with classmates. Before leaving, we were invited to have lunch in the White House Mess, another special place most visitors don't see.

For the impromptu party, the president asked me to help plan; he hoped for a simple, relaxed time to mingle with old friends. We later learned that the White House social office was displeased with the addition of this unscheduled party. These events typically take weeks to plan, and the inaugural events had already surely been a strain on staff. There would no longer be the luxury of spontaneous events; a receiving line was protocol. Movie nights in the White House Theater came closest to informal gatherings. The president's request for this party with friends put the social office staff in a tizzy, and as we entered the White House for the earlier open house reception, a staff friend approached me in tears because of the stress.

We heard later from friends that the party was a great success. They had pictures taken with the Clintons and shared inaugural experiences. The guest information I sent wasn't entered into the White House WAVE (Workers and Visitors Entrance System) security records in time, so friends gave their security information at the guard entrance window outdoors. It was raining, and friends stood in the downpour for check-in, but all agreed it was worth it. No one complained.

As we flew home, we were happy and exhausted. On the flight, we saw movie star Ed Norton, who was at the inauguration. One guy stretched across a row of seats to sleep with an airsick bag on his chest to keep others away. We laughed and understood fully. What a remarkable few days we'd had, with history and friendship all rolled together into an event of a lifetime.

It was a long time before we came down from our inaugural cloud. We were living in a dream. Letters and calls arrived to say how much folks appreciated our help. As a thank you for helping her family with an invitation to the inaugural events, my high school friend Claire Callahan Johannesen gave me a handmade quilt she created in honor of the inauguration and used the colors of deep red and white to symbolize the outfit I wore to sing at the Inaugural Prayer Service. I also received letters from all over the country from total strangers about the song *Be Not Afraid* at the Inaugural Prayer Service, with requests for copies. I hoped the song could continue to touch lives.

As I reflected on the inauguration of my friend, I realized it had all been more wonderful than I had imagined. Planning the Inaugural Prayer Service made it extraordinary, and the invitation to sing was a gift I never imagined. It was also gratifying to help friends attend. The president and Hillary made sure friends had a spectacular time. The Clintons relished every moment, and it came together perfectly. I was grateful for the experience and thankful most of all that my high school friend and neighbor was now President of the United States.

...yet the pressures and criticism made the times difficult.

We were excited about opportunities to travel to D.C. to experience the Clinton presidency first-hand and considered moving to D.C. to serve in the Clinton administration. Bill sent me a copy of the *Plum Book* with presidential appointments that might interest me. The National Endowment for the Arts has been a favorite agency since I served as Director of the Arkansas Arts Council. The National Institute for Literacy still beckoned, and I hoped those doors would open.

We followed the president's work with Congress to negotiate policies he pledged to undertake. Not everything he did was popular. Bill expected strong reactions but believed his plans would strengthen our country. One of his first decisions was to ask Hillary to lead a comprehensive healthcare task force because she had led education reform in Arkansas. He also tackled the issue of gays in the military. He found there was wide division and settled on the "Don't ask, don't tell" policy to protect military members' confidentiality. It was a controversial policy, and many wondered why he addressed this issue so early.

The president cut the White House staff by 25 percent to lower administrative costs. Reducing the deficit required a large investment of time in budget planning. His first piece of legislation, the Family and Medical Leave Act, was the highlight of his early months and made us all extremely proud. Increased terrorist activity overshadowed foreign policy work with the bombing of the World Trade Center in Manhattan and the Branch Davidian uprising in Waco. It was a tense time, and the Clintons were also dealing personally with the poor health of Hugh Rodham, Hillary's father. The first hundred days for the president were successful, yet the pressures and criticism made the times difficult. We prayed for Bill and did our best to stay in touch with encouragement.

In February 1993, just a month after the inauguration, I went to James Madison University in Harrisonburg, Virginia, to hear John Hilliard's song cycle *Beautiful Noon of No Shadow*. John had been in our high school band with the president. Francis McBeth, the president's composer-friend, was with us, and we called the White House hoping to say hello to our friend Bill. The White House operator couldn't connect us with the president's staff we asked for. I finally reached the president's secretary, Betty Currie, who told me my faxes to the president had not come through. We couldn't understand the problem, but it was nice to try to connect. It was early in the Clinton presidency, but friends were eager to stay in touch with the president. He told his staff it was important for him to hear from friends, so a system was created for sending messages using a dedicated fax number and a special zip code to direct our letters to the Clintons.

I kept hundreds of the faxes I sent to the president with news from home and reactions to events in D.C., simply to encourage him. One of the first was on February 15, 1993, after his address on the economy. I wrote, "We thought your address to the American people tonight was excellent. You very clearly and compassionately articulated the economic condition of America and the role each of us must play in its recovery. Thanks for coming to the American people with your plan. Although the details are yet to be disclosed, we felt honored as voters that you chose to share your vision with us so early. We will be certain to let our congressional delegation know we expect their support for your program. You are doing a great job! Please know of our daily prayers for you, Hillary, and Chelsea."

Two days later, on February 17, 1993, after he outlined his economic program to Congress, I wrote, "You have *never* given a better, stronger speech than tonight. It was superb, direct, and clear. You were 100% at your best. It rang to the last word as Truth! It communicated that you love your nation. You were great!"

On April 29, 1993, we sent a fax to say, "Happy First 100 Days. Congratulations on reaching this milestone! You created great expectations during the campaign and are meeting them day by day. I knew at age fifteen I'd be saying, 'I'm proud of you, Mr. President!' God bless you daily, always."

I updated him on my job interview for the National Institute for Literacy directorship and that I'd be in D.C. for interviews the following week. I hoped to get this job, which was the federal partner of the Arkansas Governor's Commission on Adult Literacy that I then held. I also hoped to visit with him while in D.C.

Phil Jamison, our class president, used the fax system to plan our thirtieth high school reunion in Hot Springs in July. He also asked the president's scheduler, Nancy Hernreich, if our class might have a White House reunion as well. Both requests were fulfilled.

Our high school class was fortunate that our Hot Springs High School 30th reunion coincided with South African President Nelson Mandela's state visit to the White House on October 4, 1994. The president invited classmates to attend a reception on October 7 to meet President Mandela. Jerry, our son, Will—then thirteen—and I attended. An official photographer wasn't present for our visit, so Jerry stood by to take Will's photo with the two presidents. What a magical, beautiful moment this was for our young son. Jerry and I went through the line, then watched as the president introduced Will to Mandela and explained our friendship. They complimented Will on his sunflower necktie, which we've kept as a souvenir. As Will shook Mandela's hand, the president beamed and looked at Jerry to signal, "I hope you get a good shot of this memory!" Bill was so happy. That photo remains one of our family's dearest White House treasures.

I faxed September 3, 1993, to say how much I appreciated being invited to the faith leaders' breakfast at the White House. I flew from Little Rock to DC for the event and was invited to stay at the White House. Bill and Hillary greeted me with warm hugs and big smiles as I met them at the receiving line to enter the State Dining Room. What an honor it was to be at the president's table with national religious leaders. It was invigorating to participate in conversations about faith in public life and hear others encourage the president's goals and present their hopes for his consideration.

On September 14, 1993, I wrote, "Congratulations on the magnificent Middle Eastern peace advancements yesterday and the masterful leadership role you played through it all. We are so proud! Thanks for letting everyone know through your comments to the press that your faith animates your life and was ever-present during these last hours. As God told Joshua, 'Be strong and courageous. Do not be discouraged, for the Lord your God will be with you wherever you go.' Joshua 1:9"

I also told him that David Leopoulos and I would be in D.C. the following week and hoped we could see him. He quickly followed with an invitation to his Joint Address to Congress on healthcare and asked us to stay overnight at the White House. What a thrill!

On October 13, 1993, I sent a note to say I'd been in touch with his mother, Virginia, and that I was trying to encourage her speedy recovery. I also told him I had lunch with his mother's friend, Marge Mitchell, and had notes of encouragement from her staff to deliver.

November 4, 1993, I sent a letter by fax to congratulate the president on the first anniversary of his election and that James Dunn of the Baptist Joint Committee had called to tell me about the passage of the "Religious Freedom Restoration Act." I also wished him a happy visit with David Leopoulos, who was coming to D.C. and joining the president for a jog with high school classmates Jim French and Phil Jamison. The president always loved to see his old friends.

I faxed to let the president know I'd been offered the position of Deputy Director of the National Institute for Literacy and would begin in January. I also shared my excitement about traveling to Russia in January 1994 to sing with Sarah Caldwell, the Boston Opera conductor.

November 17, 1993, I wrote, "Hello, dear friend. I am watching and waiting and cheering as we await the North American Free Trade Agreement

(NAFTA) vote in a few hours. We are excited and confident it will pass. So happy the Arkansas delegation appears to be with you. You are doing a wonderful job!"

These representative faxes are a reminder of the busy early days of the Clinton presidency. Once we had a communication system in place, we used it often.

I knew his support would be unwavering.

We were excited about our move to D.C. for my anticipated work at the National Institute for Literacy. My current job was with the state sister agency, so the transition would be seamless. The agency's goal made it a fulfilling place to work, as we encouraged adults aged sixteen and older who had dropped out of school to enroll in a literacy program and earn a degree. It would help their employability, give them skills to help children with homework, help them understand health information, and more. Nearly twenty-five percent of America's adult population was reading at or below the fifth-grade level. This was unacceptable, and it gave me joy to help improve lives. Sadly, that percentage remains about the same today.

My work as Executive Director of the Arkansas Governor's Commission on Adult Literacy had been rewarding. Family Literacy programs provided access to adult learning and encouraged parental involvement once the child entered kindergarten. Programs were often in public schools where parents and preschool children came for adult education for the parent and preschool for the child. They were served breakfast, went to classes, reunited for parent-child time, and ate lunch. Children then napped while the parents worked in the school office to gain employment skills or did computer-assisted classwork. The program helped parents overcome the fear of going back to school. It built relationships with teachers and paved the way for children to enter kindergarten. We also established workplace education programs where workers needing a GED could take an hour with pay each day to attend a class on-site. The benefits accrued both to the employer and worker.

I was proud that President Clinton was a supporter of adult literacy. As governor, he had seen firsthand what a difference it made. I knew his support would be unwavering and hoped I could be an effective liaison with the White House. An unfortunate tension developed between adult literacy and the new America

Reads literacy program for children. Any help to adult learners was also help for children's literacy, we argued, and the President saw the connection.

Before I was hired as Deputy Director at the National Institute for Literacy, I had calls from state directors of adult education encouraging me to seek an appointment as Director of Adult and Vocational Education. I thought having a non-appointed position would allow more freedom in a presidential friendship. The then-NIFL director thought the Department of Education appointment carried more prestige and told me I'd have a car and driver. I began to understand better how positions with power are viewed in D.C. I moved forward with the application for the NIFL director position, which required an essay about the importance of adult literacy. I did my best to be competitive. Waiting was the hard part; it was many months before the decision was announced.

"Carolyn, you ought to have this Bible for all the help you've given me."

In the spring of 1993, I went to D.C. as our literacy agency representative to the Children's Defense Fund conference. Hillary worked with director Marian Wright Edelman to create the organization. Family Literacy was a key topic at the conference, and I was honored to showcase Arkansas' programs, which were considered among the best in the nation. A friend of Hillary's, Wilma Defoggi, director of Dorcas House for women and children, was going too, and I called the president's staff to say we were coming and hoped to say hello. To our total surprise, Hillary's assistant, Carolyn Huber, called to invite us to stay at the White House and sent a car for us to the airport. We checked in and were given the special tag on a long chain printed with the words "Residence Guest." I was given the Lincoln Bedroom, and Wilma had the Queen's Bedroom across the hall. These bedroom suites were at the opposite end of the second floor from the first family's bedrooms, kitchen, and dining room. Between the wings was a large sitting area with a grand piano and bookshelf-lined walls. We couldn't believe our reception and felt highly honored. With free reign to explore the house, I took loads of pictures.

The Lincoln Bedroom served as an office for Abraham Lincoln. The Queen's Bedroom was named for the queens of Great Britain, Netherlands, Greece, and Norway who had been guests. A fascinating bit of décor was the bathroom toilet in the Queen's Bedroom, which was covered with a caned

French provincial chair. A curator offered a tour and took us behind the scenes to the laundry room where mending is done and where we learned the sheets on the president's bed are changed daily. Such a luxury, I thought, but also helpful for a good night's rest. We visited the flower shop and its deliveries of fresh flowers for arrangements throughout the White House each day. We toured the kitchen where we met pastry chef Roland Mesnier, creator of the gingerbread replicas of the White House each Christmas. On the ground floor, we saw charred residue on the walls of the fire in the War of 1812 when the British attacked and burned areas of the White House, and Dolley Madison saved the Gilbert Stuart painting of George Washington in the East Room. We toured the First Lady's offices in the East Wing, and our walk past staff offices in the West Wing led to reunions with many friends.

Wilma and I also joined a public tour of the White House to visit the first-floor state rooms, including the East Room, Green Room, Blue Room, Red Room, and State Dining Room. I recognized our guide, who had given a tour to our family a few years earlier. At that time, I had the temerity then to tell him, "One day, my friend will be president and living here." He looked stunned but I'm sure many eccentric folks take these tours, and I could've been just one more that day. As Wilma and I ended our tour, I spoke to him and said, "A few years ago, I was here, and you were my tour guide, and I told you that a friend of mine would soon be president. And now he is, Bill Clinton." He was amazed that I remembered him, and we shared a laugh and a photo.

As we waited in the Oval Office for the President, Vice President Gore came in. It was a special moment to greet him again. The Gores were very friendly and always waved enthusiastically when they spotted me in a crowd. We had a brief chat and shared good wishes for their term in office. I urged him to be a strong counselor and friend to the president, and he assured me that he would do so. When the president came into the Oval Office, he welcomed us warmly and posed for pictures in front of the HMS Resolute desk used by President John F. Kennedy. It was a gift from Queen Victoria to President Rutherford B. Hayes in 1880 and built from the oak timbers of the British Arctic exploration ship HMS Resolute.

On the credenza behind the president's desk, I saw the 8" x 10" picture Jerry took of him and Hillary with friends on our front porch on November 4, 1992, the morning after the election. I put it in a silver and gold frame and gave it to him before he moved to the White House. It was heart-warming to see it there and to know he wanted his friends nearby. Later the pictures were changed to ones of family only. Of course, it made perfect sense that the president has so many friends and can't display pictures of only a few. Later, after I started my new job and attended a meeting at the White House Conference Center, I saw a picture of the president in the Oval Office with our picture on his credenza. I mentioned its significance to the conference center director, and she gave it to me, saying the pictures were changed regularly and simply discarded. I have it in our home today and treasure it as a memory of the president's early Oval Office décor.

During my first White House overnight visit, I fulfilled a dream to play the famous Steinway grand piano given by the Steinway family to the Roosevelts in 1938. I had admired it for years as the only one I'd seen with three massive carved, gilded, mahogany eagle-design legs, squared body, and the gold leaf décor on the side depicting the five indigenous forms of American music—a barn dance, cowboy with guitar, the Virginia reel, two Black field-hands singing, and a Native American ceremonial dance. No one was around when I played, and I wondered if I was allowed to even touch it. I played J.S. Bach's *Jesu, Joy of Man's Desiring,* and the Brahms *Intermezzo in A Major* I'd been memorizing. The piano was in the main entry's Grand Foyer at the base of the Grand Staircase. It was breathtakingly beautiful and gave me pause to even sit at the keyboard. The usher's office was just next door, and I was a bit reticent to play very loudly. Still, the unmistakable tones of the renowned Steinway were unforgettable.

Our elegant White House meals were served in the East Sitting Hall outside our rooms. A small dining table was in front of two chairs at the large window, and our meals were delivered on a tray. The tray held a menu, and the presidential seal was affixed to the top of the desserts. We felt we'd caught a glimpse of meals that were served to state visitors.

One evening, the president invited me to the family residence on the second floor to say hello to Chelsea, who had invited some Sidwell Friends School classmates to spend the night. They were playing hide and seek, and Bill talked with them before suggesting it was time for bed. While there, he gave me a maroon leather Bible with his name engraved in gold on the front.

He inscribed it, "To Carolyn, you ought to have this Bible for all the help and spiritual guidance you've given me. Thanks, Bill." It is a true treasure to me.

Being a guest in the Lincoln Bedroom was so spellbinding that I couldn't get settled down to sleep. Mrs. Lincoln bought the furniture for the room. Although Lincoln is reported to have never slept in the room, he spent many hours working there. The massive carved Rosewood bed is where the Lincolns' 11-year-old son Willie was sleeping when he died in 1862. His death in this room has been documented as a terribly sad day for the Lincolns. I studied a holographic copy of the *Gettysburg Address* displayed on the desk, the only one of five that is signed, dated, and titled by Lincoln. He signed the *Emancipation Proclamation* in this room on January 1, 1863. I examined the French portico mantel clock purchased in 1833 by President Andrew Jackson, which was there during Lincoln's tenure. I listened to its rhythmic ticking and thought about how Lincoln had heard the clock as he worked.

Winston Churchill had been a guest in the Lincoln Bedroom and the Queen's Bedroom. I took a bath in the big marble tub in my room and wondered if Churchill had bathed there, too. The large closet had built-in drawers and a safe for valuables. I imagined the heads of state who had slept in the room and their belongings that had been stored there.

On the bedside table was a control for the fireplace. There was a button to ring the White House usher and a menu for ordering breakfast. I looked over the room and tried to make myself sleepy. Finally, unable to sleep, I walked to the usher's office on the first floor and saw a light on. I knocked and asked if it would be ok if I walked through the reception rooms. He nodded and gave me a flashlight. I walked through the state rooms to see what I had missed on my tour. I wondered if people passing by outside might suspect a cat burglar was afoot in the White House.

I hadn't seen Hillary but was told she was leaving early for a trip. I set the alarm to be up in time to see her and thank her for this hospitality. I saw what I assumed was an alarm clock by the bedside. I turned the dial to 6 AM and climbed into bed. As I rested, I thought the bed felt unusually warm. I wondered if the mattress was a fancy one that could sense body temperature and adjust automatically. I sat up to check and realized I'd adjusted the heating blanket and not the alarm clock. After a good laugh, I finally fell asleep.

The first evening of the Children's Defense Fund conference was a prayer service at Washington National Cathedral. Wilma and I chatted with director Marian Wright Edelman and thanked her for her work. While working in D.C., I sometimes saw Marian having lunch at the Potter's House at the Church of the Savior. We had interesting talks, and I always left motivated to do more for families.

The next morning, I watched from the Lincoln bedroom window as the president's helicopter departed. I walked through the private living quarters and saw the family kitchen, dining room, sitting area, bedrooms, and large Palladian window that looked out over the Rose Garden. I marveled at how freely I was able to stroll through the rooms. I had a rare, personal glimpse of this grand residence, the new home for my friend and his family.

Barbra Streisand said, "Carolyn Staley? You were wonderful at the inauguration!"

I returned to Washington, D.C., on May 4-5, 1993, for interviews with the presidentially appointed board of the National Institute for Literacy for the Director's position. Board chairman Badi Foster told me, "You hit it out of the ballpark." I didn't mention my friendship with the president and was told later this increased their support for me. Afterward, I walked by the agency offices across from the White House. I felt I'd done my best to compete for the position, so I prayed, "Lord, open every door if this is right, and put up every barrier if it's not."

After many months, I was offered the position of Deputy Director. I wondered and asked why the top job went to Dr. Andrew Hartman, a Republican congressional staffer. I learned that he had worked closely with Department of Education director Richard Riley and the congressional staff and was familiar with the inner workings of Congress. Secretary Riley was one of three interagency leaders of the institute, the others being the Directors of Health and Human Services and the Department of Labor. Secretary Riley felt Andy's background would be valuable for the job. Initially disappointed, I soon observed the stress of the Director's job, with Investigator General investigations into questionable purchases and senior staff dismissals. My salary was comparable and came with far less turmoil. I was free to go to the White House any time and arrange Oval Office visits for literacy bill signings and with literacy leaders. I felt I had gotten the better deal.

The day after my interview, Nancy Hernrieich, the president's scheduler, invited me to the White House for a presidential visit. Mike Willbanks, director of Arkansas Workplace Literacy, was with me. Donna Shalala, the Secretary of Health and Human Services, was at the Oval Office, and I told her she was one of the three secretaries I'd be working with at the National Institute for Literacy. I explained that literacy and health are related as adults must be able to read and understand prescriptions and health information. I was glad to have the opportunity to give her this background. The President opened his office door and greeted us with a big smile. He didn't know I was coming. Although his schedule was full, he was happy to see friends. We offered to tour the White House and return later to see him.

Betty Currie took us to the East Wing, where we saw Ann McCoy, Helen Dickey, and Carolyn Huber, Arkansas friends now working at the White House, and Social Secretary Ann Stock. We toured the First Lady's offices and saw Millie Alston, Hillary's secretary at the Rose Law Firm and now her secretary in the White House. We ran into Press Secretary Deedee Myers and Domestic Policy Chief Bruce Reed and had cordial visits with them.

Returning to the Oval Office, I was stunned to see Barbra Streisand with songwriters Alan and Marilyn Bergman waiting to see the president. I was so star-struck that I didn't speak. But when someone exclaimed, "Hello, Carolyn Staley!" Barbra Streisand turned toward me and said, "Carolyn Staley? You were wonderful at the inauguration!" Stunned, I replied, "Ms. Streisand, thank you. You were pretty wonderful yourself!" It was a thrill to meet her. I told her my daughters knew all her songs from *Funny Girl* and sang "I'm the Greatest Star" often. I showed her pictures of them and told her I was also a singer. She asked, "So, do you want an audition?" and we laughed. I told her I'd heard she slept in my bed in the Lincoln Bedroom, and she roared laughing. We had a picture taken together. What a moment! I'd been a fan since the 60s, and the president and I sang "Evergreen" dozens of times at the piano. She and Virginia, Bill's mother, became close friends and stayed in touch during Virginia's cancer struggle.

Mike and I were invited into the Oval Office for a picture with the president. We updated the president about our literacy work and life back at home. It was an honor to see him again in the Oval Office. As we left, I realized this was Mike's first visit to the White House. Since we hadn't toured the formal rooms, staff friend Wayne Skinner offered a tour. As we explored the ground floor, we ran into the President a third time on his way to have a portrait made by master photographer Yousef Karsh. We saw staff friends Robyn Dickey and Melinda Bates in the Volunteer Office, then went into the reception room and met Mr. Karsh. I told Karsh how much I admired his work, and that my husband is a photographer. He was very cordial. He told me the White House portrait of First Lady Eleanor Roosevelt is a montage of his portraits.

It was heartening to see the president again and hear his upbeat assessment about early progress while the momentum was still in his favor. We hoped the honeymoon could last, as issues were sometimes thorny and ambitious. He wanted to make the most of his time in office and honor his campaign commitments. His supporters knew he would follow through, and he always proved them right.

The President called, and it was wonderful to hear his voice.

When our daughter Sarah graduated from William Jewell in May 1993, the president had been in office only a few months. The college invited him to deliver the commencement address, but he was unable to schedule it. Instead, he called into the ceremony to speak to the graduates and wish them well. Mentioning Sarah by name in his first college commencement address as president was an honor and a grand graduation gift.

Birthdays with friends had always been a special time for us in Little Rock. For decades, a close group gathered for birthday lunches, usually barbeque or Mexican food. We met at Juanita's Mexican Café on May 20, 1993, for Joe Newman's birthday. The president called, and we passed the phone around so everyone could chat with him. He had always been there, and we missed him. We sensed his nostalgia as well.

It was a banner day in June 1993 when the president appointed Ruth Bader Ginsburg to the US Supreme Court. A progressive jurist known for her independence and open-mindedness, Ginsburg began serving in August 1993. As history has proven, Justice Ginsburg surpassed even the President's expectations, and she was considered a hero by many for her wise decisions. When she spoke in Little Rock in 2019 at the Kumpuris Lecture for the Clinton School of Public Service, the Verizon arena was at capacity with 15,000 plus 15,000 on a waiting list. President Clinton interviewed her at the spectacular event. Her service continued even during her illness. She was a treasure, and the nation mourned her death in September 2020.

The president called to say he was coming to Little Rock on July 17, 1993, for his first trip home since his election. He asked me to get friends together for a visit at our house after his golf game. I called Joe Newman, David and Linda Leopoulos, Mauria and Bob Aspell, Mary Jo Rogers, Glenda Cooper, Danny Thomason, and my mother and sisters. Everyone was ecstatic to see him. Before his arrival, we had strawberry shortcake and ice cream and saved some for him. We visited in the kitchen after he arrived. He was exhausted and sweaty from playing golf and just wanted to rest. We talked a mile a minute, and he took it in stride, good-naturedly, knowing he was a celebrity now but also just our dear friend. We moved to the dining room to hear his updates as president. We took more pictures than he probably preferred, but he was patient. Mauria and Mary Jo brought their daughters. Our children Sarah, Mary, and Will were home, and their friends Beth Buffalo and Grant Besser came. Friends Janice and Keith Sjostrand joined us. It was the first time most of us had seen him since the inauguration. He was as homesick to see friends as we were to have him with us.

Tragedy struck in July 1993 when Vince Foster, a childhood friend of the president's from Hope, took his life. Vince was Hillary's partner at the Rose Law Firm in Little Rock, and they were very close friends. The president appointed Vince as White House Counsel in 1992. He was our friend too and wrote a nice thank you note to my husband for sending pictures of his family with the Clintons at Thanksgiving 1992. We had ridden together on the friends' bus at the 1992 inauguration. A quiet man, he was well-respected. Everyone thought he liked his work at the White House, even with the many investigations into the Clintons that also affected him. He came to Washington with no political experience and found himself under enormous scrutiny. Vince's death was a terrible blow to the Clintons, and we ached for them. His death was ruled a suicide, and friends came to understand that Vince had been struggling with stress and depression. Losing Vince was devastating, but we celebrated his life and did our best to support his family.

"It is hard to live by faith without caring for the poor and downtrodden"

President Clinton invited me to attend the first White House Interfaith Breakfast in August 1993. I met the president and first lady in the receiving line and felt their warmth in our reunion as we laughed and talked about life back home. I was seated with the president in the State Dining Room with seven others around the table. Not feeling great that day, I sat quietly soaking it all in. The president told me he could tell I wasn't feeling well. Still, It was a beautiful, memorable event. I thought it must be similar to a White House state dinner with the gold and white china and table settings but without the formal dress and entertainment. I met clergy from around the nation and senior presidential advisor David Gergen.

A report on the White House Interfaith Breakfast event from *Christianity Today* in November 1993 gave this perspective: "Religious leaders who have been puzzled by their lack of access to the Clinton White House received encouraging, though mixed, signals on August thirtieth at an interfaith breakfast with the President. Nearly 100 religious leaders from across the Jewish and Christian spectrum met with the Southern Baptist from Hope, Arkansas. The President affirmed the important role that faith must play both in private lives and public policy. Freedom of religion, he said, "doesn't mean that those of us who have faith shouldn't frankly admit that we are animated by that faith … and that it does affect what we feel, what we think, what we do." The breakfast was the first such event with religious leaders since Clinton's inauguration. That lack of contact has caused some to complain about their having no access to this administration. However, Clinton's remarks and the breakfast were designed to show that he values input from people of faith. Yet the President does not seem to be wooing evangelicals or any other religious group. According to a White House insider, the administration made a conscious decision not to treat faith groups as constituencies, using religion as a political issue."[1]

I was proud the president decided not to create a liaison office for religion. Other presidents had done so, but Dr. James Dunn of the Baptist Joint Committee on Church and State warned the president that it pushed the boundaries of the Establishment Clause of the First Amendment. In addition to being constitutional, the separation of church and state is a strongly held Baptist belief dating to colonialist Roger Williams. Dr. Dunn urged Bill not to continue this practice. A strong moment for the president and Congress came with the passage of the Religious Freedom Restoration Act 1993, which ensured that interests in religious freedom and public expression in the public arena were protected. Its passage was broadly celebrated by a wide range of groups hoping to protect the First Amendment.

President Clinton built good relations with faith leaders and told them their leadership could help heal our nation. He asked people of all faiths to share how faith guides their lives openly. He said, "It is hard to live by faith without acting on the scriptural admonitions to care for the poor and down-trodden, to love thy neighbor as thyself."

He urged people of different beliefs to get to know each other, to respect one another, and to work toward mutual goals. He believed this could ease conflicts on issues like abortion and homosexuality. He told our table at breakfast about a woman who decided to host dinner parties for people with different opinions. Her only rule was that they agreed to simply get acquainted for the first hour and not discuss issues. What a difference it made, she found, when people met as parents and professionals, learned about hobbies, schools, family concerns, and simply interacted as human beings before discussing issues. The president asked us to go home and begin similar gatherings.

There were religious leaders then who wanted the White House to be a religious pulpit. They believed the White House's power was greater than their pulpits to teach God's love. They also believed that if the president would adopt their agenda, they could enjoy real power. They had a social and political agenda they believed the president could deliver. They forgot that there is no power greater than God's power, no word stronger than God's word, and that law and politics don't change hearts. Plus, it's a dangerous path to take for both church and state.

The president sought counsel from a group of trusted pastors and friends.[2] He shared his faith in press interviews. He believes God is full of second chances, forgiveness, and grace. He said he prays throughout the day for guidance, for his family, and for the ability to be the best president he can be. He has been candid about his Christian faith. He asked each person to do the same if we hoped to make a difference at home and in the world. I had great respect for him for using his personal testimony as president.

"The peace of the brave is within our reach"

September 1993 brought early achievements for the Clinton presidency in Mideast policy. President Clinton walked to the White House South Lawn with Yitzhak Rabin, Prime Minister of Israel, and Yasser Arafat, Chairman of the Palestine Liberation Organization. President Clinton introduced them and watched as they shook hands in the first agreement between Jews and Palestinians to end the conflict over shared land both consider holy, and both call home. Standing beside them were former Presidents Jimmy Carter and George Bush, who had also worked for Mideast peace. The handshake between the two former archenemies was historic and capped the signing of a *Declaration of Principles* for peace between Arabs and Israelis. President Clinton said, "The peace of the brave is within our reach. Throughout the Middle East, there is a great yearning for the quiet miracle of a normal life. We know a difficult road lies ahead. Every peace has its enemies." He praised them for "the brave gamble that the future can be better than the past."[3]

The New York Times reported, "Moments after the documents were signed, Mr. Clinton took Mr. Arafat in his left arm and Mr. Rabin in his right arm and gently coaxed them together, needing to give Mr. Rabin just a little extra nudge in the back. Mr. Arafat reached out his hand first, and then Mr. Rabin, after a split second of hesitation, received Mr. Arafat's hand. The audience let out a simultaneous sigh of relief and a peal of joy as a misty-eyed Clinton beamed and a peal of joy erupted through the crowd. "What a milestone this was for the world."[4]

I don't remember when the president was happier than on this day of Middle East peace. He sent me a photograph of the ceremony as he stood between Rabin and Arafat for their handshake. We were honored that our friend was able to preside over this historic time.

We heard Bill's voice calling, "Carolyn? David? Where are you?"

On September 14, 1993, I wrote to the president about several things. I told him that David Leopoulos and I were coming to D.C. for separate meetings and that we hoped we could see him. He said our visit would coincide with his address to Congress on healthcare and invited us to the address and to stay overnight at the White House. The first lady had led the task force, and the president had campaigned on the issue. Now, he was ready to deliver on his promise.

David and I rode with the presidential motorcade to the U.S. Capitol and were honored to sit in the president's gallery of the U.S. House of Representatives. We heard him say:

"Millions of Americans are just a pink slip away from losing their health insurance and one serious illness away from losing all their savings. Millions more are locked in the jobs they have now just because they or someone in their family has once been sick and they have what is called a pre-existing condition. And on any given day, over 37 million Americans—most of them working people and their little children—have no health insurance at all. And in spite of all this, our medical bills are growing at over twice the rate of inflation, and the United States spends over a third more of its income on health care than any other nation on Earth."[5]

David and I returned to the White House and went to our rooms, hoping to visit again with the president. Our guestrooms were on the upper floor above the family's quarters. The famous Lincoln bedroom and Queen's bedroom are on the second floor with the Clintons' family quarters. These six third-floor bedrooms have impressive furnishings with beautiful fabrics for bedding and draperies and are spacious and comfortable. The solarium, where guests often eat breakfast, is also on the 3rd floor.

David and I waited for the president to return home and finally concluded he had been delayed, so we got ready for bed. In a little while, we heard Bill's voice calling, "Carolyn? David? Where are you?" It was just the same way he had called us back in 1964 when he came home from college during our freshman year, when David and I hid in closets waiting for his arrival. I can still hear his voice calling, "David? Carolyn? Where are you?" We joined him in the sitting area outside our rooms to visit and congratulate him on his healthcare success and powerful speech. He was elated at how well it had been received. It was an historic night to share it with our friend.

Before we went to bed, he walked us through the White House to see the family residence. He took us down a back staircase and showed us where he practiced his saxophone. We marveled at works of art hanging on the walls, one by American impressionist artist Mary Cassatt. It was wonderful to see him so comfortable in his new home.

As we walked through the family residence, we spotted Chelsea in bed in her room, talking on her phone. The president asked why she wasn't asleep, and she said, "I'm getting math help." In a few more minutes, we again walked by her door, and she was still on the phone. "Chelsea, now!" he said. We shook our heads and laughed, familiar with the struggles of parenting and enjoying his experiences.

The next morning, David and I had breakfast in the solarium, and the president came to see us. He walked down the hallway with us and talked about photographs lining the walls showing many recent events at the White House. He seemed at home and happy.

It all seemed miraculous.

In December 1993, the president and Hillary returned to Little Rock to host a thank you reception for supporters at the Old State House, where he had announced his candidacy in October 1991 and where the election night celebration had been held in November 1992. Throngs greeted the Clintons at the reception and were thanked for their tireless election support. Jerry took photos of the jubilant faces of the Clintons as they greeted friends. Young and old, Black and white, all came to say hello to the president and first lady. The Clintons told their supporters they would not be in the White House without the supporters' loyal help.

As the Christmas season approached, I felt nostalgic, realizing it would be very different this year with the Clintons in D.C. I sent the president a note on December 17, 1993, to say, "Merry Christmas" and congratulated him on his many successes during his first year as president. "You operate at an energy and determination level rarely seen! The Congress, press, and public are hard-pressed to keep up with you. Those of us who know you have delighted in the amazement expressed by many we hear from." I told him our annual friend's party would be December 22nd and we would carry on, but that it wouldn't be the same without him. "We will be wistfully imagining you might ring the doorbell any minute." I regretted that our family would be unable to attend the White House party for friends because I had to leave right after Christmas for my singing engagement in Russia. Jerry was teaching, daughter Sarah had started working for Harry and Linda Thomason in California on their television hit, "Designing Women", Mary was a sophomore at William Jewell College, and Will was a 7th grader. So much had changed in our family life, but everyone was happy and thriving.

I was leaving on December 28th for Russia to sing with Sarah Caldwell, Boston Opera conductor and guest conductor of the Sverdlovsk Symphony, for concerts in January. I told the president it was an exciting coincidence that he would be in Russia at the same time meeting with President Boris Yeltsin.

I looked forward to visiting Russia and living with musicians in an orchestra apartment. Sverdlovsk, now Yekaterinburg, was Yeltsin's hometown and the burial place for Tsar Nicolas II and his family. Three weeks in residence there would be a cultural gift. Conductor Sarah Caldwell invited me to sing concerts on two Russian trips, from December 30, 1993, to January 19, 1994, and later, from May 25th to June 6th.

At the January concert, I sang *Egmont* by Beethoven, *Wedding Cantata* by Bach, *Dich teure Halle* from *Tannhauser* by Wagner, Charles Ives' *Circus Band,* and *Strike up the Band* by Gershwin. At the May concert, I was soprano soloist for Verdi's *Requiem Mass*. My agency director understood that I had these prior commitments before I took the new job.

How could so many amazing things be happening at one time? Our friend was President of the U.S., and our family was soon moving to D.C. I was going to Russia to sing, and the president was going to Russia at the same time. It all seemed miraculous and wonderful.

He raced, exclaiming, "Billie dome, Billie dome!" which is Russian for 'White House.'

While I was in Russia, Jerry faxed that the president's mother, Virginia Clinton Kelley, had died. I was so shocked and called Bill to share my grief and send my love to the family. We chatted for a long time, and I could tell he was extremely broken. He asked for ideas for music for the service. I suggested Janice Sjostrand could sing *Holy Ground* and Malvie Lee Giles, an African American singer from South Arkansas who had been on his inaugural programs, could sing *His Eye is on the Sparrow*. Bill liked these ideas. My Mother and sister went to visit with Bill, Roger, and Dick Kelley in Hot Springs. When they arrived, Bill told them, "Carolyn and I just got off the phone, and we planned the music for Mother's service." I was happy to help, but I felt so far away. I didn't know I'd be having a reunion with the president later in Moscow.

Bill and Hillary faxed a beautiful letter to me at the Sverdlovsk Symphony office to say they were thinking of me and how difficult it must be in Russia and unable to be home for Virginia's funeral. Their handwritten message meant a great deal. Mr. Koloturský, the symphony director, was stunned when he saw the letter arrive on White House stationary. He raced to find me, exclaiming breathlessly, "Billie dome, Billie dome!" which is Russian for

"White House." He asked me to speak to the symphony musicians about Virginia's death. I agreed and managed to say how much she meant to me; then I broke down.

Virginia's funeral on January 8, 1994, in Hot Springs was attended by thousands. Friends in Little Rock sent faxes to me with reports of the funeral. Barbra Streisand, who had become friends with Virginia, attended. A nice personal moment came for my mother and sisters after the funeral. My sister Deborah spotted Barbra and discreetly called, "Ms. Streisand! Ms. Streisand!" but got no response. She called again, "Ms. Streisand, I'm Carolyn Staley's sister!" Barbra turned and joined them for a long visit, which was a big treat.

Bill told me he hadn't made eye contact with any friends during the service, but when Pentecostal friend and soloist Janice Sjostrand started to sing *Holy Ground,* he turned to catch a glimpse at Barbra for her reaction. She was awestruck and later told Bill she had never heard music that made her feel that way. She recorded the song on her album of *Hymns and Spiritual Songs.* The composer Geron Davis called me to say Barbra was recording his song and played a demo over the phone. As I listened, I thought how amazing it was that this Jewish singer and meteoric star was singing a Christian hymn written by a Pentecostal choir director in Louisiana. It was truly extraordinary, and Bill Clinton had brought it all together.

I hoped I would be able to sing through the tears.

The president left on January 12, 1994, as planned, for Moscow for a summit with President Boris Yeltsin. Sarah Caldwell asked me to arrange with U.S. Ambassador Thomas Pickering's staff for the Sverdlovsk chamber ensemble to play for the president's reception. Sarah wanted to be there because we were Americans visiting Russia and wanted to greet our president. She also felt it would be good for him to hear his friend Carolyn sing after his mother's death. As he left for Russia, the president asked assistant Kelly Craighead to call from Prague to find me in Russia to say he hoped I'd be in Moscow while he was there, and I gave her the outline of our plans. It was a monumental planning effort with concerns about the number of musicians Sarah wanted to bring. The embassy staff wanted no vocal music for fear that President Clinton would stop to listen and lose time with guests, but they acquiesced.

The Sverdlovsk chamber orchestra flew to Moscow on January 13 and went to Spaso House for our concert. Our performance space was a balcony overlooking the large reception room. When President Clinton walked in, the musicians played the Bach *Brandenberg Concerto No. 2* with trumpet to herald his arrival. It was then my turn to sing *Summertime*. As the introduction began, the president looked up, smiled, waved, and blew a kiss as he continued shaking hands. I hoped I would be able to sing through the tears. This was our first visit since Virginia's death, and I hadn't seen him since our White House visit in November. I also sang *Shall We Gather by the River*, arranged by Aaron Copeland, and *Amazing Grace*, arranged by Zaninelli.

After the reception, the president met us, and it seemed to give him joy to have us there. In my journal, I wrote: "How moved to tears in awe of God's mighty hand in my life—in all our lives—what marvels God weaves through life." I continued writing a psalm of thanksgiving from a grateful heart. The many tense hours of faxing, telephoning, and working through details on top of regular symphony rehearsals had left little time for sleep for several days, but it was worth it all.

The president asked if we could visit Moscow later. He was invited to Yeltsin's dacha for dinner and asked me to come to his hotel and wait. Sarah agreed to the plan, and she and the musicians went to the motel the next morning before our flight. I went to the Moscow Radisson Hotel and waited several hours for Bill's return. I visited with friends also waiting for the president, including David Satter, a Russian expert and Rhodes Scholar at Oxford with Bill, who told me about his summers as a youth at the Indiana Dunes near where our family had lived. We talked about friendship with the president and about his book on Russia since the fall of Communism about two years earlier. Hannah and Marc Winer also waited to see the president. Marc was manager for Coca-Cola in Russia for twenty-five years and had negotiated the entry of Coca-Cola into the Soviet Union. He was now General Manager of McDonald's in Russia.

When he finally arrived, the president said he hadn't expected a twelve-course dinner and couldn't eat as much as was served. He invited the Winers, David Satter, and me to his suite. He was tired and still grieving his mother's death just days earlier. He showed us Yeltsin's gifts to him: a large antique mantel clock, a blue and white Zehl porcelain figure playing a saxophone, an antique icon diptych, and other official gifts. In the suite, we sat under a large oil painting of Tsar Nicolas II and his family.

We chatted for a long time about many things. I told Marc the musicians commented that Big Macs were too expensive, and he said he had heard that too. Bill asked him how much a Big Mac costs, and Marc said it cost about $3.50. He said the average Russian's monthly take-home pay is only $14. Hannah Winer said she was amazed that McDonald's was always full of customers. In McDonald's defense, Marc said its workers earn an average of $80 per month, and the burger's cost made higher wages possible. Bill talked about the current status of Russian life and government, the economy, and religion since the recent fall of Communism on December 26, 1991. It was a fascinating conversation.

Bill shared details of his dinner conversation with Yeltsin—how he begged Bill for advice on building a working democracy. Bill invited him to the United States to see democracy at work. Bill told him it's important to get out among the people and to learn to work with Congress. Most fascinating to me was their long talk about religion. Yeltsin asked Bill, "You're a Christian, aren't you?"

The president told him, "Yes, my faith is the most important thing in my life."

Yeltsin replied, "I have to do something about all these Protestant missionaries coming to Russia, including Pentecostals and Jehovah's Witnesses. They are ruining our country and our culture. Everyone is becoming a born-again Christian, and they are being baptized and putting crosses around their necks." He complained about the influx of the groups and said Russians were flocking to Western faith. Bill told him he shouldn't try to control people's beliefs. "Democracy doesn't work that way. Either you're free, or you're not. You can't have it both ways. You need to allow Christians into your country to preach and teach, and you have to allow the Russian people the freedom to choose their faith," he told him.

I wrote a reflection about Clinton's conversation with Yeltsin on religion that was published by the Baptist Joint Committee on Church and State (May 2007, after Yeltsin's death, April 23). I said, "What a remarkable exchange this was between Clinton and Yeltsin. In sharing his faith and belief that Christian workers should be allowed to come into Russia as missionaries, Clinton may very well have kept the doors of Russia open for the spread of Christianity beyond Russian Orthodoxy." Just months earlier, Yeltsin had considered closing Russia to missionaries, but the policy was not implemented. I said I hoped his conversation with Bill had made a personal difference for him. *Time* magazine reported on my account of the visit as well.[6]

As we visited at the hotel, I showed Bill reports on Virginia's funeral from friends and family. Bill said, "You've seen more than I have because I had to leave so soon after the funeral to get back to the White House and then two hours later was off to Brussels." I pointed out two things I thought he'd most enjoy seeing. First was the story of David Leopoulos and our high school friends racing to be on time as pallbearers for the service at Hope. They accidentally got in Vice President Gore's motorcade rather than the one with the president going to Hope. They had one hour to get there. Bill's eyes widened as he realized how this must explain why David was weeping openly when he saw him there. But Bill laughed at David's efforts to get there, jumping like a frog over tombstones only to realize he was too late. Bill said he never knew.

We also laughed until tears ran down our cheeks about the story of Barbra Streisand attending a reception at Hope's Western Sizzlin' restaurant after the graveside service. A local host opened the door and proclaimed proudly to Ms. Streisand, "I bet you don't have spreads like this in Los Angeles!" Bill loved these reports. He told his friends that I was as close to his mother as anyone he knew and that she loved me. I was very touched. He made sure I received an audio tape of the funeral and told me Janice Sjostrand's singing was tremendous.

An agitated David Gergen came into the suite as we visited. Trying to ease tension. I said, "Hi, I'm Carolyn Staley. We met at the White House." He looked at me sternly, indicating this was not a time to chat. Our ten-minute meeting with the president had stretched into more than an hour. We weren't being insensitive to those waiting but were following the President's wishes, and he begged us to stay. When I stood to try to leave, he simply said, "Sit down." Soon, others came in to try to get the president to stay on schedule. As a last desperate measure, a member of the Secret Service came in and said, "Mr. President, I just want to remind you of your early schedule and the late hour. Bill responded, "You've done your job, Steve."

Waiting for the president was PBS journalist Ted Koppel, who had been promised an interview. Our time with the president had gone over schedule, but it was clear that he was still grieving. Gergen kept popping his head in to say he needed to move on, and Bill told him he needed to be with friends. The situation became uncomfortable.

Bill eventually gave in, and we walked out to the reception area, where a large group of reporters was waiting. He waved us goodbye, shouted, "Love you," and hugged us as we left. Andrew Friendly, a presidential aide, and Kelly Crawford arrived from a walk to Red Square. I said hello and told the president he'd been out on the town touring Red Square, and Andrew teasingly said, "Thanks, Carolyn!" afraid I'd spilled his secret. Andrew sported a traditional fur hat that was his father's when they lived in Moscow. He gave me some presidential souvenirs for twelve-year-old Daniel, whose mother worked at the Sverdlovsk Symphony offices. An Embassy car was waiting to take me to the Hotel Zarya, where the musicians were staying. I had no address but was assured the driver knew the way as he ushered me into the back seat.

What was about to unfold marked one of the scariest nights of my life. It was well past midnight. Ice and snow covered the roads, and it was remarkably dark. The headlights on the car were like two dim candles lighting the January road. The driver spoke only Russian and, although I had learned a few phrases, I couldn't communicate with him. He had a vague idea of the address. I had no idea how remote the location was. The helplessness was frightening. We drove for almost an hour. We were now well outside the city limits on a deserted road in total darkness. I was fearful as the driver didn't know the location of the hotel. I was told it was in the area where all the TV reception antennas were located. "Ostenkino tower?" I asked. That was all the information I had. He stopped at a house on a remote road where he saw a light in the window and asked for directions. He was gone a long time. Here I was in the early morning on a dark road outside Moscow in a car by myself. I was completely at his mercy and could only trust he would get me there safely. I took comfort in knowing he knew I was a friend of the U.S. President and that the Embassy had arranged for him to get me to my hotel. I tried to imagine what I would do if we couldn't find the group. How would I arrange to get back to Yekaterinburg? Millions of thoughts raced through my head.

Eventually, after what seemed an eternity, he found the location. It was a campsite with lodges nestled in a forest. The innkeeper was still awake, thankfully, and showed me to my room. I was never more relieved. I slept in my clothes that night and woke up with Sarah Caldwell telling me it was time to head to the bus for the ride to the airport. I relived the visit with President Clinton and friends as we traveled. At the airport, over a breakfast of red caviar on heavy bread with sour cream, I recounted some of the adventures for the group. Mostly I was just thankful that the ordeal ended well. I treasured such a memorable encounter with the President and his experiences with Yeltsin, and to have seen him so soon after Virginia's death.

How likely was it to be in Russia and see my picture with President Clinton in the newspaper?

Many remarkable things happened on this trip to Russia. Among them was picking up a Moscow newspaper and seeing my picture with the president and friends taken on *our front porch* on the day after Clinton's election. How likely was it that I would be in Russia and see my picture with President Clinton in the newspaper? I was astonished. To sing in Russia was enough, but for my visit to coincide with the president's, that Virginia's death would come at this time, that his conversation with President Yeltsin had been so historic, that I would be there to sing for his reception in Moscow and visit afterward was all too miraculous.

When I arrived back home in Little Rock, I had only days before leaving for D.C. to begin my job at the National Institute for Literacy. I had done a great deal of packing for our coming move to DC before I left for Russia, but I would have to trust the rest would get done and that our family would manage well for these few months we'd be apart.

On Friday evening before my move to DC, friends came over for a farewell party. I showed them how to do vodka shots as the Russians taught me, and we broke into peals of laughter. The President called and said he thought it sounded hilarious, but he just couldn't "make the leap." He was still mourning his mother's passing and on his way to Camp David.

The only thing that made leaving home easier was knowing that Will would be in D.C. to visit in a week and our family would move soon to embark on a remarkable experience there. My friend since age 15, the boy-next-door, was President of the United States. We were going to experience it firsthand. We knew what a magnificent leader he would be and welcomed the coming progress for our nation and world, led by his capable heart and mind. We also awaited experiences of a lifetime. We had no idea just how remarkable it would be.

---

[1] *Christianity Today*, Clinton Meets Evangelicals, November 1993

[2] Tony Campolo, professor at Eastern College, Pennsylvania, Philip Wogaman of Foundry United Methodist Church, DC, Anthony Mangun, friend and pastor at Alexandria Pentecostal Church, Louisiana, and former pastor Dr. Rex Horn of Immanuel Baptist Church, Little Rock were among his advisors.

[3] BBC Home, *On This Day*, BBC News, London. September 13, 1993

[4] Friedman, Thomas. "Mideast Accord: The Overview; Rabin and Arrafat Seal Their Accord as Clinton Applauds 'Brave Gamble.'" NY: *The New York Times*. September 14, 1993.

[5] "Clinton's Health Plan, Transcript of President's Address to Congress on health Care," *The New York Times*, New York, September 23, 1993

[6] Staley, Rev. Carolyn, "A Reflection on Boris Yeltsin, Bill Clinton & Religious Liberty," *Report on the Capital*, Washington, DC, May 2007

CHAPTER EIGHT

Our DC Adventure Begins

We hung a framed photograph of President Clinton inside.

After returning home from Russia in mid-January 1994, I moved to DC to begin work as Deputy Director of the National Institute for Literacy. Jerry and Will remained in Little Rock to finish the school year, but we'd be reunited soon. We listed our house, and I created a brochure, "Reasons You Will Love Living at 515 W. 15th Street." We hoped for a quick sale, but it was mid-summer before the right buyer came along. Thankfully, my sister Deborah worked tirelessly to host open houses and keep the property in top viewing shape while it was vacant. We hung a Quapaw Quarter Historic Home plaque outside our front door. We also hung a framed photograph of President Clinton and our high school and college friends inside the foyer on our front porch after the election. So much history had taken place in this wonderful old house, and we wanted the new owners to know its story.

We found our new home in McLean, Virginia, outside Washington, D.C. Friends Jim and Kathy French suggested we consider the McLean Hamlet close to D.C. with access to metro stops, and near good schools. Our moving van arrived in June.

We hated to say goodbye to our grand old home on 15th Street. Our $35,000 purchase returned a nice profit and was a good investment of funds and memories. Indeed, the memories are priceless—Will's birth, Mary finishing Little Rock Central High School, Sarah in college, and all strong in faith and spirit. Jerry was doing photography and more teaching. I had experiences of a lifetime with Marilyn Horne, exceptional public service opportunities in

Arkansas state agency leadership, and singing. We enjoyed friendship with the Clintons, cherished times with old friends, sticking together through good times and bad, and seeing our friend Bill elected president of the U.S.

My job as Deputy Director of the National Institute for Literacy was to serve in the director's absence and to assist with the management of the agency. I oversaw projects, including the two-year National Literacy Public Awareness campaign entitled "Literacy: It's a Whole New World" and the National Literacy Goals 2000 Summit. The public awareness campaign was aimed at increasing general awareness of the value of adult literacy education and the locations of programs in every community across the nation. It featured an important publication, *The State of Literacy in America*, based on research by Dr. Steven Reder of Portland State University about the levels of literacy in every county in the nation.[1]

We mailed the report to every governor and mayor in the nation. It was a valuable tool for literacy leaders to take to meetings with elected officials to request increased funding support for literacy programs and adult education generally. The campaign provided camera-ready print ads and radio and television public service announcements that could be tailored to each community. The summit followed up on that work with the goal of setting attainable, measurable goals for the new millennium. After the election of President George W. Bush, the new director made the job more administratively focused on policy work and aligning our general administrative practices with our sister agency, the US Department of Education. The National Institute for Literacy also created a database of literacy work across the country with a searchable online directory of programs and services. Another program focused on the key areas of adult learning in the family, the workplace, and civic participation. A third program focused on research about learning disabilities, a key factor in assessing and addressing adult learners' needs. It was very satisfying work.

After I moved to begin my new job, we were saddened to learn that George Leopoulos, the father of one of Bill's best friends, David Leopoulos, had died. The President had been friends with the Leopoulos family since grade school and greatly admired Mr. Leopoulos. He sent a message to be read at the funeral: "George Leopoulos taught me through example to have a positive attitude about life, always to work hard, and that a customer should always be treated as family. He had a quiet optimism that pervaded everything he did. His sense of humor carried him through many days. He demonstrated fairness to all people regardless of race or status. He lived by example. He was genuinely interested in me as a young man and what I wanted to do with my life. Today, we remember George and give thanks for his life of uplifted joy and eternal optimism. We pledge we will do better to live our lives in the way he showed us. In doing so, we will bear true tribute to his life and memory."

He acknowledged Mary at the swearing-in ceremony.

In 1993, President Clinton announced the creation of the AmeriCorps national service program. It was one of his earliest, most progressive efforts and continues today. The National Civilian Community Corps was part of it. One of my first efforts at the National Institute for Literacy was to add literacy to the National Service Act regulations so that tutoring could be an AmeriCorps service area. Director Eli Segal helped create the Literacy Service Corps. This was immensely satisfying and helped to expand literacy services nationwide.

Our family was personally invested in AmeriCorps as Mary was accepted into the first class of the National Civilian Community Corps program. My dad had been in the Civilian Conservation Corps (CCC) initiated by President Roosevelt in the 1930s. I have seen the many sites built by the CCC in Arkansas and wondered which my father might have helped build.

On June 20, Mary was sworn into AmeriCorps as a member of the first class of the National Civilian Community Corps. Mary and I attended a presidential helicopter departure just after her induction. President Clinton was happy to see Mary and greeted her warmly. He was thrilled that Mary joined his flagship program for national service, and he acknowledged her at the swearing-in ceremony as she stood with her class on the White House steps. It was an exceptionally valuable program and also earned funds for her to finish her degree at George Mason University.

"That's twice now that you've played the queen on Carolyn."

On February 9, 1994, I was invited to a Razorback basketball game watch party in the White House Movie Theater. The Hogs won the NCAA championship. It was great to have this White House invitation so soon after moving to DC and to see old friends from Arkansas. The president was in high spirits as he cheered his home team and invited the Razorbacks to the White House for recognition. Coach Nolan Richardson gave the president a Razorback shirt with his name emblazoned on it, and the president was like a kid at Christmas. Our family attended another Razorback basketball game in March 1995 at the White House. Arkansas friends cheered and were grateful to the president for their time together.

On February 12, 1994, I flew home to help pack our house. The president flew home to settle Virginia's estate the same weekend. He invited old friends, David Leopoulos, Joe Newman, and me to the Kelley's Hot Springs lakeside home. Webb Hubbell and Carolyn Huber joined us. It was a happy reunion of friends, all delighted to see Dick doing well after Virginia's death.

Bill suggested we play Hearts. Webb played the queen of spades on me. Then he did it again a second time. Bill looked at Webb and said, "That's twice now that you've played the queen on Carolyn." I appreciated his watchful protection. I wasn't good at the game, but I slowly improved. I had a Hearts game nightmare on Air Force One later. The president invited me to join a game with Bruce Lindsey. On the second hand, I was dealt all the hearts but was missing the queen of spades. What in the world could I do with such a hand? In the end, I couldn't run the hearts, and I felt embarrassed. I asked how a person could win the game with all the hearts if they didn't have the queen of spades. Bill said he didn't know either. Of all the luck to have such a hand in a game with the master player of Hearts.

The next evening, the president called to invite me to fly back to DC on Air Force One. I had only an hour to meet them in Hot Springs. Jerry and Will drove me there, and we posed for photos with the president. We enjoyed McClard's BBQ on the flight. This was the smaller plane, and everyone sat in the main cabin with two seats on either side of the aisle. After reading for a while, the president slept all the way back. Ralph Alswang, White House photographer, and I sat together, worked crossword puzzles, and enjoyed talking about his coverage of the president.

Because we arrived late, presidential aide Carolyn Huber invited me to spend the night at the White House. My room was on the third floor in one of several guest rooms where David Leopoulos and I stayed for the president's healthcare address to Congress. All the White House guest rooms are beautiful, and this one had a canopy bed with lovely floral draperies and a matching bedspread. I got up the next morning, had breakfast, and walked across Lafayette Square to my office. It was convenient that my office was across from the White House. Being nearby meant I could attend state arrival ceremonies, literacy events, and other special occasions.

The Russians locked eyes with me anytime I shared what Yeltsin told President Clinton.

In February 1994, I was invited to go to Novosibirsk, Russia, with a medical mission group. I attended planning meetings where I met members of the Russian diplomatic corps. They wanted to hear about Clinton's meetings with Yeltsin that Bill had recounted to me when both Bill and I were in Russia earlier that year. I was unnerved when one of the Russians locked eyes with me as I recounted the discussions. He soaked in every word as if he were recording everything I said, either mentally or by recording device. I was nervous because a few weeks earlier, Aldrich Ames, a CIA double agent, was caught in a Russian spy ring. A Russian spy was executed, and in retaliation, Russia expelled several US agents. I read it was common practice to retaliate with the swift execution of an American agent. It was far-fetched to think, but could I be a target? I don't watch many espionage movies, but I have an active imagination. I called Mack McLarty, White House chief of staff, and told him about my experience with the Russian diplomats. Would they target a friend of the president? Mack told me I was the safest person in the U.S. and to have no worries. Appreciating that, I went home and took the trip-string off my apartment door.

It was a musical performance but also a deeply spiritual experience.

In March 1994, friends began to receive Whitewater subpoenas. I was curious because I live in Arkansas and had never heard of the "Whitewater" land development. I read later that it was a parcel of land located near Flippin, Arkansas, being developed for recreational use. The developers, Madison Guaranty Savings and Loan owners Jim and Susan McDougal, hoped the White River property would attract investors for vacation homes. It never materialized, but it certainly did create some dangerous "whitewater" currents for the first family.

White House Counsel Bernard Nussbaum resigned on April 5th after accusations that he'd participated in meetings about Madison Guaranty Savings and Loan and the Whitewater development. It was a dark, sad period, and I sent supportive letters to the President and First Lady. Critics tried to make Whitewater a larger issue than the failed land investment it was. Legal bills for staff mounted. The Clintons regretted that their friends were suffering. The press kept the story hot, and public interest didn't appear to wane.

For a more pleasant turn of events, at Easter we were invited to Roger Clinton's wedding to Mollie Martin on March 26th at the Mansion on Turtle Creek, Dallas. Jerry, Mary, and Will drove to the wedding, and Sarah flew from college to join us. The president invited me to fly on Air Force One. Tom Caplan, Congressman Martin Frost, and Sondra Seba were with us. The president was Roger's best man and helped naturally emotional Roger make it through the ceremony. As the couple kissed, a lightning bolt lit the sky outside the wedding tent, and guests cheered. The rain poured but didn't dampen our spirits. The reception was a reunion of neighbors from childhood days, including the Hassin sisters and the Shuberts. The Rev. John Miles, a family friend and pastor at Oaklawn Methodist Church in Hot Springs, performed the ceremony. We were sorry that Virginia couldn't be with us.

Following the wedding, our family drove to Alexandria, Louisiana, to attend the Alexandria Pentecostal Church's original production of Handel's *Messiah*. The president had raved about it and urged us to go. We hoped the Clintons might join us, but their busy schedule wouldn't permit it. They invited us to attend the Razorback basketball national semifinals in Dallas before we left, but we needed to get on the road. Pastor Anthony Mangun told me that he was deeply moved when the president attended Messiah. His staff members saw the impact it had on him. It was a musical performance but also a deeply spiritual experience.

The Manguns became close Clinton friends and visited the White House often. On one visit, the president asked Mickey Mangun to sing. Anthony had prayed for the president, his family, and our nation. The next morning, the president popped into the Mangun's room and coaxed Anthony to join him for a 2.5-mile jog. He tossed a cap with the presidential seal to Anthony, saying it was a small gift for all he'd done for him. As they jogged, they talked about prayer. Anthony reminded the President that prayer has great presidential precedence. George Washington was reported to have prayed so fervently on his knees at Valley Forge that the snow melted around him. Anthony also recounted the words of Abraham Lincoln about prayer: "I have been driven many times upon my knees by the overwhelming conviction that I had nowhere else to go. My own wisdom and that of all about me seemed insufficient for that day. I remember my mother's prayers, and they have always followed me." Anthony urged Bill to do the same if he wanted to know God's peace and confidence. Bill thanked him and told him he prays throughout the day and finds great strength and comfort in prayer.

On another visit, Anthony told the president that he loved and would never cease to pray for him, but would continue to disagree with him on some issues. The president told him he respected his strong beliefs but that Anthony's job as pastor is to uphold the Bible, and the president's job is to uphold the Constitution. They don't have to be in conflict, but they are different. On visits to D.C., Anthony often called me to check if we could see the president, which was usually possible. Anthony worked for his election in Louisiana and sought help from Louisiana officials on issues. But their friendship was primarily about the love and the faith they'd experienced both in Arkansas at the campground at Redfield and when Bill attended *Messiah* in Alexandria.

"Mrs. Bunny, it's time for your carrot break."

The White House visitor's office called to ask if I could take a shift as Mrs. Bunny at the annual White House Egg Roll on Monday after Easter. It sounded like fun, but I sensed from the staff that this was a serious job. They suggested I wear cool clothing because the bunny suit is heavy. I arrived at the Visitor's Office and dressed in costume. I was told that I could not speak but could only wave and hug the kids. After an hour, a staff member would say, "Mrs. Bunny, it's time for your carrot break," and we would leave. It sounded simple enough, and I practiced using waves and head gestures. My idea to chew gum to avoid dryness proved a mistake as it caught a piece of my hair. But worse was the experience of the children peering through the wire eye holes to see who was in there. Some children punched me in the stomach and hit my bunny's rear. It was tempting to swat them with my bunny paw, but I behaved. Ah, the joys of presidential friendship.

Movies at the White House were informal and fun. On April 15, 1994, I saw *Four Weddings and a Funeral* with the president and a group of friends.

The president usually wore jeans, and guests dressed casually. The president invited filmmakers to screen movies and give opening remarks. Bill sat in the first row with the actors. Others sat behind him. Movie invitations usually came with a call at 5:30 or 6 p.m. for a movie at eight. Through the years, we attended several Razorback basketball games and movies. The most hilarious movie we saw was *Naked Gun* with Leslie Nielson. We could hardly breathe for laughing. Our family loved these evenings.

I read an interview that film critic Roger Ebert did with President Clinton in 1999. Clinton had told him, "The best perk of the White House is not Air Force One or Camp David … It's the wonderful movie theatre I get here."[2] Ebert reported that nearly all the movies Clinton watched were new releases. Matt Novak, a researcher with the online magazine *Gizmodo*, obtained records on all the movies the president enjoyed at the White House movie theater and found he watched 171, including *The Patriot, Braveheart,* and many 1990s blockbuster favorites including *Forrest Gump, Enemy of the State, Jerry Maguire, Saving Private Ryan, Apollo 13, You've Got Mail, Philadelphia,* and *Mrs. Doubtfire.*[3] As I read these interviews, I recalled the many movie nights the president and I enjoyed as high school neighbors at home, and I was delighted he had the movie theater for added enjoyment and relaxation in the White House.

Hot Springs High School Reunion, 1994

In July 1994, our 1964 high school class had our 30th reunion in Hot Springs. The president invited me to fly back home to Arkansas on Air Force One. I had flown to D.C. earlier in the year on a smaller Air Force One plane, but this was my first flight on the big plane, the 747. Staff pointed out the president's sleeping and living quarters. I toured the cabinet room, galley, and press section at the rear of the plane and enjoyed dinner and a movie. The enormous plane had large, comfortable recliner seats for passengers. Guests received a souvenir trip manifest with a passenger list and itinerary, matchbooks, M&Ms, notepads, and other keepsakes. The Secret Service gave the president's guests a "trip pin" to wear, indicating we were with his party and had security clearance. I have kept several of these beautiful, enameled pins as keepsakes. The president always walked through the plane and talked with his guests. These were over-the-top experiences.

Arriving at the reunion, the president went to the new Hot Springs High

School for a service of dedication for a memorial tree in honor of classmates who died in Vietnam—Tony Fuller, Burt Jeffries, Mike Thomas, and Tommy Young. He was especially touched to see the family of classmates who died in Vietnam. Afterward, we toured the new school and enjoyed a brief program led by class officers. I told the president that elections to class offices were lifetime appointments, and he should be happy I beat him for class secretary. He laughed at that memory. School organizations came to the stage to perform songs from the 60s—cheerleaders, T-steppers dance squad, band members, and football and basketball team members. The president joined us onstage to close the fun time together.

Before the reunion dinner-dance, Arlington Hotel manager Horst Fischer and his wife Linda hosted a small reception for the President's friends. Classmates were thrilled to be reunited with the president, who generously posed for pictures. Not many high school classes have a president as a classmate, and we were proud of this distinction.

The president always looked over our way to say hello.

Mounting tensions in Haiti complicated the president's heavy workload. The White House announced that former President Jimmy Carter, Colin Powell, and Senator Sam Nunn of Georgia would lead a trip to Haiti in hopes of persuading President Cedras to step down and allow Aristide to return to power. CNN reported on July 18, 1994, that the mission appeared successful. The president addressed the nation later that evening with details.

In addition to numerous state visits around the world by the Clintons, they invited many heads of state to visit Washington, D.C. State dinners were a coveted invitation, and the guest list was dictated by State Department protocol. The guests were members of the visiting country's embassy and diplomatic staff. Also invited were agency directors who worked with the country on trade issues, and prominent residents from the country of the visiting head of state. Artists who performed after dinner attended. Guests were announced at the receiving line with the President and guest. It was one of D.C.'s most coveted invitations. A friend told me that his federal agency head asked him to write a script for his remarks in the receiving line with the president. He said that a brief minute is a unique opportunity to convey something critical. My friend would work for hours to polish those few words for his boss. I thought about the many opportunities friends have to speak with the president unscripted and how rich our time with him is from this outside perspective.

To allow friends to experience a state visit, the president invited some to attend State Arrival Ceremonies on the South Lawn. We received a souvenir program and flags of the U.S. and of the visiting head of state's country. A roped area for friends gave us a front-row view. Standing across the way were cabinet members and dignitaries. Military bands played as we awaited the state visitor's arrival. As the limousine came up the drive, the President and First Lady walked outside from the Diplomatic Reception Room for greetings, and the presidents walked to the lawn to review the troops. The Fife and Drum Corps in the Continental Army uniform of the American Revolution played. Afterward, the presidents returned to the platform for the national anthem of each country and remarks. The president always looked over our way to say hello and seemed to enjoy seeing his friends gathered there.

Of all the state arrivals we attended, none was more remarkable than President Nelson Mandela's of South Africa on October 4, 1994. It coincided with our high school reunion, and the president invited us to meet Mandela. He was elected President of South Africa on May 10, 1994, and served until June 1999. He had been imprisoned until 1990, then ran for president and was elected. President Clinton began his remarks with these words, "Now, all over the world, there are three words which, spoken together, express the triumph of freedom, democracy, and hope for the future. They are 'President Nelson Mandela.'" Clinton called him "proof that the human spirit can never be crushed." In his reply, Mandela urged Americans to "come and invest in our country."

The second favorite arrival ceremony I attended was for the Emperor and Empress of Japan earlier in June 1994. It was so regal that I wrote a poetic reflection on the other-worldly experience, and I was stunned by the majesty, the sunny day, the golden color of both the First Lady's and Empress' clothing, and the beauty of the moment. (See "Poems and Song")

I kept souvenir flags and programs for state arrival ceremonies we attended:

June 13, 1994: Emperor and Empress, Japan
October 4, 1994: President Mandela and White House reception

March 1995: King Hassan, Morocco
October 10, 1995: President Zedillo, Mexico
July 1996: President Jacques Chirac, France
April 8, 1997: Prime Minister Jean Chretien, Canada
October 29, 1997: President Jiang Zemin, China
February 5, 1998: Prime Minister Tony Blair, UK
May 5, 1998: Prime Minister Prodi, Italy
July 1998: Prime Minister Hashimoto, Japan
September 16, 1998: President Vaclav Havel, Czech Republic
June 1999: President Goncz, Hungary

Bill said in good humor, "They're just doing their job."

Our first Christmas in D.C. was thrilling. My mother, siblings, and their families came for the White House Christmas family party. There were fifteen of us and we were fortunate we had plenty of room for them in our home in McLean. The White House was resplendent for the holidays. Decorations each year had a special theme, and this year's was the *Nutcracker* in honor of Chelsea's dancing with the National Ballet. Other year's themes were the *Night Before Christmas* and *Peace on Earth*, but the most spectacular year featured artist Dale Chihuly's white blown-glass Christmas trees lining the hallways. Chihuly, a native of Washington State, created floor-to-ceiling blown-glass Christmas trees in his signature style of extended, curled forms. The effect was breathtaking. The public can see one of the Chihuly Christmas trees at the Clinton Presidential Center on the third floor, where a state dinner setting is on display.

We visited with the president, first lady, and Chelsea and saw many friends. The president's Georgetown roommates and many Arkansas friends attended, including Governor's mansion chef Liza Ashley and other mansion staff. Each state reception room held an enormous Christmas tree with unique decorations from state historical societies and children's groups. The East Room had tables for guest seating, and the dance floor was full as the Marine Corps dance band played. Silver punch bowls brimmed with egg nog. The State Dining Room banquet table was filled with beautiful dishes,[4] and pastry chef Roland Mesnier's gingerbread White House displayed on the buffet was masterful in its detail.

The highlight was visiting with the president, Hillary, and Chelsea. Choral ensembles from schools entertained us as we waited in line to greet them. Our photo with the Clintons commemorated the Christmas we knew someday would be a dream fulfilled.

We took a bag of Christmas gifts to leave for the Clintons when we went to the party, and I tried to wrap them nicely. As we arrived to go through security, I wasn't prepared for the Secret Service to begin tearing off the gift wrap to inspect each gift. Our kids told the president that their mother was distressed to see the gifts being ransacked, and Bill said in good humor, "They're just doing their job." Of course, we were grateful for their protection, but *did they need to be so aggressive* with our gifts?

Dr. Billy Graham commented that this was the most spiritual prayer breakfast in history.

In April 1995, I was invited to sing the National Anthem at the White House Correspondent's dinner. It was a thrill to be backstage with dignitaries and enjoy the program I'd watched many times on television. The audience's reactions to the host's comedic monologue and the president's reaction were always priceless, and now I was a part of it. The president served up a funny monologue and had the audience in stitches.

In addition to the president's weekly radio address, his helicopter departures from the South Lawn were another opportunity to visit with him. These invitations came often in the early years but became fewer as his schedule tightened. On the way to the helicopter, the president walked along a rope line to see friends. His staff knew seeing friends was important to him, and we loved these opportunities and the photos that followed.

As the 1995 State of the Union neared, I faxed the president to say we were thinking of him. We urged him to respond to criticism that he sometimes "waffled" and struggled with "soul" issues. We knew his greatest strength as President was his desire to serve and to leave a legacy of reform. He also has a strong instinct to win and be competitive. Those traits sometimes conflicted, but we knew he would never back away from his convictions. We urged him to stay strong, positive, and powerful. Afterward, I wrote that his speech couldn't have been better. I told him even my GOP carpool complimented him on an outstanding speech.

A good friend of the president, Lyndon Finney from Immanuel Baptist in Little Rock, called in frustration to report on criticism about the president's views on abortion and homosexuality. He hoped he would find a way to contrast his personal view with the Constitution's. I suggested to the president that the coming Prayer Breakfast would be an opportunity to encourage the faithful to be moral leaders and respect that the president must uphold the Constitution. Conservative leaders pressured him to use the presidency as a moral pulpit to pass laws to govern these problematic issues. I shared my view that laws would remove the need for individuals to struggle with personal beliefs. I encouraged him to ask the Prayer Breakfast attendees to pray for their president and tell them he drew great strength from their prayers. After the 1995 Prayer Breakfast, I faxed a letter to the president praising his remarks. Dr. Billy Graham commented that this was the most spiritual prayer breakfast in history. That was high praise indeed. The president's heart was clearly on display.

"Human rights are women's rights, and women's rights are human rights—once and for all."

In March 1995, the First Lady returned from Copenhagen to accolades for her speech. She was leaving next for Southeast Asia. I sent her information about U.S. literacy programs for women and families and noted that parents who haven't finished high school aren't able to help their children with homework. I hoped she would pass the information along and learn about literacy projects in the countries she visited.

Hillary's speech in Beijing in the fall was among her most memorable. She spoke at the United Nations Fourth World Conference on Women on September 5, 1995, condemning injustices that undermine women and girls globally. Her chief of staff, Melanne Verveer, said, "Earlier that year, Clinton had traveled to Copenhagen for the World Summit on Social Development, and she toured innovative projects and programs for women in South Asia. By the time she had gotten to Beijing, she had an awful lot under her belt—certainly, as first lady, working in the United States, and increasingly on the world stage." When she spoke these now-famous words, she launched a movement among women around the world: "Human rights are women's rights, and women's rights are human rights—once and for all."[5]

"We will stand together for as many tomorrows as it takes."

April 19, 1995, was one of the most horrific days in our nation's history. As Oklahoma City workers arrived for work, some with babies going to daycare, a truck bomb exploded and destroyed the Alfred P. Murrah Federal Building, killing 168 people. It was the deadliest terrorist act in American history. The president wrote: "Most of those killed in the attack were public servants who showed up to work that morning, as they did every morning, to do the business of the American people. We have not lost each other, we have not lost America, and we will stand together for as many tomorrows as it takes." At a service in the Oklahoma City Convention Center, he met with grieving families and helped shore up the heart of our nation. He grieved as our nation was so torn. We felt vulnerable in a new way and the President's presence brought comfort. I told him we were grateful for his compassionate response.

We visited the Oklahoma City Memorial in 2019 and read the president's words etched into the entrance: "We come here to remember those who were killed, those who survived, and those changed forever. May all who leave here know the impact of violence. May this memorial offer comfort, strength, peace, hope, and serenity." Chair sculptures on the lawn are memorials to those who were killed, including small chairs for the 19 children killed in daycare. The times 9:01 and 9:03 are etched into the entry walls to note the times the explosion began and ended. This certainly must have been one of the most trying days for our president.

He asked if we talked to reporters about Nixon and we told him, "No."

On April 24, 1995, a group of friends visited the White House and were upstairs in a sitting room with the Clintons.[6] While there, the president received word that former President Richard Nixon had died following a stroke a week earlier. The president walked to the Rose Garden to announce Nixon's death and invited Jim, Phil, and me to join him. Reporters asked to talk with us about President Nixon, but we didn't respond.

After the Rose Garden remarks, we stood in the ground floor hallway of the White House and talked for thirty minutes. It was nearly midnight. Many things were on the president's mind, including Bosnia and the NATO truce, Rwanda, Haiti, and South Africa. He was carrying a heavy load. He asked if we had talked with the reporters. We told him no, and he said that was good. Our experiences during Nixon's presidency (1969-74) had not been positive. The Vietnam conflict resulted in the deaths of four high school classmates and many college friends, and both Phil and Jim served. We didn't have anything helpful to say to reporters. But we were glad to be with the president that night.

We were proud of the president for promoting education, a goal since his college days.

In April 1995, I was invited to join Jim and Kathy French for lunch with Jehan Sadat, widow of Egyptian President Anwar Sadat, who had been assassinated in 1981. Another special event that month was an invitation to meet the Ethiopian crown prince, son of Haile Selassie. My office doorman, Alo, a Coptic Christian from Ethiopia and a friend of the crown prince, told the prince about me. The prince asked to meet to learn more about the Christian faith. We met at his home in Vienna, Virginia, where I learned he was facing death. Selassie asked me about my Christian faith and why it was important to me. He also asked how he might become a follower of Christ, as his friend Alo had done.

On May 6, 1995, Harry and Linda Bloodworth Thomason hosted a party to celebrate the 50th anniversary of Victory in Europe Day, May 8, 1945, marking the Allied victory in Europe, the surrender of Germany, and the end of WW II in Europe. Jerry and I were guests as were the president and Hillary. Among the guests at the Ritz Carlton in Washington, DC, was noted author Elie Wiesel, who wrote a moving memoir of the Holocaust. It was an honor to meet him and celebrate peace together. An orchestra played wartime and postwar tunes for dancing.

On May 16, 1995, I represented the National Institute for Literacy at the White House signing event for Education Goals 2000. The celebration was in a tent on the south lawn, and several Arkansas education leaders attended, including the superintendent of the Little Rock Schools, Dr. Ruth Steele, and Diana Sydoriak, Director of the Arkansas Department of Education programs for children with disabilities. The Education Goals 2000 were established by the president and prompted Congress to set goals for standards-based education reform. The intent was for certain criteria to be met by the millennium.

One goal was for all children to start school ready to learn. Another was to increase the high school graduation rate to at least 90 percent. This revolutionary plan was an achievement for the president, who had made our nation's educational excellence his goal since college.

This time, without the President.

On May 25, 1995, I returned to Russia for a second series of concerts with the Sverdlovsk Symphony and conductor Sarah Caldwell, this time for two performances of the *Requiem Mass* by Giuseppe Verdi. I first heard the work as a student at Ouachita Baptist University. I dreamt of singing the soprano solos and finally had the opportunity in 1982 with the Northwest Arkansas Symphony (Fayetteville) and conductor Carlton Wood. It was tremendous to sing one of the most beautiful choral works ever written, and to sing it again in Russia was a thrill.

Severe thunderstorms caused flight delays that caused me to miss the flight with Sarah Caldwell and other musicians from New York City to Yekaterinburg. The next flight was not for three days, but I finally arrived. Being in Russia in May was a far different experience than my first trip in January with sub-zero temps and frozen rivers that cars could drive across. Spring was beautiful in Yekaterinburg. The orchestra posted enormous posters with the names of soloists on the Symphony Hall and around town. The press gave the concerts a lot of coverage, and we were treated like stars. Most of all, it was a superb musical experience I will always treasure.

"He's the President!" I thought. But that's the kind of friend he is.

In June 1995, our daughter Mary was in Aberdeen, Maryland, wrapping up her year with the National Civilian Community Corps. Team experiences included the construction of bridges and clearing paths in Maryland parks, helping at a homeless veteran's project, assisting at Perry Point Hospital for emotionally challenged veterans, and working in a drug education program with students. When the program ended, she told us, "I don't think there's anything I can't do!"

One Sunday morning in 1995, Bill visited Mary's National Civilian Conservation Corps program site in Maryland at Aberdeen Proving Ground and attended church services on the base. Later, the phone rang, and the operator said, "Please hold for the president." Bill came on the line and said, "Hi! I just wanted to tell you that I was at Aberdeen this morning and I saw Mary at church. She seems to be doing well. Is she liking the program and happy she decided to take a year to participate?" I told him about some of the experiences she had enjoyed, the work skills she had gained, and how impressed we were with the program.

I was surprised that he was calling me as a parent to say he'd seen our child and report that she was fine. "He's the president!" I thought. But that's the kind of friend he is. Our children are important in his life, and he'd want a call if I had seen Chelsea away from home. I appreciated this friendly, parental report from the president.

He had his picture taken with Hillary, and it was one of his most precious possessions.

On July 17, 1995, the state directors of adult education met in D.C., and several asked if it might be possible to visit the White House because most had never had the opportunity. I contacted the White House and arranged for the group to tour the main reception rooms and the Rose Garden. We had no idea the president planned to join us. He came out to the Rose Garden from the Oval Office and mingled with the group, thanked them for their service to help adults and families lead more productive lives with improved literacy skills, and shook hands.

I was so grateful he could take a moment to make this appearance. Several had met President Bush and Barbara, as adult literacy was her key issue as First Lady. Now it was good for them to hear President Clinton speak of his support for adult education and literacy. Many said it also cemented their support for the president, so it was a win on many levels.

In August 1995, prior to the Clintons' departure for a vacation at Jackson Hole, Wyoming, the White House staff celebrated the president's forty-ninth birthday with an epic cowboy-themed party on the south lawn. Senior staff Erskin Bowles and Leon Panetta arrived on horseback wearing cowboy outfits and ten-gallon hats. Jimmy Buffet and his band performed. It was a terrific party, full of laughs, and Bill and Hillary enjoyed it immensely. We were happy that Jerry's dad, Marion Staley, and Jerry's sister, Terri, and her family were visiting from Indiana and went with us. They were huge Clinton supporters, and Marion was also a big Hillary fan. Terri and family also had pictures made with the president, now cherished mementos. Marion had his picture taken with Hillary. It remained one of his most precious possessions throughout his life.

Audience members checked the President's box to see if he was present.

A special perk for friends of the president was the opportunity to sit in the president's box at the Kennedy Center. Each theater has a presidential box that seats six to eight guests in the center of the first balcony. The box has a sitting room with a powder room and a mini refrigerator filled with snacks and small bottles of champagne with the presidential seal. Audience members looked up at the president's box to see if he was present. When he attended, the presidential seal was affixed to the box. As a performing artist with an arts-loving family, these performances were among the highlights of our time in D.C. Often, the White House staff called to invite us to go, and I could contact them when there was a performance we'd like to see.

In August 1995, Jerry, Mary, Will, and I attended a concert of *An American Requiem* by composer James DeMars, performed by the Mormon Tabernacle Choir. Commissioned in 1992 following the Rodney King trial and the Los Angeles riots, it was a memorial work to unite Americans. President Clinton wrote a dedication for the piece. Mary and Will took friends and Mary said this fulfilled her wish to attend a "fancy concert" at the Kennedy Center.

We enjoyed many Kennedy Center performances while seated in the president's box, among them:

September 24, 1995, *Hello Dolly*
September 1996, *Mrs. Klein* (stage play)
September 1997, *Phantom of the Opera*
November 4, 1997, Pianists Andreas Schiff and Peter Serkin
January 15, 1998, National Symphony Orchestra Brahms concert
July 1998, *Showboat* (I took my mother with us for the performance as well as a concert of jazz when she visited another time.)
March 23, 1999, Wagner, *Tristan und Isolde*
August 1999, *Titanic* (stage play)
January 2000, *Martin Guerre* (stage play)

November 2000, National Symphony Orchestra, Mahler, *Symphony Number 8*

January 2001, Menotti, *The Consul*

Towering over these Kennedy Center performance experiences was the opportunity to sit in the president's box for our son Will's graduation from Langley High School on June 21, 1999. Having commencement at the Kennedy Center was grand but even more special because Will was the Student Council senior class representative and was seated on stage. Will invited Federal Emergency Management Agency director, James Lee Witt, to be speaker and greeted him. Will also accompanied a vocalist on guitar. It was a day to remember, and our seats were the best in the house, thanks to the president.

She told me that the President recently talked about his funeral.

A poignant moment happened once when I went to the White House to pick up Kennedy Center tickets from Deb Schiff. She told me that the president recently talked about his funeral and told Deb he had given me a list of songs he wanted for his service. She said she wanted to share this only to say how much he loves us. I was surprised and very touched.

I knew about his wish for *Goin' Up Yonder* that a choir had sung at Hubert Humphries' funeral. I didn't recall ever receiving a list from him, per se, but imagined he would like the songs from his mother's funeral, including *Holy Ground* and *His Eye is on the Sparrow*. I also thought about ML King's funeral and Mahalia Jackson singing *My Living Shall Not Be in Vain*. He had always loved *Be Not Afraid* and *In the Presence of Jehovah*, as well as hymns *Amazing Grace* and *How Great Thou Art*. I wondered if those would be on his "list" of favorites for use someday. I also wondered what the impetus had been for this discussion but agreed it was a good idea to have a plan.

"I think I recalled about 85 percent of them," he said.

President Clinton and First Lady Hillary hosted an Arkansas Homecoming Weekend September 29-30, 1995, for supporters. The weekend kicked off with a picnic on the South Lawn. For many, it was the first time back to the White House since the inauguration. The evening was filled with pride for President Clinton and his election. As the band struck up *Hail to the Chief*, the Clintons walked onto the grounds. Bill said how great it was to see these loving faces from home. To the delight of all, the president reminisced about escapades with friends he saw. He said in October, he and Hillary would celebrate their twentieth wedding anniversary. Several present that day had been at their wedding. It was a close-knit group that had known the president and First Lady Hillary for many years.

The crisp fall day was perfect, and a huge crescent moon lit the evening sky. Festive red, white, and blue décor was used with mums and votive candles. Hundreds of white twinkling lights were strung all over the grounds, making it magical. We enjoyed a delicious buffet of barbeque ribs, fried chicken, corn on the cob, salads, biscuits, and cornbread. A separate dessert tent offered ice cream sundaes and fruit cobbler. The US Army Band and vocal ensemble dressed in khaki uniforms entertained with hits from the 40s, patriotic songs, Broadway classics, and a group of Arkansas-themed songs. The president and first lady mingled with old friends. Also, with the re-election campaign looming, the event was a perfect way to energize faithful supporters.

The reunion continued the next morning with a tour of rooms not usually open at the White House, including the Oval Office and the Cabinet Room. The weekend concluded with a "Blue Jeans Bash" on Saturday evening.

As the reunion ended, we were ushered with a few friends to the Rose Garden for a minute with the president. He pulled me aside to say he was sorry he couldn't attend my deacon ordination the next day. He also said he'd sent a letter to Sarah congratulating her on her new reporting job with an ABC news affiliate—a kindness much appreciated by her parents. The president speculated that Colin Powell would run for president and said he was probably the shrewdest and most underestimated politician in the city. The president said Powell excelled at getting his message out. I mentioned that I'd recently had dinner with some GOP friends who said they would support Powell. The president said he thought, despite many factors tugging against him, he would decide to run.

I told him how impressed people at the picnic were that he remembered their names, and he said, "I think I recalled about eighty-five percent of them." He excelled at name-recall, and it meant a lot to people. I also told him about my recent press interview about his visit with Yeltsin in Russia and how he had encouraged Yeltsin to keep the doors open to Protestant mission workers.

Many fundamentalist Christians who weren't generally supportive of the president were appreciative that he had kept Russia open to the spread of the Gospel. He said, "I did," and he thanked me for writing the story that was reprinted in many newspapers and *Time* magazine.

I was ordained a deacon at McLean Baptist Church on October 1, 1995, and honored to fulfill this dream. In Little Rock in 1979, we attended church with Bill and Hillary at Immanuel Baptist Church and afterward visited with a Clinton friend and deacon there. He said he hoped we would make Immanuel our church home. I said it was nice to meet a deacon, and I also hoped someday to be one. He replied, "Well, all we have to do is change the Bible." I was stunned, and so was Hillary. As we left, Hillary looked at Bill and asked, "Did you hear what he said to Carolyn?" Immanuel was one of many churches, particularly Southern Baptist ones, that interpreted scripture literally about women in ministry, rather than looking at it in social and historical context. These churches did not believe it biblical to ordain women as deacons or hire them as ministers. I had felt a call to full-time ministry for several years, and although there was not a nearby seminary I could attend to earn a theological degree, I believed I could serve as a deacon and be of service to a church. Thankfully, the dreams of both seminary and ordination were fulfilled in later years.

Sad news reached the White House on November 4, 1995. Israeli Prime Minister, Yitzhak Rabin, had been shot by an assassin at an outdoor rally in Tel Aviv and died a few hours later. The event was in support of the Oslo Accords, and the shooter was a young Israeli lawyer who adamantly opposed ceding any of the West Bank to Palestine as outlined in the accords. Just six weeks earlier, Rabin had been at the White House for the signing of the West Bank Accords (September 1995) that gave Palestine land formerly part of Israel. We recalled how the president had beamed as he stood between Yitzhak Rabin and Yasser Arafat on the South Lawn.

Rabin's assassination was a terrible shock. The president and first lady flew to Jerusalem, and Bill spoke at Rabin's funeral. The president sent me a copy of his beautiful remarks on their friendship and the peace they had worked to achieve in the Middle East. He reminded us that peace rarely comes without a price. We grieved with the Clintons for Rabin's widow and children. And prayed for our world.

House Speaker Newt Gingrich, a Clinton foe, had long been on a contentious path to undermine the president's budget. The midterm elections had given the GOP control of the budget process and other legislation that threatened to undo many of the president's gains. When the press asked why Gingrich and GOP members were making it so tough on the president, he replied, "Because we can." Gingrich flew with the president to attend Rabin's funeral, reporting that he felt insulted on the trip. He vowed to retaliate by piling continuing resolutions on the budget just to get back at the president. Gingrich's egocentric power motives threatened to derail critical federal services to Americans. We hoped this might be a turning point to help voters see through his actions.

Government Shutdown

Failed budget negotiations led to a government shutdown in mid-November 1995. The National Institute for Literacy staff continued to work because we were a forward-funded agency. Our staff supported the president and faxed notes of encouragement. He wrote back to say they meant a great deal. The president believed we could end the shutdown and balance the budget. He was working to do both.

On Thanksgiving 1995, our family gathered at our home in McLean, Virginia, for a family celebration. Sarah was a television reporter for ABC-affiliate WABG in Greenville, Mississippi, and traveled to New York City to report on the Granada, Mississippi, high school band marching in the Macy's Thanksgiving Day Parade. She came for Thanksgiving. Mary and Will were with us as well, and we cherished the time together.

Sarah asked the president if she could interview him for her news station, and the president agreed. We were astonished that, as part of the interview, he broke the news that he was sending U.S. troops to Bosnia. This was the lead story for Peter Jennings' ABC newscast and all major networks that evening. It was quintessential Bill Clinton style to make the announcement in the interview with Sarah because he knew it would be the lead news story and would give her national reporting exposure and credentials. Only a friend like President Clinton would do that.

At Christmas, our family went to the White House Christmas party for family and friends. It was always a joy to be with the Clintons and to spend a few minutes sharing family news. Will had reached a height of 6′2″, and the president marveled at his growth.

He said I should feel free to "keep talking to folks who call for validation."

In 1996, work was going well at the National Institute for Literacy. Helping nearly a quarter of US citizens who read below the fifth-grade level was important. The president had just returned from visiting our troops on a peacekeeping mission to Bosnia. Whitewater was in the news, and Hillary was fending off inquiries about their investment in the failed Arkansas land development. She was also saddled with investigations into the lingering White House travel office firings. Her blockbuster book, *It Takes a Village*, had just been published, and she was planning a book tour. We hoped all the negativity would end soon. The 1996 elections were around the corner, and we wished our friends a good year.

The 1996 *State of the Union* address on January 26 was a masterful speech delivered powerfully by the president. He outlined what were likely to be his campaign themes. Polls showed Clinton at fifty-eight percent to GOP candidate Dole's twenty-eight. We hoped support would remain strong.

Hillary was subpoenaed to testify before a grand jury about Whitewater. It was clear that an ugly political game was in play. I wrote Hillary with prayers and support, and she wrote back to thank me.

I also wrote to Bill and told him of our support, included some jokes, and told him about recent calls from TV and the press gearing up for the campaign. He sent me a thank you and said I should feel free to "keep talking to folks who call for validation." I never thought of myself as a validator, but I was more than happy to help. Surely, people who had no relationship with them spouting opinions and theories was getting old for the Clintons. I was eager to help people know my friend Bill Clinton and hoped to help. I gave interviews to many respected journalists, including these:

David Shribman, *Boston Globe, Wall St Journal*
Howard Feinman, *Newsweek*
Michael Takiff and Margaret Carlson, *Time*
Jeanne Cummings, *Wall Street Journal*
Susan Paige, *USA Today*

Karen Tumulty, White House correspondent, *Time*
Ken Walsh, *US News and World Report*
Peter Baker and EJ Dione, *The Washington Post*

Tragedy struck in April 1996 as the Air Force jet carrying Secretary of Commerce Ron Brown and staff crashed in Croatia. They had been promoting peace in the Balkans. Ron had been such a vital supporter, political advisor, and friend to the president through the 1992 campaign. He was playing the same role as the president moved to the 1996 election. Our hearts broke for the president and the Brown family. We were grateful for Secretary Brown's inspiring work. We also mourned the lives of staff lost in the crash and those who grieved for them.

In June 1996, the nation was stunned by a rash of Black church burnings in North and South Carolina. As young people, the president and I had experienced positive models for racial interaction and were committed to helping bring about racial respect as best we could. These hate crimes had the African American community in an uproar. Naturally, they asked for increased enforcement of hate crimes laws. Earlier defacement of synagogues had raised alerts about the state of hate in America. The president spoke at the rededication of a Methodist church in Greeleyville, South Carolina, saying that too often, the code words "America First" meant "white America" or "MY kind of America" first. I was very touched by his remarks and wrote to thank him. The President helped people confront their prejudices at home, at church, and in community.

The president wanted us to join him to view the fireworks from the White House roof.

In 1996, as the world prepared for the Summer Olympic Games in Atlanta from July 19 to August 4, the torch made its way down the East Coast toward the arena. Dr. I. King Jordan, former president of Gallaudet University, carried it to the South Lawn around 10 PM, where President Clinton, Hillary, Vice President Al Gore, and Tipper met him. Dr. Jordan and the President lit a ceremonial cauldron that would house the flame overnight.

The next morning, our family attended the Olympic Flame arrival event at the White House, where the president spoke. President Clinton said, "It is this flame that represents the best of the United States of America. The Olympic spirit is the spirit of personal responsibility and best effort, the spirit of community, the spirit of unity. The people who carried this torch all across America showed us exactly how that spirit can lift all our lives every day. This has been carried by America's best. They are everyday Olympians."[7] After finishing his remarks, President Clinton and Carla McGhee of the U.S. women's basketball team lit the torch, and she jogged off the White House grounds to continue the run. McGhee was an Olympic team member, but most who carried the torch were everyday people who wrote an essay to the United Way. They were chosen by a panel to carry the torch because they exemplified the ideals and spirit of the Olympic Games. It was thrilling to be at the White House to experience the torch's arrival. DC experienced the Olympic Games as soccer games were played at R.F.K. Stadium. To celebrate their victories, over five hundred American team members visited the White House.

ꙮ ꙮ

On July 4, 1996, we were invited to the White House for an Independence Day picnic for staff and friends on the South Lawn. As the night darkened, staff member Robyn Dickey saw our family with friends, the Frenches, and Jamisons. She said the president wanted us to join him on the White House roof to view the fireworks. That gave us the best spot in the city to view the display. We were thrilled to share it with the president. Glenn Campbell performed with the National Symphony Orchestra. I told the president I thought I'd like to be a singer of stirring patriotic songs like Kate Smith in her heyday during WWII. He nodded and said, "I think there's a market for that!" After the fireworks ended, he invited us to stay for a movie, *The Nutty Professor*. Being with the president at the White House made it a grand July Fourth to remember.

Someone Has to Say it: You're OLD!

The president's birthday was always a time for celebration, but especially so as he turned fifty. Our family attended his birthday gala in New York City on August 18, 1996. Presidential assistant, Nancy Hernreich, asked for names of friends from high school, Georgetown University, and Hope, Arkansas, saying the president was excited about this milestone and wanted his friends there. Tickets were free, and we took care of expenses. We stayed at the Sheraton New York and arrived in time for a 4:15 PM opening reception at the Waldorf Astoria Hotel. Everything was within walking distance—our hotel, the Waldorf Astoria, and Radio City Music Hall.

Because this year was his 50th birthday and a re-election year, the gala doubled as a fundraiser. The big event was at Radio City Music Hall, where three thousand people purchased tickets for $250 each. The show was simulcast to fifty birthday fundraisers across the country. Whoopi Goldberg was the gala emcee. Entertainers spanned the decades of the president's life, including Jon Bon Jovi, Aretha Franklin, Smoky Robinson, Tony Bennett, and Shania Twain. A videotaped message from our Hot Springs High School friends showed cheerleaders and the T-Stepper dance squad doing the "Hullabaloo" cheer. It was perfect.

As we left for NYC, we stopped at McLean Safeway and bought a lemon Bundt cake, candles, plates and napkins, balloons, streamers, hats, and horns for the president's party with friends the next morning in his Waldorf Astoria suite. The city streets were barricaded, and mounted police guarded the hotel. We received permission to navigate around them and reach the hotel. Staffer Robyn Dickey met us in the lobby to tell us we were invited to the birthday dinner after the gala. We could not believe it. We saw the president, Hillary, and Chelsea as they walked through the hotel lobby and told the president we would see him the next morning at a smaller party on his birthday. He gave a big thumbs-up and smiled.

The Fiftieth Birthday dinner at the Waldorf Astoria glittered with Peter Duchin and Orchestra entertaining.[8] At dinner, we sat with Olympic track and field gold medalist Carl Lewis and Kerri Strug, the gymnast. I saw opera singer Jesse Norman in the ladies' room, and we reminisced about our vocal studies at Indiana University School of Music. I asked if the president and first lady knew she was there, and she replied, "Oh, they know!" Later, at dinner, she came onstage to lead the *Happy Birthday* song.

The most special event of the birthday weekend came the following morning on his actual birthday, August nineteenth. Friends gathered in a parlor at the Waldorf Astoria. I placed the Safeway cake and decorations on a desk. The president was tired but thrilled to see everyone. He walked towards the coffee and asked wistfully, "Can I have a cup of coffee on my birthday?" He had been drinking decaf for a while and wanted to splurge on his birthday. At the gala dinner, his huge cake in the shape of the United States required several people to roll it onstage and light the candles. But his reaction to seeing our store-bought lemon Bundt cake was one of pure joy and I thought possibly even more appreciative than for the enormous one.

The president sat at the desk to open cards and gifts and roared with laughter as he read the greetings. Hillary did not come, no doubt exhausted from the previous day, but her mother Dorothy came and sat on a sofa to watch the fun. Will Staley, Patrick Campbell, and Anson Ashby presented his cake with candles lit, and the president blew them out as we sang. We wore paper hats and blew noisemakers. Mary Jo shared information about the Hot Springs High School condominiums called "Clinton Campus" for which Jim French said his brother Ed were the architects. The opening was set for September 1997, and they urged the president to attend. Mack McLarty and Joe Purvis from Hope brought a t-shirt that said, "There's Still HOPE after 50," and other nice gifts. I gave him a card that made him howl, and Jerry got a picture of his reaction as he cried, laughing. It read, "Somebody has to say it: You're OLD! And the noises your body makes are starting to scare small dogs. Happy Birthday." I also showed him a draft of a memoir I was writing at the time, and he scanned it with interest. It was certainly a birthday weekend to remember, with millionaire donors at the gala to a few friends who brought a store-bought cake.

...how grateful he was to have his friends there.

The president's re-election campaign geared up in the summer of 1996. The Democratic National Convention met in Chicago August 26-29, 1996, as a tribute to Hillary's hometown. My daughter Sarah and I went to celebrate the history.[9] There were great convention night experiences, and each day we had city tours and press events. We shared a VIP suite with Aretha Franklin and AFL-CIO chief John Sweeny. We met the Clinton staff and friends each day to get our credentials and celebrate.

Every convention day was electrifying. Hillary gave an outstanding speech one night and at a "Women Win '96" luncheon where Tipper Gore spoke as well. We went to a labor lunch with speakers Robert Reich and James

Carville. We took an architectural tour on the Chicago River and toured the Greek neighborhood where my Greek friend David Leopoulos was treated like a king! Every night after the convention, we met the Clintons and told the president what we were doing and hearing and about interviews we'd given. We enjoyed visits in the convention hallways with Vernon Jordan, Leon Panetta, Erskine Bowles, David Dinkins, Michael Dukakis, Richard Daley, Harold Ickes, and Jesse Jackson. Aretha Franklin, Phil Driscoll, and Kenny G performed. We met Tom Brokaw and Larry King. We had press interviews (but not as many as in 1992) as the president was now well-known.

The president's acceptance speech on August twenty-ninth was outstanding. He outlined his vision for the next decade: planned tax cuts for the middle class, twenty million more jobs, protecting our strong defense while making military cuts but maintaining peacemaking troops. He promised to work for welfare reform and a peaceful transition for the Middle East. The convention goers were electrified.

The morning after his re-nomination, we had breakfast with the president at the hotel penthouse. Pictures in our home remind us how grateful he was to have his friends there as he beamed. We were thankful he was poised for four more years to lead our nation as president.

The phone rang. Carolyn? Happy birthday!

The president sent a thoughtful birthday letter to me and called early on my 50th birthday, September 7, 1996. It was an incredibly special way to start the day. I made notes as we talked:

Bill: Carolyn? Happy birthday!

Carolyn: Thank you so much, Mr. President for the call and for being the first greeting by mail on my birthday! The doorbell rang a few minutes ago at 9 AM, and it was Federal Express with your birthday letter. Thank you so much.

Bill: I sent you a copy of my book, too, but we couldn't get it out in time for today's arrival. You'll get it soon. Are you doing something fun for your birthday?

Carolyn: Yes! Jim and Kathy and Phil and Susan are coming to dinner. I've also planned a party for next Saturday to celebrate both Jerry's birthday and mine and would love for you to come. Lots of neighbors, friends from church—Dems and Republicans—and it would be so great to have you with us. Or come by tonight if you can. If it would make it more fun for you, we could invite some VIP neighbors like Ethyl Kennedy and Colin Powell.

Bill: (Laughing the entire time) … he's your neighbor, isn't he? He doesn't live far from you, does he?

Carolyn: No, not at all. Lots of Senators live nearby, too, including Ted Kennedy and Alan Simpson. We're also neighbors with Terry McAuliff.

Bill: You're so funny. How are your kids?

Carolyn: Everyone's great. Sarah's planning to come back to DC and work here. Mary is doing great at George Mason University and working at Ernst and Young Technology. Will is such a fine young man, a sophomore at Langley High School, enjoying lacrosse and snowboarding, and active in school and church youth groups. We're all fine.

Bill: Great, that's great.

Carolyn: Thanks so much for your call. We love you so much.

Bill: Love you too.

Carolyn: Take care of yourself, Mr. President.

The rest of my birthday was also grand. Jim and Kathy French arrived for dinner and picked veggies from our garden for supper. We tried to cheer Phil and Susan as she was having cancer treatments. At a larger party, we had 70 friends plus Will's youth group from church. We enjoyed a buffet supper, danced the Macarena, and had a 60s sing-along with karaoke. I received beautiful gifts, including my first Hermes scarf from Mary, a Doobie Brothers CD collection and gorgeous cake from Sarah, gold earrings from my sister Deb, a Steuben glass flag paperweight from Jim and Kathy, an orchid from Phil and Susan, and a new computer from Jerry. I was happy to celebrate the big 5-0 surrounded by loving family and friends and with a presidential call.

He told me he sounded like Minnie Mouse.

The Presidential debates were in Hartford, CT, on October 6, 1996. I could not go because of a prior singing commitment. I hated to miss the debates, but Jerry, Mary, and Will drove to Hartford. White House staff Steve Goodin, Andrew Friendly, and Nancy Hernreich made their arrangements. I sent a note to the president with tips on vocal production because he'd been losing his voice. He told me he sounded like Minnie Mouse when he tried to speak as

I coached. We all hear ourselves differently than we sound, but I understood it was hard to make changes.

The second debate was held at the University of San Diego on October sixteenth. GOP nominee Bob Dole tried to make the debates about ethical lapses, but the president refused to take the bait. "I could answer a lot of these things tit for tat. But I hope we can talk about what we're going to do in the future," he admonished. A Gallup poll showed Clinton at 48 percent and Dole at 39 percent. Though the race had tightened a bit, we were feeling confident.

What a thrill it was to be with him when the voters put him over the top!

Jerry, Will, and I flew to Little Rock on November 2 to celebrate the president's re-election. It was different this time because we didn't live in Little Rock and couldn't host a post-election brunch at our house as we did in 1992. The president's staff tracked us down and invited us to his Excelsior hotel suite to watch the vote count. Campaign staff Bruce Lindsey, Doug Sosnik, Erskine Bowls, Don Baer, and Kirk Hanlin were watching, and Chelsea came in for the victory announcement. We cheered with gusto at this great news.

I helped with election night logistics at the Old State House. My task was to keep the rope line area near the stage free for cabinet members and FOBs. I didn't recognize Secretary Charlene Barshefsky, U.S. Trade Representative, and I apologized profusely. It was always a nerve-wracking assignment to try to keep people in certain areas for access to the president. Friends gathered near the location, knowing the president would come by. After he was declared victorious, we cheered for another four years. We attended the victory party at the Excelsior ballroom with friends. We re-created the 1992 front porch post-election photograph with the Clintons and stood together as we did that happy day. We were thrilled our friend Bill had been re-elected and looked forward to more progress and peace for our nation under his leadership.

I was grateful.

In December 1996, I wrote the president to urge him to include support for literacy in his upcoming radio address on work-study. The American Reads challenge had been narrowly interpreted to be for children only. Those of us in the literacy field were disappointed that it didn't reflect the national crisis of adult literacy, as well. I mentioned to the president that research shows that one-quarter of the US adult population reads below the fourth-grade level. Ninety million adults were unable to help their children with homework or read to them. How much better could children do in school if they had a parent who could help them read and write?

I had a shocking moment when I was at the White House and was called to a phone near the Oval Office. It was a mistake, as the call was intended for another Carolyn. I reached into the trash can to get a scrap of paper to take notes, and by wild coincidence, pulled out a note written to the president's staff asking that I not be allowed to speak to him before his address. What a shock it was to see my name in that memo. But I also understood the power at play to keep this issue focused solely on children. I did not feel I was asking much to include parents. I believed that parental literacy was actually supportive of children's learning. I was grateful the president decided to include those important two words "and adults" in his address. And I continued to learn about how our government works and how decisions are made, even among friends.

---

[1] *The State of Literacy in America,* National Institute for Literacy, Washington, D.C, 1998

[2] Ebert, Roger, *Q & A: Clinton on Movies.* Roger Ebert.com. September 10, 2008.

[3] Novak, Matt, *Gizmodo,* January 30, 2016.

[4] Guests feasted on lamb chops, jumbo shrimp, beef tenderloin, vegetable dishes, fruits and cheeses and pastries

[5] Chozik, Amy, "Hillary Clinton's Speech on Women Resonates 20 Years Later," *New York Times*, September 15, 2015

[6] Guests included Phil Jamison, Jim French, and Susan and Joe Purvis from Hope. Dorothy, Hugh and Tony Rodham.

[7] Brown, Jennifer, *Olympic Flame Arrives at the White House.* AP News, June 20, 1996

[8] We shared the birthday party with Jim and Kathy French, Phil and Susan Jamison, Denise and Bob Dangremond, Kit and Amy Ashby

[9] We were met by a Clinton-Gore van to the Sheraton Chicago. Staff including Deb Schiff, Laura Wills and April Springfield Arkansans gave us a warm welcome. High school and Georgetown friends of the president as well as family and Hollywood pals came for the week.

CHAPTER NINE

Clinton Presidency Second Term 1997-2000

"You started me, and you finished me."

I was thrilled to receive an invitation to sing *Be Not Afraid* once again for the Inaugural Prayer Service at Metropolitan AME Church leading up to President Clinton's second inauguration. After the event, I received a letter of gratitude from the president, who wrote, "You started me, and you finished me." The service was beautifully planned by Harry Thomason, and during the rehearsal, I had the pleasure of meeting Jennifer Holliday from Dream Girls. We immediately hit it off and became fast friends. Unfortunately, Jennifer's luggage did not arrive in time, so I offered her some options from my own closet. She graciously accepted and even came to our home in McLean to make her selections. Although we enjoyed getting to know each other, her luggage arrived just in time for the service.

When Mickey Mangun sang at the service, the Rev. Jesse Jackson stood from his seat on the dais in an act of praise. Janice Sjostrand and her choir from Lonoke also sang for the service, as did Bebe and CeCe Winans, Jennifer Holliday, Wintley Phipps, and the Willowcreek Church choir with pastor Bill Hybels, a pastor and friend to the president. Phil Driscoll played the trumpet and sang. The Rev. Tony Campolo wove his characteristic humor through his message and had the Clintons and Gores in stitches. He also spoke about our nation and prayed for their leadership in the coming years. As I walked to the podium to sing, my heel caught in the carpet, but I quickly steadied myself. Singing *Be Not Afraid* one last time for the service was a true gift, and I was grateful for the opportunity.

The second inauguration in January 1997 was again a grand event to share with the Clintons and old friends. For the swearing-in this time, instead of standing at a distance as in 1993, friends were seated beneath the podium where the president took the oath of office. We were close enough to really experience it this time. Afterward, we met movie star Kevin Costner, who posed for photos with us. We had parade seats again in the President's Viewing Stand.[1] The Clintons joined us after they walked a few blocks in the parade to greet the public. It was magnificent to share this day with them. Later in the evening, the inaugural ball was great fun with the president's Georgetown friends of the Class of 1968, who held a ball at Coco Loco in Georgetown. One of the university priests asked me to sing *Be Not Afraid* for the group before the party got underway. We were ready to party but first prayed for a great second term and were thankful our friend had been sworn in again.

"Who in the hell is Carolyn Staley?"

I opened *Time* magazine in January 1997 to find a long article, "Presidential Pen Pals," with photos of the president's friends and how we stayed in touch with him. We were interviewed by writer Karen Tumulty but had no idea the article would be so prominent. We forgot what a power-hungry city we lived in and what access to the President of the United States meant. The article said friends had a special fax number and zip code for sending notes to the president. It noted that while most of our messages were encouraging, sometimes they brought policy issues to his attention, like organ donor policies that differed widely from city to city, as explained by Georgetown classmate David Matter, and David Leopoulos' letter that told of the difficulty transferring 401(k) savings when changing jobs.

The *Time* article mentioned my fax to the president telling him his budget for adult education was lower than Bush's and urging him to increase it. I wrote, "Recent studies show that twenty-five percent of adult Americans read and write below the fifth-grade level. That hurts employability in health care because of the inability to read doctor's orders or prescription information, the ability to help children with schoolwork and civic participation in community meetings—and even voting because of the inability to read a ballot."[2]

Proof that the fax system worked came soon. In a few days, the NIFL director got a call from the Office of Management and Budget asking, "Who in the hell is Carolyn Staley?" They had received a note from the White House saying the president wanted to increase the budget for adult education and literacy by $95 million to increase it above the Bush budget level. The adjustment required an offsetting decrease from Vocational and Adult Education, but I was grateful for his response and the funding increase to support adult learning.

I drove there to try to see him.

I faxed a message to the president after his 1997 State of the Union address to tell him it was one of his finest speeches ever, both in content and delivery. When he appealed for greater bipartisanship in Congress, he received strong applause. He also quoted the fifty-eighth chapter of Isaiah about the need to be "repairers of the breach" that had been read in his first Inaugural Prayer Service. The president was indeed building bridges and repairing the broken places in our land.

In March 1997, the president attended a golf fundraiser in Florida as Greg Norman's guest. He slipped on a step at Norman's home and tore a knee tendon. Bill was flown to Bethesda Naval Hospital in Maryland for surgery. After a couple of days, I drove there to see him, but only his immediate family could visit. We sent good wishes for a full return to health.

After a few weeks of recovery, he was able to return to work. He used crutches for several weeks before adopting a cane. Phil Jamison, Jim French, and I went to the White House to check on him, and he read aloud to us jokes he'd received from Whoopi Goldberg. Sarah and I went to a movie night with him when he was on his crutches. He was traveling to Helsinki in the coming days for NATO and to meet with Yeltsin. He felt ready to travel.

My mother visited during the president's convalescence and joined us at the White House for an event. Still using a cane, he was in good spirits but continued to feel some pain. We kept our visit short but were so happy to see him. He was always delighted to see my mother any time she visited us.

The president returned to Hope in June 1997 for the funeral of his great uncle, Henry Oren "Buddy" Grisham. The press mentioned that he was still limping slightly after his surgery. He left afterward for an address to the United Nations.

April 13, 1997, was our son Will's 16th birthday. The president sent his secretary Betty Currie by Metro to meet Will with a birthday letter and a presidential pen for his celebration. What a kind gesture! We were grateful for the president's thoughtfulness of his namesake.

The *President's Summit* was held in Philadelphia on April 27, 1997. I attended because of my involvement with Literacy AmeriCorps. The summit's goal was to respond to the challenges of at-risk youth. It led to the creation of the America's Promise Alliance. In his 1997 State of the Union address, President Clinton stated the goal of the summit: "to mobilize America's citizen power in a united effort to solve our common problems, especially those that threaten our young people." Three months later, Presidents Clinton and George H. W. Bush officially convened the Presidents' Summit for America's Future in Philadelphia. Retired Gen. Colin Powell was chairman, and four living presidents attended, with Nancy Reagan representing her husband, Ronald Reagan. More than twenty governors, nearly a hundred mayors, one hundred and forty-five community delegations, and many prominent business leaders and celebrities attended, as well.

Gen. Powell agreed to lead a three-year campaign called America's Promise: The Alliance for Youth to improve the lives of two million of the nation's fifteen million at-risk youth by 2000, the target end-date of the campaign. All the former presidents spoke at the summit, as did Vice President Al Gore. TV personality Oprah Winfrey addressed the event, and Wynton Marsalis, trumpeter, performed. It was a beautiful outdoor celebration near Independence Hall.

The final dinner gave me the opportunity to speak to former President George Bush and his wife, Barbara. Mrs. Bush created the National Institute for Literacy, where I worked. I brought her up to date on the Literacy Public Awareness campaign I was coordinating and about staff friends who worked with her in the White House literacy office. She was delighted to hear about her old friends and our work to increase public awareness about literacy. President Bush was equally gracious. It was a wonderful experience to meet them at the close of this historic gathering.

"Billy Clinton" was every mother's dream date for their daughters.

In 1997, our daughter Sarah worked at the US Department of Education in media relations and met Bill Brand of the VH-1 network, who directed a music education promotion called *Save the Music*. Sarah suggested VH-1 do a program about the president, *Bill Clinton: Rock and Roll President*. They loved the idea and asked Sarah to produce it.

During inauguration week in January 1997, Sarah videotaped interviews with presidential friends for the special. Many of our high school friends in D.C. for the inauguration were at the Old Ebbitt Grill for a reception and reunion, and Sarah had the opportunity to interview many there. Randy Goodrum reminisced about "The Three Kings" jazz trio that he, Joe Newman, and the president formed during high school. Susan Boothman, Merrilyn Mann, and Gail Martin talked about dances after football games and how "Billy Clinton" was every mother's dream date for their daughters. Mike Hardgrave, Warren Maus, and Jon Springs discussed what it meant to be drum major for the high school band as Bill Clinton was. Kenny Maschmeyer, the former soloist for the Starduster Dance Band that Bill played in, sang *My Funny Valentine*, and she and Claire Callahan talked about singing around the piano at parties. They remembered the weekly dances at the YWCA. Marty Elam Walker, Joe Newman, David Leopoulos, Nancy Martin, and band director Virgil Spurlin were interviewed. Home movies made by Bill's mother, Virginia, showed several of us with Bill in their home. She also shared pictures of Bill from grade school with David Leopoulos and Ronnie Cecil. Georgetown housemates Tom Campbell, Kit Ashby, and Jim Moore said their dinner conversations often went into the wee hours of the morning, accompanied by Ray Charles recordings on the future president's record player in the background.

To cap the VH-1 production, Sarah had a compelling interview with the president about music and the impact several artists had on him. He stressed the role music education played in his life. Sarah took several albums he gave me during high school and college to the interview. He shared memories as he looked through records by Judy Collins, Ray Charles, Nancy Wilson, Stan Getz, and Joe Cocker.

A reviewer of the documentary wrote: "The President mused, 'I still think *Eleanor Rigby* is one of the most powerful songs I've ever heard.'" The hour was not devoted simply to one genre of music. The president's love of gospel music was also examined. "To me, there's nothing more emotionally healing," he said. He called a Mahalia Jackson concert "one of the most memorable concerts I attended in my entire life."

The President pitched increased funding for school music programs, calling them "very, very important." "I think all young people should be exposed to music and the arts," Clinton said. "Everything we can do . . . to save these programs should be done." Most of the hour was taken up with reminiscences of and by the president. Old friends were interviewed and spoke glowingly about Clinton's musical interests. Old photos and home movies of Clinton, including a bit of him at a high school dance, lent visual emphasis to the documentary, which also included newer clips of the president with his saxophone, playing on "Arsenio" and "The Tonight Show starring Johnny Carson."

There were also interviews with various singers and musicians mentioned by the president, ranging from Ray Charles to Peter, Paul, and Mary, to Nancy Wilson talking about how thrilled they were to make an impression, to Judy Collins saying how honored she was that the Clintons named their daughter for *Chelsea Morning*.[3] VH-1 hosted a documentary screening at the Hay-Adams Hotel in D.C. on June 2, 1997. It aired on June third and fourth and was replayed many times. The president loved it and said he didn't realize it would be so excellent. It was a trip down memory lane for friends who loved the same music Bill did. It was also a powerful message of support for music education and the importance of access to the arts for all young people. When the credits ran, tears rolled down Sarah's cheeks. This had been a massive undertaking, and the result was spectacular. The president was happy, Sarah was glad, and Jerry and I were enormously proud of her.

One photo shows him being crowned the "most beautiful baby."

The president's boyhood home in Hope, Arkansas, was opened to the public in June 1997. The house has thirty-five hundred visitors a year from around the world. Bill spent his first four years of life there with his mother and his maternal grandparents. Items on display include his childhood books, toys, and photographs. One photo shows him being crowned the "most beautiful baby" at the Hope Watermelon Festival. The designation of his home as a National Historic Landmark has been a boon to Hope's tourism.

In September 1997, the president's school, Hot Springs High School, was designated a National Historic Landmark. Now known as the Clinton Campus, the school has been renovated as condominiums. The president and first lady attended the event, and high school friends gathered to share memories. We raised the flag again over the school, and I led the *National Anthem*. Carolyn Wilson's portrayal of our high school principal, Johnnie Mae Mackey, was epic. The president spoke, toured the building, and then had lunch in the band room with pals.

On July 17, 1997, I faxed the president a congratulatory note on his historic NATO expansion trip to Spain and Copenhagen. Europeans greeted him with cheers, waving our flag. He and his family toured Mallorca. When he returned home, he played his first eighteen holes of golf since surgery in March. I told him our family was traveling to Cancun, Mexico, to tour Chichen Itza and the Yucatan and relax during his diplomatic visit.

Each year, the president wrote a proclamation for National Literacy Day. In November 1997, he invited the National Institute for Literacy board members to the Oval Office for the proclamation signing. He also recorded an outstanding radio address underscoring support for adult education and literacy programs. He urged all adults without a high school diploma or lacking literacy skills to enroll in classes. I appreciated the president's television message for the national literacy public awareness campaign I was leading, *Literacy: It's a Whole New World*. The campaign provided literacy programs with television and print ads to promote literacy programs. Leading the campaign was one of the highlights of my work at the agency.

A business card pushed under the door from a Kenneth Starr attorney.

On October 28, 1997, Chinese President Jiang Zemin came to D.C. for the first state visit of a Chinese leader in twelve years. Hopes were high that there might be a nuclear agreement as well as an agreement to address China's air pollution from coal-fired power plants. Progress on economic understanding was a breakthrough of the meeting.

Dissidents were highly visible during China's visit, calling attention to human rights violations in their homeland. Many Chinese in exile in the U.S. had been exercising the right of free expression taken from them eight years earlier when Jiang's government violently suppressed the student-led demonstrations at Tiananmen Square in Beijing in 1989.

As we approached the White House for the state arrival ceremony, we were met by large groups holding "Free Tibet" signs. Hundreds of protestors swarmed sidewalks, streets, and Lafayette Park. Jerry and Will photographed them. The protesters staged a "stateless dinner" with activist Richard Gere that evening. Because free speech, human rights, and religious freedom are core American values, U.S. officials didn't curb the protests. Organizers said the protests were the largest in decades directed at a visiting foreign leader.

President Clinton and President Jiang Zemin set up an around-the-clock phone connection to strengthen their relationship. At the meeting's close, President Clinton said, "As we look ahead, the United States welcomes China's emergence as a full and constructive partner in the community of nations, a great nation that joins its strength and influence to our own to advance peace and prosperity, freedom and security."

In January 1998, I arrived home and found a business card pushed under the door by a Kenneth Starr attorney asking me to call. I couldn't believe they showed up at the door, but this was their confrontational approach. I called back just to get it out of the way. The attorney started listing women's names and asked if I knew them and whether Clinton had a relationship with them. I didn't have any information to share. Then he asked if I had ever been involved with him. Outraged, I told him that I was highly offended. He said he understood and was sorry he had to ask. This brief encounter with the Starr team gave me a clear sense of what it must be like for the president and others who were being grilled.

Later, I was interviewed by a lawyer for the Paula Jones team who wanted to know if I "traded favors for my job or could I see a pattern of how women who work for Clinton got jobs through favors." I participated as long as I could stand it— to take notes and know what they were asking. It was truly sickening but revealed their tactics of intimidation.

In January 1998, Jerry and I attended the swearing-in of our friend and the president's Georgetown roommate, Kit Ashby, as U.S. Ambassador to Uruguay. Kit and his wife Amy were a marvelous choice to lead U.S.-Uruguayan diplomatic relations and a credit to the administration. We lunched afterward in the Indian Treaty Room. Kit and Amy have been steadfast friends. Friendship with the president has also led to close ties with his friends.

He said he kept his distance to protect us.

January 17, 1998, was the day of the president's deposition with the Starr team. It lasted nearly eight hours. We knew he was under immense pressure and felt the process was unfair. Feeling helpless, we prayed for his strength and wisdom—and for the family through it all.

In April 1998, the president and Hillary led a delegation of private citizens and bipartisan Congressional members to Africa for visits to Ghana, Uganda, Rwanda, South Africa, Botswana, and Senegal. It was the most expansive trip ever by an American president, and a major success. I wrote to him about how thrilling it was to see him amid the reactions of the people. The Secret Service had grave concerns about the visit to Rwanda after the ethnic cleansing in 1994 and criticism that the U.S. had not done enough to curb genocide. The president visited with families directly affected and heard their stories. He vowed to do all he could to support the war crimes tribunal. Later, in South Africa, the Clintons visited Robben Island, where Nelson Mandela was a prisoner for eighteen years.

April 1998 was also a time of elation for the president. On April tenth, all parties in Northern Ireland agreed to support a plan, *The Good Friday Accord*, to end more than thirty years of sectarian violence there. The president, himself of Irish descent, worked with leaders through the night to reach the agreement. He credited them for choosing the path of peace. This enormous breakthrough gave the president great joy. Again, he was living his hope to be a bridge-builder.

We attended the arrival of the Italian Prime Minister on May 6, 1998, and faxed the president beforehand to say we hoped to see him. We hadn't visited since Christmas due to the Starr investigation. We exchanged smiles and hellos from a distance, but no visit was possible. He knew his friends were pulling for him. He said he kept his distance to protect us.

Later in the evening, I watched *Hardball* and was relieved I had turned down a request to be interviewed for the program. Host Chris Matthews unleashed a bombastic Clinton-bashing tirade. When I heard author David Maraniss was to be a guest, I declined. Later, I was thankful I had done so.

We continued to despair about the Starr investigation. Starr was determined to limit the president's executive privilege and would not disclose whether Bill would be called to testify before his lawyers. I often saw Starr's wife, Alice, in the grocery store. Each time, I walked the other way. She was a high-profile civic leader in McLean and active with the Chamber of Commerce. Our family just prayed for the president and hoped for this to end well and soon.

In June 1998, we were invited to the White House for the taping of a PBS special, *In Performance at the White House: An Evening of Gospel Music*. Our friends Mickey Mangun and the choir from the Pentecostals of Alexandria, Louisiana, were performing with trumpeter Phil Driscoll. Gospel recording artists Bebe and CeCe Winans were emcees, and the Morgan State University Choir sang. Janice and Keith Sjostrand and singer Wintley Phipps and his wife sat at the table with Mary and me. The taping was inside the enormous tent used earlier in the day for the arrival ceremony of Kim Dae-Jung, President of South Korea, which I attended. It was also used for that week's thirtieth reunion of the Georgetown University class of 1968. Happy events were taking place at the White House. We hoped they filled the president with joy and were a distraction from the Starr tribunal.

At the PBS taping, Mary and I enjoyed visiting with Mickey and Anthony Mangun and Phil and Lynn Driscoll. Mickey sang powerfully. Phil began playing the shofar, then moved to trumpet for *You Got to Serve Somebody*. The Morgan State University Choir sang *Ain't Got Time to Die*, and the program ended with all artists singing *Amazing Grace*. After the taping, Mary and I chatted with the president for the first time since Christmas. He was happy to be reunited and congratulated Mary on graduating from George Mason University in May. We told him that Will appreciated his letter about his selection to Virginia Boys State. Janice had an encouraging chat with the first lady. The evening of powerful music was a gift to the president and first lady and lifted everyone's spirits after such gloomy weeks.

Tension filled the room because of his impending grand jury testimony.

Our family was on vacation at the Outer Banks in Duck, North Carolina, in August 1998 when we learned the president had volunteered to testify before Starr's grand jury. His August seventeenth testimony was videotaped in the White House map room with only the president's attorneys and Starr's team present. CNN gave regular updates, and I traipsed to a local store every morning for a newspaper. The president's planned testimony was little known, and we were concerned for him. On Friday, the *New York Times* reported he would change his story to admit to an improper relationship with an intern, say it was wrong, and that his testimony might differ from his January denial. Hillary had strongly denied any wrongdoing, and there was concern that she would feel betrayed.

The president felt pressure to confront al Qaeda as national security indicated Osama bin Ladin was planning an attack on the U.S. embassy in Albania. The president assured leaders that he would do whatever was necessary. There was so much on his shoulders.

Prior to the president's grand jury testimony, the White House staff hosted a birthday party for him. My daughter, Sarah, and I attended the party in the East Room with staff and Cabinet members. Tension filled the room because of the impending grand jury testimony. John Podesta tried to boost spirits with humorous remarks. He presented a symbolic birthday gift check to the president from his staff. The president thanked everyone and said, "I hope you will always tell people what you've worked for." Sarah and I visited with him. He said Pentecostal pastor and friend Anthony Mangun had been there and promised to pray all night for him. I took some banana bread as a gift, and we shared hugs. We visited briefly with Hillary and told her we loved her.

Every day, I faxed a note to the president and sent some small gift—a rustic apple pie, a book to encourage, or some possible scenarios for his testimony. He said it meant a great deal to him; he had read my note often and would continue to do so in the days ahead. I just told him to be truthful and trust God to guide his thoughts and words.

August 17, a Monday, was testimony day. I awoke at 6:30 a.m., praying. Still in North Carolina, I walked along the beach to quiet my mind. We followed all the news possible. I tried to reach David Leopoulos. His wife Linda said he appeared on the television program *Extra* the night before to talk about Bill. He wanted to get friends together for a TV roundtable, and I agreed to help.

Friends started calling us at the beach, and a steady stream of calls continued all day. The day was heavy with anxiety; we needed to be in touch with each other. Phil Driscoll called to say he'd gotten through to the president the night before. David Leopoulos called with news of the *Extra* TV interview. Phil Jamison spoke with the president and shared Isaiah 57:15, which says, "For this is what the high and exalted One says— he who lives forever, whose name is holy: 'I live in a high and holy place, but also with the one who is contrite and lowly in spirit, to revive the spirit of the lowly and to revive the heart of the contrite.'" Phil hoped the president would be humble, repentant, and trust God totally. The president told Phil it meant so much. He said the prayers of his friends and their letters had strengthened him during this time.

I found it amazing that most of our friends shared scripture and prayer with the president. That might have been expected from me as a preacher's kid but not from most other old friends. In my darkest moments, I have always found that little is more uplifting than a spiritual word of support. I was happy our friends felt the same way. Few of us had ever prayed together or shared Bible verses, but now we were all counseling and supporting.

Jim French called me and suggested that we pray together for the president. Rabbi Joe Edelheit asked him to read Numbers chapters 13 and 14 about Moses and to resist the temptation to strike the rock in the desert twice angrily. Anthony counseled him not to repeat King David's mistake of taking a census and mustering his army when God told him not to. Jesse Jackson shared Psalm 51:10 about David's prayer after he was confronted about his relationship with Bathsheba, "Create in me a clean heart, O God, and renew a right spirit within me."

At 10 p.m., we watched Bill's speech. CNN showed a stopwatch with seconds passing as the president testified. After being advised it was "too dramatic" and in poor taste, CNN took the clock down later. When the president began to speak, I thought he looked pale and stiff, his eyes weak. He was like a scared, trapped animal. He wasn't himself. We all felt he had been entrapped, and the Starr inquiry was purely a political game. While he is a master competitor, he knew from the outset that no answer he gave would end this. No strategy could save him. I hoped he would come across as warm, penitent, and honorable. He appeared deeply angry, as he had every right to be. We were told he had written his own speech, but that David Kendall and Hillary thought it didn't express enough outrage. In his speech, Bill implored, "This all must stop so we can get back to the important work of our country." I wrote to him that he'd done an excellent job, entirely credible and personally touching.

On Tuesday, August eighteenth, the Clinton family left for Martha's Vineyard. All who saw the images of the Clintons walking across the White House lawn to the helicopter—with Chelsea between them holding hands—were touched to see how Chelsea was the glue that held the family together at this difficult time. Hillary has since said that staying with Bill was a personal choice and, while not right for everyone, she loved him and wanted their marriage to work. No doubt, Chelsea encouraged and helped their reconciliation. Bill told friends he was relegated to sleeping on the sofa for a while.

The Clintons were met at Martha's Vineyard by friends Carly Simon and Vernon Jordan. We learned that the intern, Ms. Lewinsky, had been called again by the grand jury. On his birthday, August 19th, the president had dinner at Vernon Jordan's home. He was photographed walking on the beach with his dog, Buddy. The next day, the president ordered a missile strike on Osama bin Laden's campsites in Afghanistan and Sudan. As expected, many questioned the timing of the strikes. Thursday, he traveled to the White House for briefings with the State Department, then returned to Martha's Vineyard. What a week it had been.

Congressional reaction to the president's testimony and the strikes on bin Laden was swift. Senator Orin Hatch initially called for the president's resignation, but after the missile strikes, he was complimentary. It was whiplash. Bill told Jim and Phil at his birthday party earlier in the week that he thought his vacation might be interrupted by Russia's possible economic collapse, plus problems in Africa. We knew bin Laden was also planning more terrorism. We wondered how the president could possibly have a relaxed vacation.

On August 26, Anthony Mangun called to say he'd spoken with the president to tell him to remember that he had asked for and received forgiveness from God. I sent a note saying that "as far as the east is from the west" and "70 x 7," as scripture says, you are forgiven. (Jesus said to him, "I do not say to you, up to seven times, but up to seventy times seven" (Matthew 18:22). Anthony told the president that fifty of his church members had stayed all night at church to pray for him before his testimony. From six to eight p.m., five hundred gathered in the church to pray.

On August 28, we watched the president speak at Union Chapel in Oaks Bluff, Massachusetts. Finally, we saw the man we knew. He was animated, comfortable, genuine, and eloquent. He was attending an observance of the 25th anniversary of Martin L. King's "I Have a Dream" speech and was joined by Congressman John Lewis. Lewis embraced the president, called him his brother, and said that he had been with him when he was up and would stick with him when he was down. It was a healing balm for the president's spirits.

Starr's 450-page report and thirty-five boxes of materials were delivered to the House of Representatives at 3:00 p.m. on September 9, 1998. His spokesperson said the report contained evidence that could lead to impeachment. White House lawyer David Kendall said that there was no impeachable evidence.

The president attended a Democratic campaign event in Florida and commented again on how sorry he was for all the nation has been through. He said he had just met a boy who reminded him of himself as a youngster and told him he wanted to be president someday. Bill said he hoped to restore the office to one parents would like their children to hold. He looked sad as he spoke but was strong, holding on. It was hard to know how to be a friend at this time, but we hoped he felt our support.

On September 11, the president spoke at a Prayer Breakfast at the White House. "I have sinned," he said, adding that repentance, a contrite spirit, and a renunciation of pride and anger were areas he was working on in his life. He thanked them for their prayers and said he intended to continue to work hard to lead our country and world toward peace and freedom. He quoted from the Yom Kippur service about the need to turn and repent. "Now is the time for turning." The group responded with tears and "Amens." It was a sincere outpouring from the president's heart and the faith leaders present.

Later that day, the Starr report was posted to the internet. I read parts of it and felt disgusted by what I saw as Starr's emotional manipulation and shrewd legal maneuvering. It was draining to read and more so for the president to have lived through.

I wrote a sermon, "A Faith Response for Our Time," and sent the president a copy. The following Sunday, I sang *Lead the Way* by Ken Medema about how impossible it is for any of us to be the kind of person we want to be, so we can only rely on God to lead the way. I saw tears on many faces. Friends expressed support for the president and said they were praying for him. They knew that this was a difficult time for our friendship.

Several rabbi friends sent sermons for Rosh Hashanah, just a few days away. All planned to preach about morality and how recent events had challenged our hearts and spirits. My friend, Rabbi Joseph Edelheit, reminded his Minnesota congregation that Rosh Hashanah is a celebration of hope and an expression of faith in the future. Once we celebrate this, we can better deal with our past failings, saying, "Hope is fundamental for finding the strength to face our failures." Friend and Rabbi Gene Levy of Temple B'nai Israel, Little Rock, sent a prayer he would use and wrote a powerful article for the national Jewish press.

Efforts to embarrass the president continued. During a family birthday dinner for Jerry on September 14, 1998, our daughter Mary took a call from the *London Daily Mail* asking her to look at a photo they'd just faxed to see if it showed her jogging with the president in August 1993. Mary said she'd never jogged with the president, and the photo wasn't of her. The reporter pressed her, and Mary insisted, "It's not me!" The media had a voracious appetite for new female links to the president. Mary set the reporter straight, but we were sorry she got badgered.

On September 18, 1998, the Judiciary Committee voted along party lines to release the president's videotaped grand jury testimony. The White House argued that the release was meant strictly to embarrass the president. The discussion of possible presidential censure now had moved toward impeachment, and some were demanding his resignation.

I sent the president a draft speech he might give asking the American people to join him on a journey to higher moral ground as a nation, to "do justice, love mercy, and walk humbly with God" (Micah 6:8). I told him that I saw renewed peace and confidence in his face at the state arrival ceremony for Czech President Vaclav Havel.

I taped interviews for the television programs *Extra* and *Dateline NBC* to support the president and share my respect for him. A reporter asked if I was aware of any abuse the president experienced as a youngster, and I said I had never heard the slightest suggestion of such. He wondered if he had grown up without having a childhood and was forced into adulthood too soon or if he had a dysfunctional home. I said that, as his neighbor, I never saw that. One reporter wondered about reports of spousal abuse, arguing, and fighting, and I had no knowledge of such. The media was working every angle, and I tried to validate our friendship since age fifteen truthfully.

On Monday, September 22, 1998, the president's four-hour grand jury testimony was played on all major networks and streamed online. The release of secret testimony was unprecedented, and there were strong overtones of partisanship as impeachment chatter increased. The Judiciary Committee didn't respond except to release the president's sworn, secret testimony. It had all been terribly disappointing and was clearly aimed at defeating the president. The public largely continued to stand by him, which was heartwarming. People saw his love for others, his desire to make life better for all of us, and his commitment to do all he could to that end. His centrist politics and popularity with voters enraged his foes. We just had to hold on and stand firm.

The president's testimony was outstanding. He was calm and poised, eloquent and respectful. Aside from the few times he was provoked, he kept his cool. His brief moments of anger were justified, anyone would argue. The lawyers were, in my view, ruthless. In his opening statement, he said he had made an error in judgment, that he was sorry, and took full responsibility. But that didn't stop the hammering barrage of humiliating questions they had prepared to ask.

I was relieved when this chapter was over. The president's poll numbers went up. He spoke at the United Nations the day after the testimony aired and received a standing ovation in an amazingly strong show of support and respect from world leaders. It was as if the entire world was standing with the president. It made the Republican congressional members appear mean and hard-hearted, with a desire only to undo the election. It wasn't going to happen, and they knew it.

"Fire Ken Starr. Do it tonight!"

October 8, 1998, was a somber day. The U.S. House of Representatives voted to impeach the president. What started as an investigation into the Clintons' failed investment in the Whitewater land development in Arkansas resulted in a "fishing expedition" for anything potentially unsavory they could find about the Clintons. Staff and campaign volunteers were subpoenaed, and their attorney bills were devastating. I sent a steady stream of faxes to the president to encourage him and made suggestions like "Fire Ken Starr. Do it tonight!" Other messages were more realistic. I sent him copies of letters that friends sent me to support him.

On Sunday, I sang in worship at McLean Baptist Church. So many were hurting for our president and our nation. Many in the congregation wept openly. God's presence felt near, and many commented on the song. Jerry Harvey told me I was "on fire." Bill Lowe, who was at the president's inaugural prayer service, said he didn't want the song to end. A woman told me she cried throughout; another said she'd never heard a more beautiful message. I hoped to bring some healing as people were weary and hoping for the best. The president's approval rating remained high, and we hoped for a good outcome. We didn't talk to him because he told us we might be subpoenaed if he spoke with us. He knew we were standing with him through it all.

Life moved on, and we celebrated many events with the president. One of the most outstanding was on October 24, 1998, when Benjamin Netanyahu of Israel and Yasser Arafat of Palestine signed a new Middle East Peace Accord. President Clinton and King Hussein of Jordan stood with them, looking on. The signing was a diplomatic victory for the president and a highlight in his presidency overall. The world watched in awe as the accord was signed. The hope and pride the president felt were etched on his face. He had worked hard to bring this about. I wrote to congratulate him and said that Shabbat services around the world that evening would celebrate this achievement for shalom and peace.

In October 1998, the adult education and literacy field celebrated a twenty-million-dollar funding increase for state programs. The Reading Excellence Act was also announced. The National Economic Council was working with our agency on a new policy for basic education for America's families. It would acknowledge the need for better screening for learning disabilities and address the impact of poor literacy on Hispanic and Non-native English speakers. It predicted workplace productivity would increase with better skills, and healthcare costs could decrease as Americans could better understand doctors' instructions and prescriptions. Civic participation would increase as voters understood ballot initiatives and felt confident of their voice in the community. We were elated at this major progress.

The Starr investigation had settled down a bit. We awaited the midterm elections on November 3, hoping Democrats might win more congressional seats. Many viewed the election as a referendum on the presidency. In the end, while the GOP held control of the House, Democrats made gains, and the outlook was brighter. Overall, voters did not support candidates who pushed for impeachment.

The president made impressive progress in his second term. Public opinion generally held that he didn't deserve impeachment. Voters appreciated his determination to keep working for the American people, and the president was grateful for the significant gains Democrats made despite the distractions. Weeks later, Newt Gingrich announced his resignation as Speaker of the House. David Leopoulos and the president's friends cheered the news. I congratulated the president and said the election victories were a vote of confidence in him.

A shocking event came on December 17, 1998, when Congressman Robert Livingston of Louisiana, speaker-designate of the House, resigned at the impeachment hearings, admitting to an extramarital affair. Just a few days earlier, he had called on the president to resign and was one of Clinton's most outspoken critics. The *Washington Post* reported, "In a year of bizarre political turmoil, the spectacle of a speaker-designate resigning on the same day the House voted to impeach the president over alleged lies in sworn testimony about sex with an intern left even the most seasoned veterans gasping and shaken."[4] It seemed the fiercest critics often had issues of their own. I attended church with Livingston's chief of staff. We never talked about this and maintained a friendly civility. He was a native Kentuckian, as am I, and he and his wife invited me to play the piano for their annual Kentucky Derby party. We just knew where to draw the line in political discussions.

On December 19, 1998, the U.S. House of Representatives voted to impeach the president. The Senate believed the trial would end in acquittal on February 12, Lincoln's birthday. The Senate trial began, and the House managers presented their case for three days. The White House attorneys followed with three days of arguments.

The president's *State of the Union* address on January 19, 1999, was powerful and uplifting. The Starr investigation still swirled, but Bill kept his focus on the good that was happening and his administration's accomplishments. Bill was inspiring. He remained calm, positive, and strong.

"This is a case of wanting to win too badly."

I attended the last day of the Senate impeachment trial on January 21, 1999. At 8:00 a.m., I decided I wanted to go, so I called Betty Currie, the president's secretary, and asked if I could attend as a show of support, although I knew the president wouldn't be there. She called the senate office for a ticket. Upon arrival at the Capitol, Senate staff led me to the gallery. The bright yellow ticket read, "The Impeachment Trial of President Clinton." I sat in the VIP gallery with a few other Clinton supporters. Whoopi Goldberg was there with security. My seat directly faced the speaker. Strict rules included no standing at recess and no note-taking. I sat with Arkansas Senator Blanche Lambert's cousin, David, who worked at the New York Stock Exchange. When Senator Pryor's son, Dee, came to say hello at recess, I borrowed his pen to send

Whoopi a note that read, "Thanks for the jokes you sent the president when he broke his tendon. He read them to friends." She flashed a big smile.

I witnessed Dale Bumpers, a beloved and respected former Senator from Arkansas, make his eloquent closing statement at the trial. He spoke as the president's friend and why he opposed the whole, sordid process. "Why are we here?" he asked. "This is a case of wanting to win too badly. Every trial lawyer knows that feeling." Bumpers spoke calmly and clearly. He chastised the House managers for being insensitive to the Clintons.

It was spellbinding to be seated in the front row in the Senate chamber with a commanding view. I witnessed this moment of history in the life of my friend and our nation, and it felt bizarre. I had tears in my eyes as Bumpers spoke. He remembered his trip to Little Rock for induction into the Marine Corps. He said he knew something about what a person fights for—not necessarily "the rule of law," which Rep. Henry Hyde said the men and women in Flanders Field had fought for but for love. David Kendall, Clinton's lawyer, refuted the impeachment managers' testimony. His remarks to the committee were superb, as were those by lawyers Greg Craig and Cheryl Mills. The trial was recessed at 5:00 p.m.

Seated across from me in the press gallery was a familiar face, *Wall Street Journal* reporter Jeanne Cummings. She had interviewed me, and I respected her. She called later to say she saw me there and wanted to write an article about my friendship with the president and why I attended the proceedings. I agreed to speak with her about what watching a friend go through impeachment meant. She wrote the article and said the editors liked it, and it would run on the front page on January 28, 1999. She sent an artist to take my picture for a pixilated illustration.[5]

I could hardly sleep worrying about the article, but I knew Jeanne was fair. I got up early to buy a copy. Reading Jean's story, my faith in her fairness was affirmed. It was positive. Jeanne also quoted old friends Jim French and Skip Rutherford.

Calls began to pour in. Jan Piercy, a close friend of Hillary's working at the World Bank, called first to say the article was a coup because the *Wall Street Journal* was not supportive of the president during the Starr investigation. Many friends called, and I had emails and letters from people I didn't know. TV personality Diane Sawyer's staff asked me to be on *Good Morning America*.

I checked with White House political advisor Doug Sosnik, who discouraged it because of potential editing tricks. He suggested I wait until after the trial to do the interview.

The Senate announced it would hear witnesses Vernon Jordan and Sidney Blumenthal on January 31, 1999. We hoped they would give balance to the house's hearings. Starr admitted in his testimony that he had found no wrongdoing by the president in his investigations into the travel office and FBI files. He also admitted talking to the press, which was against grand jury rules. I hoped this would stoke as much outrage in the Senate as it did with the public.

Friends went to the White House after the impeachment vote for a rally for the president. The president and first lady greeted us on the White House lawn. They were obviously in a great deal of pain. He thanked friends for their support, adding that the experience had been extremely difficult for their family.

February 1, 1999, Joe Newman came to D.C, and we had lunch with *US News and World Report* reporter Ken Walsh at the Oval Room in my office building across from the White House. A White House intern came across the street to tell us the president wanted to see us after lunch. Ken was amazed and said in all his years of White House reporting, he had never witnessed anything like that. I told him Joe's friendship was special, and his D.C. trips were rare. Joe and I enjoyed time with the president as we laughed, shared jokes, and caught up on the news. Joe and I knew the president had lived through a nightmare. It meant a lot to be together and for him to feel our unconditional support and love.

David lifted his finger bowl for a sip.

On February 12, 1999, the Senate voted to acquit the president on both articles of impeachment, allowing Bill to remain in office. We were relieved and grateful. The president went to the Rose Garden to speak to the American people. He asked us "to rededicate ourselves to the work of serving our nation and building our future together. This can be, and this must be, a time of reconciliation and renewal for America," he said. We breathed a sigh of relief on this warm winter day, thankful that the president would continue to serve his term.

On April 28, 1999, the president invited a group of old high school friends, including Jim French, Phil Jamison, and David Leopoulos, for lunch at the White House in the family dining room. It was our first visit to this area, a room rarely seen by the public. David lifted his finger bowl for a sip but noticed the president dip his fingers in the bowl and quickly set it down, and we laughed. He was always great comic relief and appreciated the president's quick lesson in table etiquette. The elementary school buddies who walked to the Polar Bar in Hot Springs after school hadn't used finger bowls there.

The situation in the Balkans was very tense, and the president was feeling the stress. After years of ethnic cleansing by Serb forces, a war had broken out in 1998 in Serbia's province of Kosovo between ethnic Albanian rebels seeking independence and Serbia's armed forces. The fighting ended in 1999 after an 11-week NATO bombing campaign. In June, a peace accord was announced in Kosovo.

On June 21, 1999, our son Will graduated from Langley High School in a ceremony held at the Kennedy Center. The White House invited our family to sit in the president's box. As Student Government Senior Representative, Will was on stage to make presentations and shake hands with graduates. Will had successfully invited Federal Emergency Management Agency Director James Lee Witt to give the commencement address. Will also played guitar for a classmate's vocal solo. We were very proud of him.

In June 1999, Will appeared with the president and first lady on *Good Morning America* with students to discuss gun violence. As Langley High School senior class representative, he developed a program called SAVE: "Students/Schools Against Violence in Education" and got approval from the Student Government Association. Its goals were that every student would pledge to live nonviolently and respect others as equals, a confidential hotline number would be established for students to alert counselors and teachers about suspicious behavior, and the school would plan assembly programs about respect for cultural differences and anger management. The president and first lady shared the program and expressed pride in Will's leadership.

The president toured the U.S. Delta region to promote business investment in July 1999. Andrew M. Cuomo, Secretary of Housing and Urban Development, said, "Now is the time for the Government to tap those markets." He said the president waited to make a significant push for inner-city and rural economic development until he had the political clout to pull it off. Also, the electronic revolution had changed the nature of business, making it possible to conduct commerce remotely from anywhere globally. "He couldn't have done this six or seven years ago," Cuomo said. "He has the economy at his back, he has credibility in his government, and business is more mobile. These high-tech guys can go anywhere." The president had the Delta's needs at heart and was eager to help the region.

In October 1999, our Hot Springs High School class of 1964 went to the White House to celebrate our 35th reunion. Phil Jamison, class president, worked with White House staff for dinner and an extravagant cake by White House pastry chef Roland Mesnier. Nearly 100 classmates purchased dinner tickets to celebrate with our classmate, President Bill Clinton. We had held an earlier reunion in Hot Springs in August, but being at the White House was a highlight. Five years earlier, we had our thirtieth reunion at the White House and knew a second visit would be a thrilling opportunity to celebrate the president's second term.

The president traveled to Greece, Turkey, and Kosovo in November 1999. He was only the third U.S. president to visit Greece. U.S. relations had been tense in the region, and rioting threatened to hamper the president's visit. The president talked about our responsibility to Greece and said, "We are all Greeks." He talked about his childhood friend David Leopoulos, who sent him emails about Greece each week. The speech was an enormous success, as tensions with Turkey eased and the country changed its constitution. Serbian President Milosevic was brought to justice with help from Greek diplomats. Greece played a pivotal role in aiding Kosovo civilians. The Clinton family joined Madeline Albright and General Wes Clark for Thanksgiving dinner with U.S. troops in Kosovo. Clinton thanked all who had worked for peace. And, of course, our high school friend, David "the Greek," felt elated.

At work, I was busy organizing the National Literacy Summit 2000. The goal was to adopt a set of benchmarks for adult learning in the new millennium and ensure that adult literacy education remained a priority for the president and Congress. The summit coincided with the release of national literacy goals for the new millennium, building on the work of the *State of Literacy in America* report released earlier. We distributed the report to Congress, governors, mayors, and federal agencies. The report included a map of every state with percentages of literacy in each county as reported in U.S. census data. The high percentage of adults reading below fifth-grade level was discouraging. The National Institute for Literacy hoped to urge attention and increased funding.

A regional literacy summit led by Congressman Tom Sawyer of Ohio in December 1999 was held at Kent State University. It was my first visit to the campus, and I walked the sidewalk where students protesting U.S. involvement in Vietnam were shot on May 4, 1970. To quell riots, the National Guard was called and opened fire on a crowd of protestors. Four students were killed, and nine were injured. It remains a painful memory in our nation's history.

The culminating National Literacy Summit 2000 produced excellent recommendations for states, communities, and national leadership. The president increased funding for adult education to its highest level, with an increase of $100 million over 1999 funding levels. It was a proud moment as the president made clear he understood our nation's literacy crisis.

In December 1999, our family enjoyed the family White House Christmas party and visited with old friends from Arkansas and Georgetown. We had an historic family picture taken with the Clintons. Mary was engaged to be married, and the president lifted her hand for the photo to display her engagement ring. It was fun for him to celebrate with us. It had been a difficult two years, and it was finally time for some joy. We hoped the painful days were over because there was much work remaining for Clinton's presidency. We were eager to see it through. We looked forward to a wonderful wedding, too!

The President reached out to Will and pulled him towards the stage with Bono.

January 2000 was a remarkable time for the world and the dawn of the new millennium. Having our friend as president compounded our joy as the world welcomed the year 2000. Jerry was in London doing photography and unable to attend the White House celebration, so I invited friend Martha Child, Jerry's photography employer, and our son Will invited friend Chris Grindler.

The White House Millennium Gala was spectacular. Our seats were center stage at the Lincoln Memorial, with the reflecting pool behind us. Actor Will Smith was emcee. Performers included Kenny Rogers, Tom Jones, and opera singers Renee Fleming, Kathleen Battle, and Jesse Norman. Producer Quincy Jones presented a musical montage from opera to rock and roll that also included dance, readings, and video tributes. The mall was teeming with people. The gala ended with a fireworks display that showed the sun rising on a new millennium. It was like nothing ever seen before. The night was also extremely cold, but we were thrilled to have this historic experience as our world turned 2000. Thinking the fireworks were over, Martha and I left to catch the trolley back to the White House to beat the crowd and get warm, but Will and Chris stayed. As we reached the White House for the New Year's Ball and dinner buffet, we heard a thunderous noise. We realized it was the fireworks finale. We were able to see the display from a distance and happy the guys were there to witness it.

The Marine Corps orchestra played for dancing in the East Room, and a resplendent dinner worthy of a millennium year awaited in the State Dining Room.[6] Will and Chris joined us at 2:00 a.m. after the fireworks. Our car pickup was set for 3:30 AM, but we had time to visit with the president, which was extra special for Martha, who hadn't met him.

The president and Chelsea walked to the East Room for a dance, and we followed. Will called out to get the president's attention, and the president reached out and pulled him and Chris to the stage. Meeting the president was momentous for Chris, who said it was the highlight of his life. The guys met Bono and had pictures made. The president's thoughtful gesture made the evening unforgettable.

Will and Chris stayed until the end of the party and took a taxi home. Guests received a gift bag as they left the White House with a medallion of President Clinton and John Adams (1800-01) and William McKinley (1900-01), who were presidents at past millennia changes. Will and Chris were home at 6:30 a.m. We watched the television reports of the millennium's arrival first in Australia and New Zealand. Tears filled our eyes as a chorus sang the *Hallelujah Chorus* from Handel's *Messiah.* We had lived the millennial moment in history to the fullest. I was sorry our family couldn't be together. Jerry was in London, Sarah was in California, and Mary was in Kansas City, but all seemed right with the world.

The much-anticipated "Y2K Bug," which was predicted to disrupt computer systems, didn't happen. There were a few blips, but thanks to careful national planning, nothing happened on the scale feared. While it would be a year before we officially entered the 21st century, we were grateful for our president's leadership to see us safely across the transition to the year 2000.

He was mowing the lawn, trimming the hedges, and chasing the First Lady's limo.

In January 2000, we attended President Clinton's final *State of the Union* address and White House reception. It was thrilling to hear the president's address and cheer him on at this moment in our history. It was his best address to Congress, and it would be his last. He had just one year remaining in office to complete the tasks ahead, and we sensed it would be memorable.

The president's weekly Oval Office radio addresses were always a special opportunity to see him. These were generally on Saturday mornings, with groups of ten to twelve present. Guests sat on the sofa or stood behind it, and the president entered and sat at his desk for his address. Afterward, the president greeted everyone, and a photographer took pictures. The president took time to visit with everyone. He was genuinely happy to hear guests' stories, what they were celebrating, where they lived, and all about the children with them. He liked having an audience for the address. Being with "regular" people invigorated him.

In April 2000, we attended two radio addresses. On April 7, I took my cousins from Philadelphia, Kathy and David Broll, and children, Steven and Kelsey, to the address. On April twenty-eighth, Bob and Leslie Barry, friends from McLean Baptist Church, and their children Bobby and Krista attended. The president was in rare form both times, and they were amazed by the time he spent with them. Being a gregarious person, the president found the White House confining.

The president held a fascinating press conference in February 2000 as the last year of his presidency began. The press praised his candor and good humor. He underscored the important work still to be done as outlined in the *State of the Union* just weeks prior. The president had strong words of support for Al Gore in his anticipated race for president. Hillary had recently decided to enter the race for U.S. Senator from New York to fill the seat of Sen. Moynihan and wanted to remain active in politics. The president predicted she would do well in her race. He was comfortable chatting with the press in a way that reminded me of our living room conversations when he was home from college.

We also enjoyed a screening of the movie *The Height of the Sky*, directed by Lyn Clinton, and thought it was a beautiful depiction of the rural South. It reminded us of the power of Dorothea Lange's depression-era photos for the Farm Security Administration of the poor in America.

The annual White House Correspondents' Dinner 2000 in the president's last year was great fun. The highlight was a video that the *Washington Post* called "a triumph," portraying the president coping with boredom as a lame-duck. He was shown mowing the White House lawn, trimming the hedges, doing laundry, and chasing the first lady's limo with a lunch sack in hand. He was shown answering calls at the White House call center and washing the Secret Service presidential limo. The scenes didn't surprise me because I'd seen him wash the family car and mow the lawn when we were neighbors. I also watched him fold the family's laundry and celebrate when all the socks matched. Jay Leno was the guest host; critics called it the funniest correspondents' dinner in history. The president closed by saying, "I've had a wonderful time. It's been an honor to serve and fun to laugh. I only wish we had laughed even more in the last eight years." With the impeachment behind him, it was a poignant time, and we could all breathe.

On June 26, we got the sad news that Diane Blair, a dear friend of the president from their years in Fayetteville, died after a long struggle with cancer. The Clintons visited her as her health failed. She taught law at the University of Arkansas with the Clintons, and she and her husband Jim were at Clinton's wedding. She was an important Clinton historian, and her papers are a valuable part of the Clinton archives. Her friendship was uniquely special in their lives. Her work continues to live for all who research the Clintons and Arkansas politics.

Our family was invited to the White House to enjoy the 4th of July, 2000 celebration. We took Corrie White, the daughter of our former pastor, with us. She lived in our home while interning at the U.S. State Department. We visited with the Clintons at the diplomatic reception and knew our time with them in the White House was drawing to a close. They had generously given us so many historic opportunities.

On July 5, 2000, President Clinton invited Prime Minister Ehud Barak and Palestinian Authority Chairman Yasser Arafat to Camp David to continue negotiations for Middle East peace. On July 11, the Camp David 2000 Summit convened. The president had high hopes for the outcome and told me later he felt optimistic. Israel was ready to make concessions on Jerusalem's boundary lines, which had been a sticking point. No official proposal was adopted, but enormous progress was made. The president told me after he left office how disappointed he was that President Bush was unable to build on their progress. He believed we had gotten so close and hated that later efforts didn't lead to an agreement.

In August 2000, we were invited to visit Camp David. Jim French and Phil Jamison joined us, and Ann McCoy led our tour. We missed the "no photography" sign, so we snapped photos all day. We saw the golf course, putting green, chapel, president's house, guest cottages, and more. The camp lodge where meetings took place was cozy and comfortable. We toured the president's office, and I saw a photo of us on his desk taken the day after the 1992 election. We thought of meetings with world leaders that had happened here. Israeli and Palestinian heads of state had walked these sidewalks in July. It had also been a retreat for the president and a Thanksgiving dinner site. One sensed the comfort in which world leaders could sit and work through problems. The absence of big conference tables and the casual dress made discussions comfortable.

The president's 51st birthday, August 19, 2000, featured a big party at the White House with entertainment by Jimmy Buffet and his band. Jim French, Phil Jamison, and I also attended another party for the president with Cabinet members and donors at the White House swimming pool and gardens.[7] The president was in great spirits and introduced us to other guests. We had a beautiful supper, and the summer night was perfect for the president's last White House birthday. It was so typical of our old friend to include us at a party with the cabinet and major donors.

The president's final official address to the Democratic National Convention was in August 2000 in Los Angeles, where he nominated Al Gore for president. It was a powerful message that summed up the accomplishments of his presidency over the past eight years and urged Americans to keep the momentum going. He expressed confidence that Gore would continue the progress. Our nation was in a much stronger place than when they took office in 1993. He urged us to keep putting people first, to keep building bridges, and to never stop thinking about tomorrow.

Senator Hillary Clinton of New York!

During these final months in the White House, Hillary had begun to assess her next steps in professional life and service. When Senator Daniel Patrick Moynihan announced his retirement, she moved to announce her candidacy for the seat. She had never lived in New York, but I remember her telling me and my friends that she would love to live there one day. She bought property in Chappaqua, where the Clintons still live. She campaigned in all 62 counties even as her husband's impeachment trial was still in the news. "I may be new to the neighborhood, but I'm not new to your concerns," she promised. She won with 55 percent against Rick Lazio on November 7, 2000. Hillary's election made her the only first lady to hold elective office. While the news of her election was wonderful, it was also bittersweet, as now the Clintons would be moving to New York to live rather than back home to Arkansas. We hoped we would often see them to visit, but we knew times together would be rarer than if they lived in Arkansas.

We were in shock about the very close 2000 presidential race between Gore and George Bush, and that the Supreme Court had to decide the outcome as late as December. Bush was declared victorious even as votes were still being counted. It was a deep blow to our democracy and seemed fraught with missteps. We had to accept the outcome.

"This is not a day to be sad but to be happy for all our experiences. We did a lot of good."

January 17, 2001, the president flew to Little Rock for a farewell visit to Arkansas and invited friends Phil Jamison, Jim French, and me to make the trip on Air Force One. It was a cold, icy day. On arrival, we saw old friends David, Glenda, Mary Jo, and Danny Thomason. We accompanied the president to the State Capitol, where he addressed the legislature. He acknowledged those with him, and I felt honored as he noted my work in adult literacy. He later sent a transcript of his speech.

Back aboard Air Force One we chatted about the Hot Springs High School Clinton Campus project to convert the school to condos. He was pleased to see the Peter Max poster fundraiser designed for it. I took an envelope inscribed with Virginia's handwritten note, "Bill and Young Friends," that she'd given me years earlier with photos of Bill, David Leopoulos, and Ronnie Cecil at about 10-12 years of age. He treasured these photos his mother saved and gave to me.

Trips aboard Air Force One were among the most special experiences for a friend of the president. Whether aboard the 747 or one of the smaller planes, there were always conversations with the President, friends, and staff, and an occasional card game. I appreciated the president's thoughtfulness in inviting me to fly with him several times.

On Inauguration Day, January 20, 2001, friends were invited to Andrews Air Force Base for a farewell sendoff for the Clintons after they welcomed the Bushes to their new home at the White House. We met in the visitor's lounge at 11 AM with Phil Jamison, Jim and Kathy French, other Arkansans, and White House staff to watch Bush's televised swearing-in and Clinton's departure from the U.S. Capitol.

After Bush's swearing-in, we took a shuttle to the hangar, where hundreds gathered for a ceremonial farewell. We sat in the second row behind Janet Reno and Madeline Albright. I wound up standing because the Secret Service needed my seat. The Clintons would fly to New York City to be greeted by another rally, primarily of Hillary's senate supporters.

Bill spoke to the crowd and said, "This is not a day to be sad but to be happy for all our experiences. We did a lot of good." I took a large Clinton-Gore campaign sign I'd saved, and the Clintons posed by it with friends as they left. That sign had seen us through two successful elections. These had been incredible years for our nation, our president and family, and for all fortunate enough to call him a friend. We hated to see the eight years of his presidency come to an end, but knew their years of service were far from over.

---

[1] Cabinet members Madeline Albright, Bill Richardson, Robert Rubin and Janet Reno sat with us. Staff members Bruce Reed, Gene Sperling, and Erskine Bowles were there. Barbara Walters and Sen. John Warner smiled for our cameras. Rev. Jesse Jackson, Harry and Linda Bloodworth Thomason, and National Institute for Literacy board member Lynn Waihe'e and husband Gov. John Waihe'e and the president's pastor Dr. Rex Horne and family were also there.

[2] Tumulty, Karen, *Presidential Pen Pals, Time Magazine*, January 27, 1997

[3] Scott, Tony, *Variety* magazine, *Bill Clinton: The Rock and Roll President*, June 3, 1997

[4] Pianin, Eric, "Livingston Quits as Speaker-Designate," *The Washington Post*, December 20, 1998

[5] Cummings, Jeanne, "Hell or Whitewater, She Isn't Ashamed to be Called an FOB," *The Wall Street Journal*, January 28, 1999

[6] The State Dining Room table featured lamb chops, boiled shrimp, crab cakes, pizzas, and a vast array of canapes, tarts, fruits, plus another dessert buffet with pies, mousses, trifle and assorted masterpieces. Stars attending, including Jack Nicholson who dashed past us. We saw Bono, Will Smith and other celebrities. We chatted with Senator Chuck Robb and wife Linda, Mrs. John Glenn and Vernon Jordan. Friends Phil and Susan Jamison and Jim and Kathy French attended.

[7] Georgetown friends Tom and Jude Campbell, Tom Caplan, and Tom and Debbie Siebert and Joe and Kathy Baczko were also there.

CHAPTER TEN

Life in DC after the Clinton Presidency

The former director told me I was "radioactive."

Life in DC felt vastly different after the Clintons left the White House. We stayed in touch as they began life in new homes in New York and DC, opened the Clinton Foundation offices, and as Hillary served in the US Senate. We missed visits to the White House and other related events and perks of having our friend in the Oval Office. It had been quite an amazing eight years.

My work continued at the National Institute for Literacy as Deputy Director and as Acting Director until my contract ended in 2002. The work was fulfilling, but the new administration had me in their crosshairs, and the former director told me I was "radioactive." I served until my contract was not renewed. Jerry continued architectural photography around the globe with Sunrise Living, traveling the U.S., Germany, and England. Our children's marriages, college, and careers thrilled us.

While living in DC, I fulfilled a long-held dream to attend a theological seminary. The John Leland Center for Theological Studies opened in 1998 for progressive theological education as an alternative to historic Southern Baptist seminaries that had grown more conservative and didn't support women in ministry. It also had the mission to offer theological education to international students who pastored churches in the area. Having student colleagues from Vietnam, Africa and the Middle East enriched the experience greatly. I entered the graduate theological studies program. I was also delighted to have several female classmates during my two years of seminary.

The Masters in Theological Studies curriculum was rigorous. I expected it to be a little easier because I'd been in Sunday School and church programs all my life, studying scripture, Paul's missionary journeys, and listening to my Dad's excellent sermons every Sunday. However, I was not prepared for the depth of theological thought and history I would study. I took Old and New Testament, Introduction to Theology, Historical Theology, Systematic Theology, Hebrew, Missions, Global Church History, Introduction to Christian Ethics, Philosophy of Religion, and other courses and seminars. A thesis and two on-site ministry experiences were required. My primary theology professor was a Ph.D. graduate of Catholic University in Washington, DC, and expected his students to be thoroughly trained in classical theology. We studied the early First and Second Century church councils, how the understanding of God the Father, Son, and Holy Spirit was determined by the Catholic church as *homoousios*, how schisms and controversies developed and were settled, how Holy Communion was understood as transubstantiation and consubstantiation, and how the early church fathers and mothers gave their entire lives to these matters so that Christians could have the understanding we enjoy today.

The classes were at night, so I was able to continue work at the National Institute for Literacy during the day until my contract ended. I took a full load every semester for two years to complete the degree as quickly as possible. I had started late in life and was already serving in church ministry at Briggs Baptist, Bethesda, Maryland. I slept with my books piled all around me and studied endlessly. In one semester, my studies spanned from Old Testament creation to Twentieth Century Black liberation and feminist theology. I was so tightly wound and excited about all I was learning that our daughter Sarah said she wasn't coming home for Christmas unless I settled down. It was arduous, but I am grateful for the fine education I received.

It may be difficult to understand how my life led to ministry, but I realized my entire path had led to this focus. My childhood as a preacher's kid, an early interest in theology, a desire to attend seminary from young adulthood, a passion for justice and service to others, time spent in the pulpit as a singer and lay leader, and interest in public service all culminated in seminary and my ordination to ministry. My friend Bill observed, "I believe this is what you were meant to do."

As my ordination approached, my mother, a member of a Southern Baptist church in Mississippi, began to be asked by women about my plans. "What do you think about Carolyn being ordained, Mrs. Yeldell? Do you think that's Biblical?" My mother often replied, "I believe that is between Carolyn and God." She quoted Joel 2:28, which is requoted in Acts 2:17, "And it shall come to pass in the last days, saith God, I will pour out of my Spirit upon all flesh: and your sons and your daughters shall prophesy…" She had little patience with those who viewed scripture literally rather than through a social and historical context, particularly St. Paul's teachings about women not speaking in church. I was grateful for her support and felt my Dad would have also been proud of me.

In 2000, I joined the staff of Briggs Baptist Church in Bethesda, Maryland. Pastor Dr. Bob Maddox was the religious liaison for President Jimmy Carter and a staunch supporter of President Clinton and Hillary. I was licensed to the ministry there, and Jerry was ordained as a Deacon. I served Briggs as Associate Pastor until we moved back to Little Rock in 2005, when I became Associate Pastor at Pulaski Heights Baptist Church. I was also a professor of voice at the Washington Conservatory of Music housed at Briggs Church. It was a richly rewarding experience. The churches I've ministered in have been progressive, racially integrated, welcoming, and service-oriented. My churches have been primarily in urban settings but also in rural Arkansas. I've been blessed.

"I am accustomed to the rough and tumble of politics, but…"

As President Clinton left office, he received criticism for the pardons he granted. The press always scrutinized pardons, but this was unusually tough. The President wrote an editorial in the *New York Times* to explain his decisions. He noted that, during his presidency, he had issued about 450 pardons—in line with Carter and Reagan pardons (Carter 566, Reagan 406). The President said his pardons went largely to unknown people, many to people he believed had served long enough under mandatory drug sentencing laws. Others were nonviolent offenders. Most went to people who had been convicted and served their time. The pardon restored their fundamental civil rights. Many had vigorous bipartisan support. We wondered about a pardon for our Little Rock friend, Webb Hubbell, a Rose Law Firm associate and a good friend of the president's. As part of the Whitewater investigation, Webb pleaded guilty to one count of wire fraud and one count of failing to disclose a conflict of interest. He was sentenced to 21 months. We later learned that he was not eligible for a pardon at the time. The president said in no case had there been a quid pro quo in his decisions. "I am accustomed to the rough and tumble of politics, but the accusations made against me in this case have been particularly painful because, for eight years, I worked hard to make good decisions for the American people. I want every American to know that, while you may disagree with this decision, I made it on the merits as I saw them, and I take full responsibility for it."

The Clinton Foundation started in 1997, and President Clinton began fundraising efforts for his library. The foundation opened its offices in Harlem at 55 W. 125th Street. In 2011, the offices moved to 77 Water Street in the financial district, but President Clinton kept his office in Harlem. We visited his office, and Hannah Richert, secretary to the president, gave us a tour. We saw Arkansas friend Helen Robinson, who worked there and met director Laura Graham and chief of correspondence Stephen Rinehart. We enjoyed a visit with Bill in his office. We saw our picture on the window ledge with other photos and awards. Bill was in good spirits and encouraged by how well the foundation work was going.

In 2005, the Clinton Global Initiative (CGI) launched and continues today to bring together leaders of major corporations to commit to improving our country and world. CGI programs raise and donate billions every year. As the CGI began, access to HIV/AIDS drugs was a high priority, and the foundation made them available in Africa and around the globe. Earthquake relief to Haiti and tsunami relief in South Asia were high priorities. Former presidents Clinton and George H.W. Bush worked closely on these areas through their Clinton-Bush Foundation. Their partnership highlighted the strength of bipartisanship and was a model of hope to people who regarded politics as a big slugfest.

Esquire magazine's *The Impossible Issue*, 2019, examined Bill Clinton's support for rebuilding Haiti after devastating earthquakes in 2010. The Clinton Foundation provided earlier help as well. The president was appointed UN Special Envoy to Haiti in 2010. The Clinton Foundation raised over $16.4 million for assistance. Since then, over $30 million has been raised for health care services, childhood education, reforestation, the reduction of carbon emissions, and aid to farmers. *Esquire* writer Tom Chiarella wrote, "While most of the world has stopped paying attention to Haiti, Bill Clinton is the de facto leader of the efforts to rebuild the country after the historic earthquake. The problem is, there wasn't much there to begin with. A story of looking for hope in the dirt."[1]

The Clinton Foundation's work on HIV / AIDS has been one of its longest commitments. The Clinton Health Access Initiative was formed in 2002. At that time, people with HIV / IDS in poor countries did not have access to treatment. The Clinton Health Access Initiative brought drug company executives together to commit to making drugs more affordable. In just ten years, the Clinton initiative provided eight million people with drug treatment for HIV / AIDS and turned the AIDS epidemic around.

When I worked later in Africa on literacy projects in the summers of 2003-2006, I found that people were aware of the HIV / AIDS drugs provided by the Clinton Foundation but had no way to get to the drug dispensaries except on foot. Often, it was a full day's walk to a nearby town. They had to tend their crops and families, and being gone for so long was difficult. Additionally, the drugs could only be distributed to the individual who came to the clinic and not to other family or community members. I shared that concern with the president, who said he was aware of the issue. We discussed the possibility of mobile health clinic vans to get to rural areas.

The Clinton Foundation has other goals, among them giving children access to education, combatting the opioid epidemic, and tackling childhood obesity. Listening to the president talk about the foundation's work is always fascinating. He cares about people worldwide who lack basic needs of clean water, food, education, and access to healthcare. He's thrilled when financiers agree to invest and retool their work to help the Clinton Foundation achieve its goals. He gives full credit to all who support the foundation and the leaders who accept his challenge to work together.

In addition to the Clinton Global Initiative and the Clinton Health Initiative, several other programs were started by the Clinton Foundation, among them the Clinton Climate Initiative and the No Ceilings Initiative in partnership with the Bill and Melinda Gates Foundation. Our family supports the work of the Clinton Foundation and considers it a ministry of hope. We are as proud of Bill Clinton's work as we are of his years of service as president and governor. He sees the work as fulfilling his legacy, and he continues to use friendships he made to leverage good in our world. We cheer for him, Hillary, Chelsea, and all who lead the work.

September 11, 2001, rocked our country as never before.

Jim French, Phil Jamison, and I were enjoying supper on our patio in McLean on Memorial Day 2001 when David Leopoulos called, sobbing. His seventeen-year-old daughter Thea had just been killed in a car accident. She was a new driver out with her best friend when she spotted a speeding car approaching and driving erratically. Thea overcorrected and lost control of the car. We were all terribly shaken. I made reservations to visit Little Rock the following day to be with the family. Bob and Mauria Aspell and many friends surrounded them.

President Clinton learned the news while golfing at St. Andrews, Scotland. He flew to Little Rock to be with David, Linda, and sons Thaddeus and Nick. David and Bill have been neighbors and friends since third grade. The president and Hillary came to the funeral, and he delivered Thea's eulogy. He told how Thea had been in touch with him when he was president and how much her letters meant to him. He spoke of his friendship with David since childhood.

I began thinking about how to honor Thea's life. Thea's unique set of interests made her an incredibly special person. Two stood out: her love for art and her ability to build relationships. Her art skills brought her recognition in high school. Her counseling gift became apparent as she visited with friends' parents to help them understand what kids were going through. She was a remarkable young woman and peacemaker.

When David and Linda learned that Thea had made an A in trigonometry, they were astounded because math wasn't her strength. Her journals revealed she had gained confidence in difficult subjects because of her success in the arts. Their hope to help other students find the same success soon led to the formation of the Thea Foundation. I was honored to serve on the first board of directors, which at the start had a dual focus (counseling and arts) but later focused solely on the arts. Millions of dollars in college scholarships have been awarded through a competitive process that recognizes top young artists in Arkansas. The grants are given regardless of college major. The foundation also provides art supplies to classrooms and has been a tireless advocate for the importance of arts education.

David retired from directing the foundation in 2021. His son Nick is now the director. The Clinton Foundation has been a major supporter of the Thea

Foundation, and the president has hosted dinners. Out of tragedy was born a beautiful and ongoing tribute to Thea's life.

ꕥ ꕥ

September 11, 2001, rocked our country as never before. As events were unfolding, President George W. Bush learned that the Islamic terrorist group al-Qaeda had flown planes into the World Trade Center towers and the Pentagon and planned to attack the White House before the aircraft was brought down by passengers in Shanksville, Pennsylvania. Nearly three thousand people died, and thousands sustained long-term health consequences. It was the deadliest terrorist attack on American soil in U.S. history.

Our family was in Hot Springs, Arkansas, for a family wedding on September 7-8, 2001. Our friend Phil Jamison, who worked in the Pentagon, said he likely would have been in the area that was hit if he had been at work. I was still employed as Deputy Director of the National Institute for Literacy and in my office near the White House when the planes struck the Twin Towers. A staff member was watching televised congressional testimony when the news broke. We wondered if it was an accident, but the second plane confirmed it was a targeted attack. Staff left because we heard a plane was heading to the White House. I was the senior staff in the office and stayed until everyone left. It was late evening before clogged traffic opened, and I could leave. Thousands walked for hours to get home because of the traffic deadlock.

Several weeks later, my daughter Mary and I went to Ground Zero, where the World Trade Center towers had stood. We walked around the misty, hazy site where the building's twisted girders stood, still visible amid smoldering embers. Next to the site, we signed a banner at the Episcopal Church that miraculously escaped damage. The area was eerily quiet. It was a sacred, hallowed place of death for nearly 3,000 people. A friend in our church who worked in the towers got out before the second plane hit and was able to run through debris and smoke-filled air. By a miracle, she was able to run out of danger, but the emotional scars lingered.

I participated in several interfaith dialogues after 9/11 to help build trust and understanding between Muslims and other faiths. We worked hard to quell mistrust and hate. The images of 9/11 are still etched in our shared psyche and hearts.

"I believe this is what you were meant to do."

In 2001, the National Institute for Literacy's public awareness campaign I directed was completed. Materials were in the hands of literacy agencies to boost enrollment in literacy and adult education programs. I was enormously proud of this work and the National Literacy Summit that followed it in 2000. I was happy I could continue my contract after President Bush's election to complete this.

On May 19, 2002, I was ordained to the ministry. It was unique that two churches ordained me, McLean Baptist Church and Briggs Memorial Baptist Church. Pastors Dr. Michael Catlett and Dr. Robert Maddox suggested this because I was associate pastor at Briggs and had also been on staff and chair of Deacons at McLean Baptist. Both churches were pivotal in my recent ministry experiences. I went before an ordination council to answer questions on various theological topics.

The ordination service at Briggs Church was profoundly moving. President Clinton sent a beautiful letter that read, "Your commitment to serving the spiritual needs of others and celebrating God through music is invaluable in fostering an atmosphere of compassion and fellowship. By embracing this profound challenge, you are helping to shape a part of our world for generations to come." He added a handwritten note saying, "I am so proud of you. We have been friends for nearly forty years, and I believe this is what you were meant to do." As the culmination of a life of church work, public service, singing, teaching, and volunteering, church ministry emerged as the nexus of this experience and training. Everything had been linked all along.

In 2002 Will traveled to Europe with his design program at Kansas City Art Institute for a study tour entitled *Art on the Edge of Politics*. President Clinton was fascinated by the course outline about how art had influenced and been influenced by the politics of war and turmoil in the mid-Twentieth Century. The group toured Warsaw, Poland, and took an Alexander Schindler-inspired tour of Kazimierz at the National Gallery of Art. They toured Auschwitz-Birkenau, and Will wore a special yarmulke sent to him by his namesake, Rabbi Joseph Edelheit, for the occasion. The tour also included Prague, Weimar Germany, and the Bauhaus Museum, among several sites in Berlin.

At the end of the study tour, Jerry and I met Will. We traveled to Milan, Italy, from different directions—Jerry from England, where he was doing photography, and I from D.C. We were relieved when it all came together, and we met at our hotel in Milan. We toured Milan, Rome, Florence, and Venice. It was a dream trip for Jerry and me because we met in a graduate course entitled *Art and Architecture of 17th Rome*. We had always hoped to visit Rome to see the art and architecture we studied of Michelangelo, Bernini, Caravaggio, and many other masters. It was a spectacular trip and finally justified our saving of two massive, twenty-pound textbooks we used to plan our trip.

I traveled in 2003 and 2005 to Angola to start adult learning centers in churches. I was asked by Cooperative Baptist Fellowship mission worker and director of HIV/AIDS projects in sub-Saharan Africa, Lonnie Turner, to go because of my experience in literacy. I went July 10-27, 2003, and August 5-19, 2004. After we moved to Little Rock, I went to Zambia in 2006 for the same literacy work and building wells. The native language of Portuguese in Angola was a challenge, as were villages where indigenous languages were spoken. Blessedly, I had excellent translators for my classes. The students were thrilled to hold pencils and paper to learn literacy basics. They wanted to learn practical words and words they used in church. Watching their profound joy as they learned to write their own names was exciting.

In both Angola and Zambia, women were recruited for our new literacy classes because they were the family teachers. Tradition did not allow them to speak to their husbands about marital fidelity. It was commonplace for men to have numerous sexual partners and to frequent brothels in neighboring countries. AIDS had claimed the lives of millions. I saw young children who were raising their siblings. The problems of malnutrition and poor education were rampant. The lack of clean water exacerbated the health crisis.

The goal in Angola and Zambia was to start literacy programs for women so they could learn the basics of reading to understand HIV/AIDS leaflets. Churches made sets of alphabet flashcards. I donated literacy books and collaborated with pastors to begin programs they would operate after we left. I also asked African friends at seminary to write sample sermons about HIV/AIDS for pastors to use. It was interesting to me that the male pastors had trouble preaching about HIV/AIDS. I attributed this to the endemic practice of having multiple sex partners outside marriage. The women were willing to talk openly about HIV/AIDS and how it was impacting their lives and their children. A pastor's daughter in one village was a nurse, and the pastor prevailed on her to talk about HIV/AIDS in worship. She explained the protection condoms give and demonstrated how to use them by taking a broom to the pulpit and putting a condom over the end of the broom handle. I admired her creativity.

These trips to Africa were life-changing for me. Jerry and our kids shared my excitement. I felt a kinship with the loving people I met. We sang, danced, and celebrated in worship. We enjoyed meals, and they taught me their traditions of cooking and crafts. I tried carrying large baskets on my head as they did, hearing the peals of their laughter. We built bonds of friendship and understanding. The work was very satisfying. I remember imagining that I could live there.

❧ ☙

The president and I hoped we might sometime work together in Africa. I was also happy that my first visit took us to Johannesburg and Cape Town. I visited the Robben Island prison where Nelson Mandela had been held. I saw his cell, the garden in the courtyard where he planted crops, and the rock quarries where he was forced to labor. In Johannesburg, I visited the ornate capitol and saw the chambers where the vote to end apartheid had happened.

I traveled to India in 2003 with a team from the Baptist World Alliance to visit and particularly to lend support to the Christians in the remote northeastern states of Mizoram, Manipur, and Nagaland near the border of Myanmar. It was a dangerous, arduous trip to the northeast because of one-lane roads around mountains on one side and steep cliff drop-offs on the other. I was prepared to die at any moment. The Indian army was stationed along the roads to quell protests for freedom from Indian rule. The people of the northeast are more culturally aligned with China, plus India had made Hinduism the national religion and outlawed Christianity. Armed guards with machine guns stood guard in our hotel lobby. It was fascinating, but I was relieved to return to Calcutta, Hyderabad, and Delhi.

I was in Delhi when Bill was there for a Clinton Foundation meeting. It was good to be there at the same time, but we regretted being unable to connect. He launched an initiative to make anti-retroviral drugs available at one-third the existing market cost. He announced an agreement with four pharmaceutical companies, including one in India. He was meeting with Prime Minister Atal Bihari Vajpayee, hoping to work with the Indian government for local patients. It was a worthy undertaking.

On September 6, 2004, we were stunned that Clinton required quadruple coronary bypass surgery. My next-door neighbor called to me from her driveway, "Hey, I just heard that Bill Clinton had heart surgery today. Did you know about that?" I hadn't heard this news, so I thanked her and learned he was at New York Presbyterian Hospital. He did well but developed a rare lung complication that required another operation 6 months later. He said it really changed him, and while he felt more relaxed, he also was more tired. In February 2010, he had two mesh artery stents inserted. He adopted a vegan diet and got down to his high school weight. He read it is possible to heal the body from the inside out through healthy eating. He's a true inspiration, and I have moved to a plant-based diet. In 2009 he wrote, "I like your diet. I still eat some chicken, turkey, and occasionally buffalo (better) but mostly fish, vegetables, fruits, and non-wheat grains." He looks wonderful and is healthier than ever. We need him at work in our world for a long time.

"We all do better when we work together."

I served on the Central Arkansas Presidential Library Study Committee to encourage Clinton to build his library in Little Rock. He was considering other sites, including multiple locations around the state. We were elated when he settled on Little Rock. Not only did he build the Clinton Presidential Center in Little Rock, but he also selected a site on the Arkansas River in a neglected warehouse district where few went. The 30-acre center has given new life to the area. The President approved the design in mid-June 2001, and architects and landscapers were impressed by his detailed questions about the plans. He asked that the Oval Office be lit with natural light to make it more like the White House. The Clinton School of Public Service also opened in the former Choctaw Railway Station next to the Clinton Presidential Center. Skip Rutherford, Dean of the Clinton School of Public Service, commented, "We've changed the way presidential libraries are built, and we'll change the way they are looked at in years to come."[2]

We flew to Little Rock for the dedication of the William J. Clinton Presidential Center. On November 18, 2004, at 10 AM, the center was dedicated, one of the most significant events in the state's history. It was also Clinton's first event following his heart surgery.

President George W. Bush and former Presidents Jimmy Carter and George H. W. Bush spoke at the opening ceremonies. President Bush praised Clinton as "an innovator, a serious student of policy, and a man of great compassion." He added, "The collections here record the dedication and hard work of thousands who brought talent and idealism to public service. And at the center of that era, at the head of that administration, was an able and energetic American." Former South African President Nelson Mandela sent a videotaped message. Former President of Colombia, Ninos Vallenato, spoke of his friendship with Clinton. Hillary introduced the president and was cheered for her leadership. As the president spoke, he said the center "represents what I tried to do but also what I want to do with the rest of my life. Building bridges from yesterday to today, building bridges across racial and religious lines, and ethnic and income and political divides." He said, "We all do better when we work together. Our differences do matter, but our common humanity matters more." Chelsea presented the key to the center to the U.S. national archivist John Carlin, Mickey Mangun sang *The Battle Hymn of the Republic,* and Tony Campolo gave the benediction. It was a miserably rainy day, but our spirits were not dampened thanks to presentations by the African Drum Ballet, Hot Springs High School Marching Band, River City Men's Chorus, and the Philander Smith College choir. Our seats right down front allowed a perfect view.

Before the library dedication, the city and state bustled with extraordinary events honoring the president. Exhibits, poetry readings, a theater event with Al Franken, a concert at Robinson Auditorium by Aretha Franklin, tours at Little Rock Central High School, and Clinton staff reunions filled the calendar. "Arkansas' Largest-Ever Fireworks Display" kicked off dedication eve at the Clinton Presidential Center and Park.

After the dedication, the center opened for tours. I was honored to find the picture of our family with friends taken on our porch the day of the 1992 election included in the photo wall display on the third floor. Another of my husband Jerry's photos showed Virginia cradling Bill's head in her hand at the brunch in our home after the election. There is also a display case of items from the president's high school years. Our yearbook is there, opened to the page of us meeting John F. Kennedy in the summer of 1963. I was also so happy that a video shown in the cabinet room included images of me standing at the pulpit at Metropolitan A.M.E Church, singing at the Inaugural Prayer Service. The center features a heavy use of technology with an interactive timeline of events during the Clinton presidency. The archives contain the most presidential material in the National Archives system and required eight C-5 cargo planes to transport the collection to Little Rock.

We attended a gala lunch set like a state dinner. It felt wonderful to reunite with friends from home and DC. Barbra Streisand and Morgan Freeman spent time visiting with us. We had a photo together, and I also chatted with Senator John Kerry. Foreign dignitaries joined cabinet members and White House staff for a celebration to rival all others, and worthy of the stunning accomplishments of our president and friend, Bill Clinton. Even better, the center would continue to provide inspiration, education, and opportunities for continued good work for decades to come.

"You need to register those squash as weapons"

Time was nearing our move back to Arkansas. Working at the National Institute for Literacy was a rewarding experience. I had also attended seminary, been ordained to ministry, and worked in two wonderful churches in Virginia and Maryland. Jerry taught school and worked as a photographer for Sunrise Living in a dream-come-true job. Sarah worked in communications for Secretary Riley at the U.S. Department of Education and was now employed in communications at Apple, Inc. in California. Mary graduated from George Mason University, studied acting at the American Academy of Dramatic Arts in New York City and was married to Doug and living in Kansas City. Will was studying design at Pratt Institute in New York City. We were thriving because of the opportunities we had here.

We enjoyed proximity to the White House, monuments, concerts, and the opportunity to experience the presidency of Bill Clinton firsthand each day. We had super parties with friends and White House staff at our home. We loved our house in McLean and our large garden, which was made memorable in 1998 when Mother and I took a big bag of vegetables to the Oval Office.

The president could not believe the size of the squash and said, "You need to register those squash as weapons." We discussed likely targets, all in playful fun. The president never visited our home, although we invited him often. He said his visits caused chaos in neighborhoods. He preferred us to come to the White House, and we made the most of his countless invitations.

Our experience in the nation's capital from 1994 to 2005 was monumental and enriched us in ways we will always treasure, with friendships that remain dear today.

---

[1] Chiarella Tom, *Esquire* "The Impossible Issue", January 2001

[2] Architect James Polshek of New York City designed the building to resemble a glass bridge leading to the 21st century to play off the "bridge to the 21st century" theme used in the presidency. The exhibit area was designed by Ralph Appelbaum who created the Holocaust Memorial Museum exhibit space. More than $1 billion has been invested in the warehouse area since the Clinton Presidential Center opened November 18, 2004. Heifer International built their global headquarters nearby. The Central Arkansas Library System built new headquarters blocks away. The Arkansas Studies Institute of the Central Arkansas Library system built a beautiful research study center that houses the papers of many Arkansas leaders and a gallery of Arkansas artists' work. The University of Arkansas at Little Rock opened a campus on President Clinton Avenue. Condominiums, hotels and businesses opened. The President Clinton Avenue district is now the city's most popular area for dining and night life. The Clinton Presidential Center has been a spectacular addition to the state and region with changing exhibits, service projects, a popular speaker's series, concerts, a venue for conferences and weddings, and tours for visitors from around the world.

CHAPTER ELEVEN

Move Back to Arkansas, Continued Clinton Friendship

President Bill and First Lady Hillary Clinton made our time unforgettable.

In 2005, we moved back to Little Rock, where I became Associate Pastor at Pulaski Heights Baptist Church. Living in the DC area was an incomparable experience watching my friend preside over our nation's business. Many personal goals and dreams were fulfilled, and we were grateful for the experiences. We were now ready to put to work what we learned and experienced. Returning to Arkansas had always been the plan, to minister, maybe to run for office to fulfill a long-time personal goal, but primarily just to be back home. Jerry retired from teaching and photography and began living the good life.

Life in DC was a treasure-trove of experiences. Countless opportunities to celebrate former President Clinton in the White House still hold deep memories. White House visits for policy signings, state arrival ceremonies, helicopter departures, radio addresses, Christmas parties, Easter egg rolls, movies, July 4th fireworks from the roof of the White House, birthday parties, and more were such a gift. Exceptionally special memories were overnights in the White House, trips with the president aboard Air Force One, Oval Office visits, lunch with the president and friends in the president's private dining room, the Millennium Gala, and sharing these events with our family. The president and first lady helped make our time unforgettable.

There had been sad days, too, upheavals and turmoil as we watched the politics of DC play out. But our friends had always landed on their feet, bravely facing any obstacle, and we were thankful they were in the White House. They ushered us into a new millennium with strength and hope.

Most of all, the Clintons had given us an incomparable chapter of life and friendship. We had witnessed history and been part of it in a way few people experience. The friendship that began in high school with an early glimmer of my neighbor Bill Clinton's White House potential had come to fulfillment and he took us along to enjoy it.

"The President wants you to come for supper."

Today, one of our greatest delights of living in Little Rock is that the Clinton Presidential Center is home for the Clintons when they are in town. Their beautiful residence on the top floor has a breathtaking view of the Arkansas River and woodlands. It is filled with art and travel keepsakes and has a beautiful grand piano I have enjoyed playing. The residence has become our meeting place with the former president. We love getting a call to say, "The president would like friends to come for supper." These visits give us an opportunity to catch up with our friends and a chance for Bill to talk about what is on his mind and to unload a little. We usually start our visit in the kitchen enjoying some vegan dishes from Café 42 in the presidential center and follow up with apple or cherry pie. We play Hearts, share pictures of family, and make silly jokes. We mostly listen and share unconditional love. On Saturday, August 19, 2006, the Clinton Presidential Center hosted a 60th birthday celebration for Clinton. He was unable to attend but was the center of memories as panels of friends discussed their relationships with him. I participated in the morning panel entitled "The FOBs Turn 60" with friends David Leopoulos, Mauria Aspell, Rose Crane, and Joe Purvis. We relived memories about growing up as friends of the president. We also talked about early signals that we noticed that foretold his life of public service and eventual presidency.[1]

On October 28, 2006, friends and Clinton Foundation donors gathered for a 60th presidential birthday party in New York City. Jerry was away on photo business, so Will and I attended. I flew to NYC, where Will was a graduate student at the Pratt Institute in Brooklyn. The main events were a dinner on Saturday night at the Museum of Natural History and a private Rolling Stones concert at New York's historic Beacon Theater on Sunday. Dinner Saturday night at the museum was spectacular. On Sunday night before the Rolling

Stones concert, we enjoyed dinner at the Loeb Boathouse in Central Park. The view across the park was spectacular as the sun was setting. Friends celebrated with the president before dinner. As we left, we received a gift bag with a vintage Rolling Stones t-shirt and handy earplugs. Buses took us to the Rolling Stones concert at the Beacon Theater in Gramercy Park. The small venue gave us an intimate concert experience with an excellent view of the stage. Friends Tom Caplan and Mauria and Bob Aspell joined us in the balcony with the president and family. Mick Jagger was on fire. He told the president, "Thank you, President Clinton, for bringing along your husband," as the house cheered, and Clinton himself leaped to his feet to applaud his wife, Hillary, a potential presidential candidate. The *New York Times* reported on Clinton's speech about the work of the Clinton Foundation in the areas of AIDS and green environmental jobs.

"Thanks for giving our mother the 12 most secure, stable years she ever had."

On January 31, 2007, Dick Kelley, the husband of Bill's mother, died, and his funeral was held on Saturday at First United Methodist Church in Hot Springs. His casket was brought to the church in the Presidential limousine recently used for President Gerald Ford's funeral. Dick and Virginia were married in 1982. Former President Clinton spoke with deep affection for Dick and all the care and love he gave his mother. He said, "I am very thankful to him for many things, but most of all for giving our mother the 12 most secure, stable years she ever had."

In March 2007, the Clintons endowed a chair at the University of Arkansas Medical Sciences in honor of the former president's mother, Virginia Clinton Kelley, who died in January 1995. The chair was established with over $1 million in donations from friends, the Barbra Streisand Foundation, and the Arkansas Breast Cancer Act of 1997.[2] This profound and lasting gift in Virginia's memory honors her life of professional service in medicine.

Proud news for our family was that our son Will graduated from Pratt Institute with a master's degree in industrial design in May 2007. Students designed thesis projects and most designed furniture. For his thesis, Will designed a solution to poverty in the Arkansas Delta. He called it Thrive, Inc. The non-profit would offer design services to Delta businesses to keep them competitive, train design entrepreneurs in design skills, and slow the outward migration of young talent. He hoped to increase Delta residents' pride in their culture of music, arts, food, dance, and literature. After graduating from Pratt Institute, Will worked for the Clinton Foundation on the Clinton Climate Initiative. The president wrote to us that he was hearing good things about Will's work at the foundation and was happy to have him on the team. In 2008, Will moved to Helena, Arkansas, to lay the groundwork for his non-profit, Thrive, Inc. He sent the Thrive proposal to the president for comment. The president wrote in October 2006, "Will's proposal is very good. I'll be happy to be listed as a reference and advisor. I have some ideas, and he can see me when he returns to New York. In 2009, Will started Thrive Inc., and the non-profit celebrated its 15th anniversary in 2024. Thrive continues to mentor hundreds of young people. Thrive offers professional graphic design and community branding as an income stream. Thrive is grateful for the Clinton Family Foundation's support. The former president and Hillary are proud of Will for his ground-breaking work in the Delta. The President recently wrote to Will, "You deserve our support. Press on!"

He added, "I'm so proud of her."

In 2007 Hillary announced her campaign for President of the United States. She was the junior Senator from New York. She was an immensely popular candidate and campaigned hard. She lost the nomination to Barack Obama but won the popular vote among delegates. She suspended her campaign in July 2008 and endorsed Obama. We felt sure she'd be our first woman president. When those hopes dimmed, we decided this was perhaps a trial run, and that 2016 would be our year. We saw a very rustic "Hillary for President" sign on Highway 10 near our home and took a picture of it for Hillary. She loved it and said it was one of the best she'd seen. We were downcast when she lost the primary and felt our nation had missed an opportunity to experience her outstanding leadership. We supported our party and Obama and hoped she'd have another opportunity to serve in the future.

In February 2008, former President Carter convened the progressive New Baptist Covenant in Atlanta. We met to define ways to confront and combat social injustice in our country and world. I enjoyed sitting next to Carter at lunch and chatting about our hopes and about my neighbor and friend, Bill Clinton. Clinton spoke at the meeting and delivered a beautiful, personal message about his hopes for the organization's work, and his own life as a Baptist. He talked about going to church as a boy in Hot Springs and doing what he could for people in need in the community. As he grew older, he discovered the connection between his faith and his call to public service. He said he was dismayed by Baptist's drift to the right.

Boston Globe writer David Shribman wrote in January 2010 about *Presidents and Prayer*. He commented in-depth about Clinton's spiritual life and the importance of faith in his life and leadership. Dr. Rex Horne, former pastor to the president at Immanuel Baptist Church in Little Rock, said they talk by phone every week and said, "The President knows how to pray. He understands the Bible teaches he has a right to go to God in prayer without a mediator. He knows that God hears us when we pray. He prays freely and frequently."

Secretary of State Hillary Clinton

Just months after his election to the presidency, Obama began talking with Hillary about serving as Secretary of State in his administration. She had proven a strong opponent in the presidential campaign, and he knew she had valuable skills to offer. She accepted his nomination and, in January 2009, was confirmed by the Senate and resigned her Senate seat to take the post. She served from 2009 to 2013. She is also the only former First Lady of the United States to become a member of the United States Cabinet. We were grateful that Obama wanted to put her talents to work and that neither of them harbored ill-will following the arduous campaign for the nomination. We were enormously proud of Hillary as our Secretary of State and felt her presence made our nation safer, stronger, and more respected than ever on the world's stage.

"What would I do without you?"

In almost every letter I sent to the former president, I tried to include a few jokes. I knew he enjoyed a good joke and loved sharing them with others. In January 2009, the President thanked me for the jokes. "What would I do without you? I enjoyed the jokes you sent. As always, they gave me a good laugh, and I truly appreciate the time you take to bring a smile to my face." He added a note at the bottom of the letter, "See you soon. Keep the jokes coming. In this economy, we all need them." In November 2009, he again thanked me for sending jokes, and added, "As they say, 'A day without laughter is a day wasted!'"

Running for office was something I wanted to do since being inspired in high school. When we lived in DC, I hoped one day we would return home, and I could fulfill this dream. Our high school principal taught us that politics is public service, and that we need people willing to serve. My grandfather, E. J. Boswell, was Land Commissioner in Daviess County, Kentucky. My great aunt Katherine Griffin served as County Clerk in Daviess County, Kentucky. I enjoyed Girls State and Girls Nation and ran for office. I ran for Student Council in high school. I wanted to run again in Arkansas. I believed I could be a voice for the marginalized, work for education and literacy achievement, and bring fairness and justice to our citizens.

At an interracial service in March 2010, state legislator Fred Allen approached me and said, "Did you know that your congressional district has no Democrat running against the incumbent? Would you consider running?" I was stunned because I had dreamt for years about making a political race. Jerry and I discussed it, and I filed the next day before the deadline closed, March 8. I was very excited to take this step. My legislative District 32 had voted Republican in recent years, but I hoped voters would give me an opportunity to serve.

In May 2010, the Clintons sent me the maximum campaign contribution, and Bill offered to do a fundraiser in the fall. Our son Will created a beautiful campaign logo and website for me, and we printed signs and t-shirts. Bill wrote, "Your campaign materials are really good. I like the specifics and the general themes. If you print stuff it has to be shorter and geared to what your voters care about a lot. Keep going!" He came to Little Rock in September 2010 for a fundraiser at Doe's. We had a standing-room-only crowd, and it was a big success. He spoke about our call to service and how I'd served in the arts and adult literacy education and was highly qualified to serve.

I enjoyed campaigning and worked hard. My manager said I knocked on more doors than anyone she'd ever worked for. I did my best and, although I made a good showing, I lost the race. I was grateful to fulfill this lifelong dream. I knew the ministry was my way to make a lasting difference in people's lives. The idea of public service had been implanted early in my heart and mind, but politics had changed dramatically.

The former president was so pleased with my political campaign and that I'd taken this step. He wrote to Jerry and me in December, "I'm proud of you both for making that race."

"America has never been a retirement party. It's time to 'suit up and play again."

The 20th anniversary of Bill Clinton's 1991 campaign announcement and election in 1992 was celebrated on September 30, 2011, at the Clinton Presidential Center. Campaign staff, White House staff, and old friends attended.

Saturday, October 1, 2011, the party continued on the Old State House lawn, where Clinton made his Presidential announcement in 1991. The band "Chicago" played for the crowd. An announcement day 1991 video was shown. Rodney Slater and James Carville spoke. Bill thanked Chicago and Fleetwood Mac and thanked Vice President Al Gore for calling in. He commended President Obama for appointing the best Secretary of State possible. He said, "When I met Hillary forty years ago, I thought she was the most gifted person of my generation, and I still think so today." He said he was feeling nostalgic and said this day was a thank you to all who supported him and gave him a chance to serve. He said someone once told him he may be the only president elected on the strength of his friends. He reassured all young people present that we can still be better than ever.

Bill also reflected that his administration decided early to be guided by the motto of *Putting People First*. He outlined accomplishments he was proud of in education, trade, health insurance, improving the environment and the economy. He said much of his administration's success was a result of building networks of cooperation around the world. He said it is possible to have both national prosperity and human dignity. "In the second 4 years of my administration we had the bottom 20 percent see their income increase as much as the top 20 percent of earners, and that's because we had a partnership between a smart government working with the private sector." He said we needed now to have three things: a short-term growth strategy, a long-term plan to deal with the debt, and a plan to deal with housing. He reminded us that the Razorback football victory earlier in the day had not looked very promising at halftime. "But someone forgot to tell the players that," he said. "America got to this point through cooperation. I'm not pessimistic. I still believe every place in America can be a place called Hope." He added, "America has never been a retirement party. It's time to 'suit up and play again,' to give future generations the world they deserve." His powerful speech revved up the crowd and inspired us to keep working.

June 10, 2012, the Clinton Presidential Center showed an exhibit honoring the mothers of the President and Hillary, "Dorothy Howell Rodham and Virginia Clinton Kelley: Remarkable Women, Extraordinary Lives." It was one of the best exhibits, I believe, the Clinton Center has produced. The exhibit showcased keepsakes from both women, collections they had amassed during their lives, and many photographs.

I was personally thankful for the ways Virginia touched me as a young woman. I recently found a note she sent me in January 1992 saying, "My dear Carolyn, your visit was so important to me yesterday that I determined you would be my first correspondence in 1992. Once again you taught me how much meaning life holds. Every friend should take the time to sit down at the end of the year and talk about times past. It's important. Thanks for everything you and your family mean to me. I sure love you, Virginia." I was grateful she had lived to see her son elected President of the United States. She saw the difference his life was making in our troubled world that she talked about so many years ago to friends gathered at her dining table. She worked tirelessly to help elect him attorney general, Governor of Arkansas, and President of the United States. The exhibit honored these women's lives beautifully.

In 2013 President Obama bestowed the Presidential Medal of Freedom on former President Clinton in the 50th year since its creation by President John F. Kennedy. The nation's highest civilian honor, it is given to individuals who have made especially meritorious contributions to the security or national interests of the United States, to world peace, or to cultural or other significant public or private endeavors.[3] The *Arkansas Democrat-Gazette* interviewed David Leopoulos and me on August 9, 2013, about the award. We said how fitting it was for him to receive this recognition. David spoke of the thrill of seeing him rewarded for his effort at home and around the globe. We went to the Clinton Presidential Center to view the awards ceremony on a large screen television in the Great Hall on this enormously proud day.

"I'm inspired by your dedication .... I'm so proud of you."

I enjoyed serving as Associate Pastor at Pulaski Heights Baptist Church and started my ministry there in 2005. In June 2014, I resigned at age 66 to make room in the budget for a youth pastor. I enjoyed preaching, leading Bible studies, and assisting our missions and ministry programs to serve the needs of our community and world. One of the outreach programs I was most proud of was the Hillcrest Farmers Market. We started the market to meet our community neighbors, offer healthy food, care for creation, and give farmers a place to sell. Our market is the only one open year-round on Saturday mornings. The market remains strong, and I serve as the communications manager, posting about vendors each week. Former President Clinton sent a kind note on my semi-retirement, and said he knew I wasn't planning on slowing down any time soon. "I'm inspired by your dedication to community outreach, youth development, and to your family." He added a note, "I'm *so* proud of you." The letter was read at my last service at the church.

On February 15, 2016, our precious grandson, Freeman Ellis Staley, the son and only child of our son Will and wife Misti, died at 10 months from pulmonary hypertension. He was born April 25, 2015, and spent all but a few weeks of his life at Arkansas Children's Hospital. We spent every day with Freeman at Children's Hospital, holding him, loving him, talking, reading, and singing, and encouraging his team to do all possible to help him heal. We hoped so much that he would be able to recover and were devastated when he died.

The president called and spoke to me and to Will and Misti to express his sadness at the news. He received word about Freeman's death earlier in the day. He told them, "I couldn't breathe when I heard." It was a deeply loving call, and the president's grief was very real. Freeman's life led to the creation of the Freeman Playground in Helena, the only handicapped-accessible playground in the area for 70 miles. Misti created a mural along the playground fence depicting many animals in the region and created a picture book to sell for the playground's upkeep. The Freeman Playground keeps Will and Misti surrounded by "adopted" children who enjoy the playground just a block from their home. Misti and Will also designed and manufactured the Free-Arm Tube Feeding Assistant that helps families and caregivers. Misti serves as the CEO of the company and employs staff in Helena and elsewhere to assist her. Freeman's life certainly continues to inspire and serve others. We grieved again at the premature death of Will and Misti's daughter, Pearl Luna, in 2023, caused by a rare genetic syndrome.

We glimpsed again what might have been.

Election night, November 8, 2016, is still almost too painful to write about. It seemed impossible that America would be deprived of Hillary's leadership as our president. The exhilaration we felt when she was nominated as the Democratic Party's candidate was still palpable. She was the first woman in U.S. history to be nominated by a major party. She was our country's best hope. The campaign was difficult with unfathomable hurdles, from the difficulty in gaining traction with young voters who "felt the Bern" to the hurdle some had imagining a woman president. We were grateful to Hillary for making such a major effort in the presidential race and for continuing to lead.

Former President Clinton came to Little Rock on September 26, 2017, for the 60th anniversary of the desegregation of Little Rock Central High School. Eight of the nine students who integrated Central High in 1957 were at the event to reflect on this defining moment in our nation's history.[4] Melba Pattillo Beals, Elizabeth Eckford, Ernest Green, Gloria Ray Karlmark, Terrance Rovers, Carlotta Walls LaNier, Minnijean Brown Trickey, Thelma Mothershed Wair attended. Jefferson Thomas died in 2010. The President and Harvard University professor Henry Louis Gates Jr. spoke. Clinton said, "I wanted to stand up and say a lot of simple bromides… and make everyone feel good and tell them to sit down. I wanted to say, 'You did 60 years. Take a victory lap. Put on your dancing shoes. Have a good time.' But instead, I have to say, "You've got to put on your marching boots." He went on to remind everyone, "We're all 99 percent the same genomically." He continued, "We have to reject the sentiment and the anger in favor of answers. We have to reject polarization and demonization in favor of racial respect."

The Little Rock Nine said they are fighting a war against the force of inequality. They asked for a new generation of activists to help now as many helped them then in 1957 to break the school's color barrier. Ernest Green spoke about the current state of race relations in America, with police brutality, protests, and the 2015 killing of nine black churchgoers in Charleston, South Carolina by a white supremacist. "The Little Rock Nine turns to the Charleston Nine, paying the ultimate sacrifice," he said. Elizabeth Eckford said, "I hope someday that opposing sides can have nondiscriminatory dialogue. The only way we can have true reconciliation is if we honestly acknowledge our painful but shared past."

He's started texting now, which is a delight.

In May 2018, my husband Jerry suffered a stroke. Former President Clinton sent Jerry notes of encouragement and hope. He told us to stay optimistic and to keep working hard. I appreciated him saying he'd been touched by the love and grace I'd shown in caring for him. We were adjusting to our "new normal" and moving ahead in life. Each time a letter or note arrives from Bill, it's a real gift. He laughs about his handwriting, but I think it's beautiful. I do, however, take time to type the letter's contents before I file it in case someone tries to read it in the future and needs a little help. He is wonderful at sending thank you notes, birthday notes, well wishes, and follow-up notes after visits. If his note is type-written by staff, he adds a few personal lines at the bottom. He's started texting now, which is a delight. I have been able to send him some video podcasts that our family has done about their work and pictures along the way. He has sent videos as well of things he knows we will enjoy. We have entered a new tech age in our friendship.

Bill calls sometimes and we enjoy catching up. I try to make notes as we talk to remember everything he said. His insights about current events are worth going back to revisit afterward. I think everything he says is worth treasuring and keeping. After several messages, I transcribe them with other notes I've saved. Sometimes, our exchanges are brief, and other times, as in the case of our discussion about the Supreme Court's overturn of Roe v. Wade, they are longer.

Bill is a thoughtful friend. When he learns about the death of a friend, he often asks for the phone numbers of family members. When someone has had surgery or needs a word of encouragement, he is thoughtful to call. We exchange Christmas gifts with the Clintons, and they are generous friends. Recently, Bill and Hillary sent a beautiful silver piece made from large serving spoons and fashioned into an angel that he found in a small shop in Chappaqua. He likes to shop and visit shopkeepers, and he selects unique items that have a personal connection. The Clintons sent an inscribed copy of Harry Thomason's recent book, *Brother Dog*. I also love that he wraps his Christmas gifts and writes a note on the tag. It makes the gifts extra special to see his handwork.

In 2020 I found a vintage Dryden pottery mug made by Dryden Pottery in Hot Springs in the 1950s etched with the name BILL on it. I sent it to Bill as our birthday gift. His mother, Virginia, had a set of Dryden pottery in the same glaze, and I knew he would enjoy it. He texted that he loved it. Simple things are the best gifts sometimes.

"It's just what we have to do now. It's the only safe way to live."

The coronavirus Covid-19 rocked our world in early 2020. It began in China and quickly spread around the world as a global pandemic. The president called me after Easter 2021 to talk after reading a few chapters of this book and asked if we were doing ok during the pandemic. He knew that Jerry was in physical therapy to regain walking skills after a stroke in 2018. I told him we were staying active at home. He said, "It's just what we have to do now. It's the only safe way to live."

Bill told us Chelsea and her family moved into the house next door in Chappaqua during the pandemic because it was safer than living in New York City. He said they spent Easter afternoon 2020 putting together a trampoline for the children. Bill said he climbed on it himself to try it out. Chelsea's family moved back to their apartment in Manhattan as schools reopened. Bill reported missing them terribly. They missed their "Pop Pop" too, no doubt.

"No one deserves to die the way George Floyd did.

Just as my college friend Bill Clinton had worked to integrate the Boys Club swimming pool in Hot Springs and worked as governor for racial equality, now, in 2020, as former president he tried to bring peace during a time of racial tension. Racial attacks were on the rise in our nation and sadly seen most recently in law enforcement. On May 25, 2020, George Floyd, a Black man, was killed while in police custody in Minneapolis. He died from asphyxiation as a white police officer pinned him to the pavement with a knee on his neck for 8:46 minutes. Floyd begged for his life, saying, "I can't breathe." Floyd's death sparked outrage at the brutal use of police force. Former President Clinton wrote about Floyd's death, saying, "No one deserves to die the way George Floyd did. And the truth is, if you're white in America, the chances are you won't. That truth is what underlies the pain and the anger that so many are feeling and expressing—that the path of an entire life can be measured and devalued by the color of one's skin. Fifty-seven years ago, Dr. King dreamed of a day when his "four little children would be judged not by the color of their skin, but by the content of their character." Today, that dream seems even more out of reach, and we'll never reach it if we keep treating people of color with the unspoken assumption that they're less human."

A Glimpse at Personal Staley Family Life

Jerry has worked hard to recover from his stroke in 2018. He continues therapy to learn to walk, and we hope he will realize that dream. He is physically and mentally strong, and we enjoy life each day. We took a 3000-mile driving journey to the Grand Canyon in 2019 and enjoyed it fully. I often tell people how easy Jerry is to live with and what a positive and supportive guy he is. When we were dating, he told me that he believed that when you love someone, you set them free to be all they can be. I have experienced that fully as he has encouraged my work in the arts and literacy agencies, as a professional singer, a theology student, and ordained minister, traveling to sing in Russia and Europe and to begin literacy programs in Africa and India, running for office, and being fully engaged in life outside our home and family which has always been the top priority. He leans toward quietude, while I am often the gregarious one. He compliments me when I play the piano and sing at home. He is easy to please with meals and we just get along splendidly. This memoir has been possible because he's been excited about it all along the way.

Our children Sarah, Mary, and Will and their families are doing wonderfully well. They continue to build on these opportunities and are grateful for what we have had the privilege and proximity to experience. Each is making a significant contribution to their community and workplace. We treasure the time we get to spend with them when we can be together. Our grandchildren, Georgia, Scarlett, and Timothy, continue to amaze us with their academic and athletic skills. We are thankful for their kind, servant hearts and the strong faith of all our family members.

Conclusion

I continue to ask: How is it possible to describe a friendship like the one I've been so blessed to enjoy with Bill Clinton? He is an exceptional friend. I have often wondered and prayed, "God, what were you doing when Bill Clinton and his family moved next door to us in Hot Springs? It's a gift to have been Bill Clinton's next-door neighbor and friend through all these years. The friend who was next door is still my friend.

I sensed from the moment we became friends that Bill Clinton would not only become one of my best friends but that his life was destined for greatness. His deeply caring heart, his commitment to justice and fairness for all people, his charisma, intellect, and personal drive showed me that he was an extraordinary man. He is able to look into the eyes of a person and see into their heart. One of his most remarkable attributes is that no matter where he has traveled or what he has accomplished, he has remained the same person I have known from the beginning. He is humble and awed by the opportunities he has been given. He believes he has a responsibility to help make life better for all people.

Bill Clinton's life has been marked by struggles, both personal and professional; however, both have served to strengthen, refine, and mature him, and to add wisdom and renewed vision for service to our country. I am thankful he was elected be President of the United States, as I believed one day would happen. He saw the needs of people and felt called to serve and lead. He had the desire to renew America's hope in our government, education, cities, and the economy. He wanted, most of all, to give families everywhere the chance to achieve the American dream of a job, a home, healthcare, opportunities, and a future of peace. I am honored to be Bill Clinton's friend. I knew he would be a great President. He will continue, God willing, to inspire and lead in the years to come as one of the world's most admired people. I believe this because I have experienced it firsthand. He has been a caring, devoted friend to me. I am grateful for his family and their friendship. I pray we have many more years to celebrate our friendship and to serve and make a difference together in any way we can.

I will always be grateful to the Clintons for the experiences they have allowed us to share. My life would have been full if these had not happened, but how blessed and thankful I am that we have shared historic times with them. I have dozens of binders filled with photos and keepsakes of our years with the Clintons throughout our lives. How did I know to save all these letters, mementos, and souvenirs? What made me want to preserve and organize these memories? All I can say is this: somewhere along the way, incredibly early, in fact, I realized I was truly blessed. I knew that unfolding before me, year by year, was an uncommon story that needed to be lived fully and recorded to the best of my ability. I've tried to be faithful and true to that calling and to the extraordinary gift God has given me to be at this place and time.

Someday indeed, I hope I will truly fully understand how it is that such a friendship came to be, how neighbors became lifelong friends, how we shared so much growing up, and how we continued to celebrate the joy of serving others all through our lives. Bill's work in public service through elected office in Arkansas and as President of the United States, followed by the founding of the Clinton Foundation, and its work around the globe continues to be a guiding light where needed most. My work in public service through the arts and literacy, through singing and teaching, and through ministry has been the way my calling has been born out. We've both traveled to India, Russia, and Africa to try to help, and that has been an interesting parallel.

Most compelling and telling is that, regardless of his rise to power, his stellar trajectory, and seemingly endless gifts and energy for good, Bill Clinton has never lost touch with the people he loves. I am just one of many who are privileged to call him a friend. We all hold one thing in common: we have each experienced his presence firsthand in our lives and are better for it.

Our life story remains intertwined with our dear friend, President Clinton. Our journey is inextricably linked to a friendship with the boy who moved next door to the pastor's parsonage in Hot Springs in 1961.

Thank you, Mr. President, Bill, my friend, for this journey of friendship with you since we were age 15. As life continues to unfold, I have little doubt that the story will continue to hold new joys along the way as we celebrate a truly exceptional, rich story of friendship. I hope it continues for many more years. May there be many new experiences and happy times, adventures in service to others, and opportunities to laugh and enjoy life. I pray for you and your family daily and ask God's best blessings on all you do. I will continue to be right where you can find me when you need an old friend to call on.

---

[1] The afternoon panel entitled "From Tricycles to Bicycles to Air Force One" was moderated by Bobby Roberts and panelists were Patty Howe Criner, Bob Nash, Carol Willis and Betsy Wright. The event closed with a supper of McClard's Barbeque and birthday cake. Visitors viewed an exhibit of hundreds of documents and memorabilia from the Clinton administration. Musical groups entertained all day and 3000 people attended.

[2] The first recipient, Dr. Laura Hutchins, doing breast cancer research at the UAMS Cancer Center, was on the caregiver team for Virginia when she was a patient at UAMS.

[3] Also honored at the 2013 ceremony were Oprah Winfrey, Daniel Inouye, Ben Bradlee, Sally Ride, Richard Lugar, Gloria Steinham, Ernie Banks, Bayard Rustin, Daniel Kahneman, Loretta Lynn, Maria Molina, Arturo Sandoval, Dean Smith, Patricia Wald, and Rev. C.T. Vivian.

[4] The nine African American students, or the "Little Rock Nine" as they became known, attended their first full day of classes on September 25, 1957, under the protection of the 101st Airborne Division activated by President Eisenhower. They were initially being barred from entry by the Arkansas National Guard under orders from Gov. Faubus.

Bibliography

Agee, James and Evans, Walker, Let Us Now Praise Famous Men, Ballantine Books, New York, 1966

Baker, Peter, *The Breach*, Scribner, New York, New York, 2000

BBC Home, *On This Day*, September 13, 1993

Chiarella Tom, *Esquire* "The Impossible Issue", January 2001

Chozik, Amy, "Hillary Clinton's Speech on Women Resonates 20 Years Later," *New York Times*, September 15, 2015

CNN television, *Evans and Novak*, December 1992

Cummings, Jeanne, "Hell or Whitewater, She Isn't Ashamed to be Called an FOB," *The Wall Street Journal*, January 28, 1999

Dillard, Tom, *Arkansas Democrat-Gazette*, Opinion, "Hot Springs' Notorious Casinos", April 2019

Dumas, Ernie, The Clintons of Arkansas, The University of Arkansas Press, Fayetteville, 1993

Farrar, Clay, "The Heyday of Casinos," *The Amateur Historian*, April 2018

Greenburg, Paul, editorial, *Arkansas Democrat-Gazette*, November 3, 1992

Scott, Tony, *Variety* magazine, *Bill Clinton: The Rock and Roll President*, June 3, 1997

Staley, Rev. Carolyn, *A Reflection on Boris Yeltsin, Bill Clinton & Religious Liberty, Report on the Capital, Washington, DC*, May 2007

Taff, Russ, *We Will Stand*, Word Music, 1983

Takiff, Michael, *A Complicated Man*, Yale University Press, New Haven, Connecticut, 2010

The New York Times, Thomas Friedman, September 14,1993

The State of Literacy in America, National Institute for Literacy, Washington DC, 1998

The Traveling Church, Center for Baptist Heritage & Studies, Richmond, Virginia, 2007

Tindley, Charles Albert, *By and By*, written 1905, *New Songs of Paradise*, 1916

Tumulty, Karen, Presidential Pen Pals, *Time Magazine*, January 27, 1997

Wenner, Jann, "Bill Clinton: The Rolling Stone Interview," *Rolling Stone*, December 2000

Wikipedia, Hot Springs National Park, 2022

Original Poems and Songs by Carolyn Y. Staley

August 1968: For Bill's birthday I wrote a poem and framed it as a gift:

Why ask now how it came to pass
Or why or when 'twas known,
The seed for questing the uncommon life
Into his life was sown.
Not uncommon for uncommon's sake
Or that his name should provoke recall,
One life to live, why then should it fare but so far as men past were called?
    Where are you going, my wandering love,
    As you search for the road untrod?
    Where will it lead you, this virgin path
    As you brave the untouched sod?
Reverie of brotherhood
The mirth of peace untold
The pleas of love for all mankind
Still ringing, haunt the soul.
The vision, not a maiden one
May you strengthen the old as you pass,
Then leading, unfold
And make new dreams of old
Help find a better world at last.
    Where are you going, oh wandering love
    As you search for a road untrod?
    Where it will lead you, this virgin path
    That nobody knows but God?

February 1981: A Song for Chelsea

We welcome you Chelsea to our great big world, welcome with love and with pleasure
We've already had so much joy in our lives, but your life's a new gift we treasure,
We tried to get ready, we tried to prepare,
One day you're a dream, and the next day you're there
Looking at us with your beautiful eyes,
And we know we're not worthy, but we hope we'll be wise.
Refrain:
'Cause child you're a natural joy full of natural laughter
Your tears are natural too and we'll wipe them dry after,
Your days are so young and so free, full of promise of what you will be,
And child you're a natural wonder to me.
2. You'll find lots of things are important in life, some more important than others,
But one of those things stands above all the rest, and it's learning to live as brothers,
Your life's a book and the pages are clean,
There's so much to do, there's so much to be seen,
And it has to be wonderful, it has to be good,
And we'll try to lead you in the way that we should. (Refrain)

For Roger in prison (1983): *I Believe in You*:

I know you've been down, your chin on the ground
The weight of your life's taken hold,
You're looking for hope, trying to cope, this old world seems so cold,
I wish there's some way I could change things, I pray each day to heaven above,
But here in my heart all I can do is love.
    All that you are, all you will be, all that has been you're special to me,
    What's in the past is forgotten and forgiven, now it's time for loving and living,
    And start each day brand new, I believe in you.

June 13, 1994: After attending the White House arrival ceremony for the Emperor and Empress of Japan, I wrote this reflection:

Emperor and President, esteemed golden friend
First Lady and Empress resplendent in gold
Regal, majestic, glorious!
Sunny summer day, warm and golden.
  Bands resounding hear them come!
  Hearts are pounding with the big bass drum
  Saucy piccolo, spritely fife,
  Plucky tunes breathe a fresh new life!
Military in full dress, sober, serene,
  Precision, perfection, pride.
Twenty-one guns
BOOM quiet BOOM, heart-stopping display
  Of awesome grandeur, power, golden glory: America!
National anthems waft o'er the scene
  Amid the smoke of canons,
  Tears start to stream.
Where do tears come from? Surprise me, oh heart.
From deep within a place, an inner-most part,
  Love, pride: renewed belief!
  For a moment, back where we came from,
  What we knew we were preparing for in our youth,
  A calling forth to lead when the time was ours:
  America!
    Suddenly time seems to stop
    And we remember who we are,
    Who we have been, who we might yet become.
    Hope upon hope, for all the people, all lands, all creation.
    Renewed promise!
Golden president, golden friends,
  Reviewing troops, flags in the wind,
Past stars and stripes with hand over breast,
  Golden friend, above all the rest!

Golden fanfare, golden trumpets salute a golden heart, spirit, intellect,
Man, friend, president, and his partner and honored guests.
Fifteen, sixteen, forty and seven,
See you now, standing there, Mr. President,
All the plans, all the dreams, all the hope and vision,
All the toil and struggle, all the planning and running,
THERE YOU ARE! Dearest friend. Sacred, unspeakable moment.
Thanks be to God for this golden day.
Thanks be to God! God and ancestral sun goddess,
For gold, upon gold, upon gold.

Index

G

H

I

J

K

L

M

N

O

P

R

S

T

This page is intentionally blank.

This page is intentionally blank.

This page is intentionally blank.

This page is intentionally blank.

This page is intentionally blank.

This page is intentionally blank.

This page is intentionally blank.

This page is intentionally blank.

This page is intentionally blank.